BANKING INDIA

BANKING INDIA

Accepting deposits for the purpose of lending

Harihara Krishnan

PARTRIDGE

To order additional copies of this book, contact
Partridge India
000 800 10062 62
orders.india@partridgepublishing.com

www.partridgepublishing.com/india

CONTENTS

Acknowledgement.. ix
Preface.. xi
Introduction... 3

1   Money Lending..11
2   Banks in India so far..19
3   Banks Today 27
4   Changes in Banking 31
5   The Underwhelming Scenario...45
6   Juggernaut of Processes..61
7   Securing Bank Loans 128
8   Legislation 136
9   Recent Initiatives from the RBI...150
10 Uncertainties...158
11 Competition 173
12 Top Ten Indian Banks..183
13 Case Studies..222
14 Models 237

Tables 249
Glossary 259

TO
MY PARENTS, FAMILY AND LOVING FRIENDS

ACKNOWLEDGEMENT

Book cover design: Ms. Anisha Kotibhaskar

PREFACE

Does the Indian banking system fall short of expectations?

Banks are the conduit for mobilising individual savings from households to provide capital for enterprise in a country. This function of banks boosts employment opportunities, accelerates the growth of GDP of a nation and improves the welfare of its people. Appallingly, out of 247 million households in India, according to the 2011 Census, only 145 million avail themselves of banking services. This means that more than a 100 million households are deprived of banking services in their daily lives. Their earnings and savings do not enter the capital building process of the country. While bank loans form capital for industries, commerce and investments by banks in government bonds, forming part of Statutory Liquidity Ratio (SLR) or Non SLR investments, are used for infrastructure development in the country. In spite of being aware of the significance of having banks in remote areas, arguments such as: government or planning officials not giving sufficient thrust; extension to these areas not achievable; or "unbanked" poor not providing an economically viable proposition, have been put forward. These arguments and views can be proved as unfounded when one delves deeper into the various aspects of banking in India.

When the people of India inherited the country from the British Administration in 1947, the new rulers did consider the development of banking as important for economic growth and the social welfare of the country. One of the major initiatives taken by the new government after independence was to set up the State Bank of India in 1955. In fact, the preamble to the State Bank of India Act 1955 states unambiguously the urgency of spreading banking to rural areas:

"To constitute a State Bank for India, to transfer to it the undertaking of the Imperial Bank of India and to provide for other matters connected therewith or incidental thereto.

Whereas for the extensions of banking facilities on a large scale, more particularly in

the rural and semi-urban areas, and for diverse other public purposes it is expedient to constitute a State Bank for India, and to transfer to it the undertaking of the Imperial Bank of India and to provide for other matters connected therewith or incidental thereto."

This bank later acquired eight large princely state banks as its associates. Evidently, the state bank group was to spearhead the task of extending banking to remote areas as well as to serve as banker to the government.

After fourteen years of setting up the SBI, fourteen banks were nationalised by the government by an act of parliament – The Banking Companies (Acquisition and Transfer of Undertaking) Act, 1969 (5 of 1970). The preamble to the act provides the reason for bringing banks under government control as follows:

"In order to serve better the needs of development of economy in

Conformity with national policy and objectives".

This was followed by the nationalisation of six more commercial banks in 1980. By virtue of that, more than 95% of the banking business was under the control of the Indian government. However, by 1990 it was observed that these banks were not as competitive as foreign banks operating in India. Therefore, the government embarked upon liberalisation of the bank licensing scheme, so as to let in private sector banks and inject competition and at the same time improve the efficiency of the banking system.

Looking at the present banking scenario in India, the following questions may arise in the minds of anyone who is interested in areas such as banking, politics or investments in the country.

- How these ambitious banks in the private sector competed with large government-owned banks and foreign banks over the last 25 years
- Why then, did these new private banks, supposedly designed to operate freely, also leave 100 million households outside the banking system?
- Whether government banks, in spite of having traditional practices, change themselves to adapt to the recent stimuli of globalisation and IT

This book attempts to find answers to these questions, on the basis of my operational experience in banking and related areas for more than three decades.

The book is divided into three sections. The first section explores the inheritance of Indian banking and the changes that have taken place in banking the world over. It also outlines the expectation of today's customers from banks and how the banking scenario in India interacts with government, the central bank and judiciary.

The second section discusses topics such as the operations and processes carried on in banks, the uncertainties in the industry, the non-existent competition and significant legislation that plays a critical role in shaping the country's banking system.

The third section features an analysis of the top ten banks in India in terms of assets and their potential to assume a dominant role in Indian banking in the future. The topic of improving banking in India is hotly debated nowadays and the RBI has already taken some major initiatives towards this goal. The impact of these initiatives is discussed in this section. Before drawing to a close, in order to comprehend the difference between the 'theory and practice of banking', two case studies have been presented. I consider the case studies essential in order to comprehend the realities "on the ground" that usually get filtered out in communications to the board, the regulator or the government.

SECTION 1

INTRODUCTION

'Relationship of society and banks'

Banks are very important for all economic activities and a sound banking system helps nations in improving the wealth and welfare of their people. Development of banking in India, despite banks being in existence for more than 100 years, is not comparable with banks the world over. Indian banks are similar in stature to the legal and political systems of the nation for their lack of determination to reform.

Banks are often viewed by people in India, especially in rural and semi-urban places, as the resort for 'big money', while in order to save small amounts they resort to a close circle of friends, family and well-wishers who for them constitute a mutual private bank. The arrangement does a wonderful job of banking for the common man and forms a block on the development of banking. This approach results in a promotion of thrift that empowers the saver with a capital sum, for any medical emergency or purchase of white goods, clothes, gold ornaments, etc., without burdening the earning member of the family. Albeit being at a disadvantage in terms of the interest received on their savings, people opt for this network because of poor accessibility to mainstream banks, their need for privacy and wish to keep the tax authorities at a distance. There are other factors also that prohibit them from going to mainstream banks.

People do not appreciate the interest offered by banks on savings accounts. The interest amount offered by banks for small savings may not be economical when it is compared with the cost of travel, time lost for visiting banks, etc. Incidences of deceit by the door-to-door collection agents of banks may also linger in their mind. Proliferation of round-the-clock banking facilities through ATMs, online transfers, mobile banking, etc., have tried to address the issue of access and have shown promising signs, especially in urban areas and to some extent in semi-urban areas.

In the case of loans too, banks have been incapable of inspiring confidence in people, particularly family-run business establishments. Despite having the potential to grow manyfold and increase their profit with the support of banks, many of these second generation business owners rely on personal finances, local money lenders and friends. The underlying factor in these relationships is trust, procedural simplicity and non-interference in their business operations. Conventional business folklore continues to influence many decisions, especially in brick-and-mortar establishments. They are abundant with nightmarish tales of those who abandoned tradition and willy-nilly partnered with banks but went down after a brief honeymoon with the mainstream banks. They perceive the causes for the unsustainable long term relationship with commercial banks are the missing elements of non-interference and privacy enjoyed with money lenders and the inability to trust the ever-changing and unknown officials in a bank. Many such entrepreneurs, who take bank finance when unable to reconcile financial losses in business and their image in society, try to salvage the damage by challenging the bank for their discretionary move against them in a court of law through political influence. Even if they do not expect to win the battle, the time provides them succour. Thus the role of the judiciary in banking becomes significant in an under-banked scenario. Those who do not like to be dragged to court avoid banks in preference to usurious money lenders for finance.

How can the nation provide banks that can be trusted, ensure privacy and lure those who live their life without getting into the banking system? Perhaps the uncertainty coming from various discretionary activities of bank officials may have to be addressed first. Lack of discretion causes a conflict of interests. The less discretion there is, the more unstable the institution will be. Scientific systems offer a higher level of predictability to the banking process. The uncertainty is also caused by the banks' culture of frequently changing banking policies. The management's inability to streamline business processes and set up an enterprise-level decision support system can also become reasons for uncertainty. Certainty enforces good discipline in the banking system and encourages naysayers and fence-sitters to join the mainstream. Penetration of Information Technology (IT) into the system has also laid the way for virtual anonymity that plays an important role in this behavioural shift.

When can we say that the banking system is sound and well-developed: if people think of banks as their first choice for keeping their savings, to raise funds in an emergency, or as the safe, secure and fast method of making payments to others. Further, to obtain currency notes of their desired denomination, they prefer to visit a bank or an ATM. Even entrepreneurs count on banks as the smart way to raise finance for making up their shortage of capital to expand their business. Affluent citizens look upon banks as the best and easiest way to grow their assets. Thus banks can become an integral part of a society. They will be able to mobilise surplus by way of savings from all people, and lend to those people who need money. Thus enterprises are not held back from growth for want of capital. Flourishing enterprises create job opportunities for people and education systems comprising schools, colleges and universities in the country gear up to provide the skills needed by the enterprises. Resulting opportunities for good education and earnings improve the demand for other services such as medical, transport and habitation and thereby increase the overall welfare of the people. Socially and politically, proper perspective on Time and Money will energise people to lead their lives more intelligently.

Developing banks to make them people's first choice evolves from the legacy a nation inherits. The pace of change is affected by other systems like the political and economic systems espoused by each nation. Ultimately the banking system occupies a particular level in each country. People with plans to improve the pace of evolution therefore need to begin with steps to take care of the banking needs of the people.

Firstly, from the customer's point of view, banks must be capable of being accessible, providing a quick and safe service. There should be sufficient incentives in the system for depositors to save their money with banks without depletion in the value of the amount they save. Secondly, banks must have interconnected systems that facilitate payments and transfer of funds safely within a reasonable timeframe across banks, including remittances to overseas destinations. Thirdly, bank loans must become attractive by an emphasis on privacy and less cumbersome processes. The charges, including interest, should be affordable to people from different strata of society. For example, the potential to gain from loans taken for procuring consumer goods, education, trade or for manufacturing, impact the borrower differently. Fourthly, banks must provide knowledge and information on avenues for investing in the tax-saving schemes provided by government. Fifthly, they must also have arrangements for providing value added services such as safety deposit boxes or lockers for keeping valuables and custodial services such as the safe custody of important documents. On the whole, features such as safety, security, privacy, personal attention, reliability, certainty and above all transparency, gain the trust of customers in banks.

From the nation's perspective, the banking system must actively engage in the building of the nation by the government. Banks must attract and encourage entrepreneurs who espouse advanced technology for large scale production so that products and services can be provided to citizens more economically than in other countries. As demand goes up more employment opportunities are created. They must play a pertinent role in fostering an environment that improves the socio-economic lives of poor people through education and employment, and encourage small enterprises to scale up sustainably with financial discipline, from safe and low risk activities to high risk, high returns ventures, where the risk can be mitigated with the support of the banks. They must communicate well and educate entrepreneurs on aspects of banking so that the latter do not become victims of ignorance. Business plans of banks have to include schemes that are designed to encourage education and setting up of educational institutions, hospitals and other infrastructure, such as hotels and other hospitality centres that can provide employment for local people. Banks have to become a conduit for those members of the public who are interested in investment in government bonds and help them support the government in their mission to develop infrastructure for industrial growth such as development of roads, transport, power generation, supply of water, etc. Government also would expect banks to play a responsible role in the government revenue collection system.

Banks must design their organisational systems to strike a balance between customers' expectations and government expectations, with the objective of making profit. Their systems should have fool-proof mechanisms to prevent misuse by customers, employees and the government. Customers with malafide intentions try to deceive the bank (in collusion with the banks' own employees or otherwise) by engaging in fraud, forgery, even in mob behaviour, etc. All of these lead to wastage of time and resources. Governments also intervene in the procedures of the bank at times using their authority, disturbing the flow of bank's activities. Good housekeeping, clarity of instructions and a sound audit system can frustrate such misuse of the banking systems. The responsibility of bank managements in moving banks from a position of dependence to a position of command, depends upon how strongly banks are structured to stonewall any attempts at defamation or false allegations by a few evil-minded in society.

Banks are energised by their stakeholders viz. the shareholders, customers and employees. It is necessary that all of them are taken care of properly by the system. On one hand, it is important to recruit well-trained employees with service skills to secure business, and on the other, it is equally essential that the management encourages the public to become their customers through their decisions and actions. Customers are numerous, heterogeneous in behaviour and their expectations change with the times. Bank managements have to adopt the latest systems to address their changing requirements. Shareholders expect banks to be at the right place at the right time to seize opportunities for making profit, both from within the country and beyond.

Government may have great expectations for banks and they have a significant role to play in the development of a sound banking system in the country. Excessive emphasis on control of banks can be burdensome and damaging to the government. Ideally, banks and government must be kept at arm's length from each other. This thought was put into practice in India when the State Bank of India was set up and also the Reserve Bank of India. Indirect control with sufficient regulation to control excesses committed by banks and to protect the interests of the customers provides safety to the economy.

Ensuring the perfect working of these arrangements is the responsibility of the personnel who are appointed to manage banks and administer the regulatory institutions. However, if the required professionalism is found wanting in the officials, this arrangement will flounder and banks will be named for all the wrong reasons.

Banks in India are alleged to eat up to 4% of annual GDP on account of bad loans, which is indeed worrisome. The amount of bad loans does not lead one to infer that these are the result of a few poor credit decisions. On the other hand, it would be reasonable to surmise that the system is not watertight and that loopholes are plentiful. Processes are substandard giving rise to regular wastage of energy and effort. It is not that all banks behave badly every year. That leads to one or two options to discover the reason for the present scenario of banks in India: the quality of leadership of the captains of these banks and their difficulty in leading them in India.

The leaders are appointed by the government. The intention and commitment of governments over the last six decades to install a sound banking system in India is unquestionable if one goes by the steps initiated by various governments. But there have been many factors that have prevented banks in India from meeting the expectations of the government. Some of them are: the legacy of money lending and features of British colonial rule, and lack of faith in proven banking models which are successful elsewhere in the world. Ultimately the features that the public look for are missing from banks. Consequently a large portion of the population stays away from them.

A common adage in banking circles is that 'the theory and practice of banking are different'. Over the years, there have been several models introduced to face the challenge. On one hand, there are large, government-controlled banks that are run with a deliberate and conservative outlook engendering slow growth, while on the other hand there are ambitious private banks that mushroomed when licensing was liberalised. Irrespective of their priorities and approach, neither has been able to push banking forward dramatically. In fact, their lack of success has forced several small private banks to merge with larger ones. Government-supported Regional Rural Banks began operation with a hybrid model but many of them still continue with hand-holding support from their sponsor banks. Most of the foreign banks operating in the country do so, on a limited mandate.

All of these circumstances point to the conclusion that there are some serious challenges to be tackled by banks in India at a basic level and realistic comprehension of the functioning of banks is necessary to find a pragmatic solution. Inasmuch as the nation is under-banked, it offers a great deal of scope for growth in the banking business. The challenge can be worth taking, especially if the Indian economy is growing quickly and going global.

The challenge can be illustrated with the analogy of the conversion of a library into a bookstall. Banks in India operate today like libraries. Libraries have a large collection of books stacked in a particular order and members are expected to help themselves with their requirements. The librarian is only a passive facilitator and guide, having no interest in promoting the habit of reading among the people, even though that may be the prime objective of setting up a library. On the other hand, someone at the bookstore may be particularly keen to see that more and more people take up reading books regularly. The types of visitors to libraries and book shops are also very different in terms of their desire to acquire a particular book as well as their willingness to pay for it. Libraries regularly lose more books from readers than a book shop loses from its stocks. For librarians, books are at the centre of their business while for the book shop, customers are at the centre of business.

How can banks in India be changed from a 'library model' to a 'bookshop' model? Banks need to focus on the customers rather than on the systems they have. They should reorient all systems to make them simple, comprehensible, usable and helpful. Everyone needs banks. But banks need to differentiate themselves by their quality and unique value. Proper branding reinforces that differentiation in service. It forces its employees to follow a discipline and a set of traits, therefore developing branding. Marketing is essential for embedding a competitive environment and efficiency in the services banks offer.

This book places before the reader the task of grasping the deeply entrenched unhealthy features of money lenders in Indian banking and thereafter gleaning information surrounding the functioning of banks, in the hope of future improvement of Indian banks for the people and the government.

1. MONEY LENDING

'Deep in their heart'

The legacy of money lending is deep rooted. It continues to influence the modern banking system in many ways. In India, this is visible in almost every core banking transaction. To understand this distinguishing feature better, let us travel back in time to the early days of money lending in the country and the evolutionary course of modern banking described in a book entitled 'Banking in India' by S G Panandikar[1], written in 1934, that is, thirteen years before India's Independence and the end of British rule.

The book commences: 'Although the earliest reference to the existence of money lending operations in India region is found in the literature of Vedic times (i.e. 2000-1400BC), no information is available regarding their pursuit, as a profession by a section of the community, till 500 BC'. Since then, 'India possessed a system of banking which admirably fulfilled her needs and proved very beneficial to her, although its methods were different from those of modern Western banking'. The book mentions the existence of money lenders called *'sresthis'* whose activity was 'to lend money to traders, merchant adventurers who went to foreign countries, explorers who marched through forests to discover valuable materials, and sometimes to kings who were in financial difficulties (mostly during wars) against the pledge of a movable or immovable property or personal surety'. Usury was practiced but held in contempt. Kautilya's Arthasasthra laid down 15 per

---

[1] Book titled 'Banking in India' written by Mr. S G Panandikar and published in 1934

11

cent for secured loans per annum and 60 per cent for unsecured loans but permitted a maximum of 240 per cent if the risk was especially heavy.

One can also understand from the book that money changing came into existence with metallic money as the means for trade settlements. This opportunity was kindled by the use of different types of coinage in the various parts of the country. They succeeded in getting deposits regularly and giving loans to friends and neighbours. But the book mentions that these indigenous bankers could not succeed as bankers as they combined trade with banking business, which according to the author reduced the stability of their banking business. When some of these businesses failed, they would write off the loans, resulting in liquidation.

Relationships with money changers even today begin with the help of locally well-known or seemingly rich families. People usually do not doubt their ability to return the savings. Though the money lending business is theoretically profitable, unforeseen events can cause their business plans to fail. For some of them who commence money lending it is a dignified employment of resources and time with good scope for wealth accumulation. They run the show without forsaking their social status. In fact, many money changers sell their ancestral property and settle with depositors just to keep their honour in society. Some good and some bad experiences made a number of money changers maintain their profession with its inherent advantages of proximity, privacy, and quick finance management in emergencies to all classes of people in India.

Despite the appearance of joint-stock banks and state-run banks, money lenders[2], indigenous bankers who run chit companies or local savings companies attract public savings by offering higher rates of interest. Farmers and small entrepreneurs who fail to break the vicious circle of poverty in farming or other traditional jobs, continue to look upon indigenous banks for timely financial assistance. They obtain funds at the beginning of the production cycle and return them with interest at the end of the cycle. Having relied on nature for the means to repay the funds, some end up losing their means of making a living - the land they own. Farmers and people engaged

---

[2]   Usually restrict their lending to their own surplus funds

in such traditional professions have failed to take up crop insurance, due to ignorance and rampant illiteracy. The procedural inconvenience and implicit hesitancy of commercial banks to welcome farmers provides a niche market for the indigenous bankers.

These indigenous bankers and money lenders often exist with local support. Mostly, the unemployed people in the locality have no known source of regular personal income. They offer help and assistance to these indigenous bankers in organising the transfer of properties held as security for loans given to farmers and others. They do it by accepting some remuneration by whatever name one may refer to it. Whether anyone really becomes better off by accepting such petty sums is doubtful. The law intended to prevent corruption provides to proceed against the giver who can be proved by their own complaint while the person who has demanded, has the advantage of time till he is proved guilty.

The ruthless behaviour of money lenders caused the less-privileged borrowers often to commit suicide or run away, leaving their families in utter despondency. The government sometimes cracks down on these bankers but some of them overcome the troubles. They survive and prosper further. As long as the absence of an alternative short term financing option from state-run banks for small scale entrepreneurs and farmers remains, such banking ventures will co-exist with commercial banks.

There are also some other players in the market, like credit card companies, who are not labelled 'indigenous bankers' or 'money lenders'. But features like: high interest, lack of transparency and criminal onslaught on defaulters by taking the law into their own hands, make them similar in operation. Sometimes, inappropriate handling by officials from commercial banks gives an impression similar to these indigenous bankers.

Features of money lending practice that continue to exist in banks

Tradition and practices continue for years without change unless some intervention with the purpose of change takes place. Some deep-rooted traits of such money lenders stay the same, perhaps in a different style in commercial banks. The following are some of those functional areas where commercial banking apparently features money lending practices.

Gold loans

Banks encourage loans against gold ornaments on easy terms and conditions. If the purpose of the loan is to finance agriculture, it is still cheaper with a government subsidy on interest and it also gets classified under the 'priority sector[3]'. The probability of such loans going bad is less except when the gold ornament pledged is spurious or there is a steep fall in the gold price. If the gold value falls below the loan amount along with accrued interest, borrowers do not turn up at the bank but forfeit the loans. Gold ornaments are publicly auctioned by banks and money lenders quite easily. While money lenders charged higher interest rates and took greater care about the quality of gold collected as security against a loan, inadequately skilled bank employees sometimes end up with the custody of spurious gold ornaments that cannot be sold. The preference the commercial banks show in providing gold loans instead of loans based on activity and project plans to the people features the money lending embedded in commercial bank operations. It is easy to get bank loans against gold. The regulations provide ample opportunity for the public to obtain loans at a cheaper rate of interest than is normal for bank loans. Gold ornaments can be easily melted and sold. The high realisable value often of a small chain, a bangle or even a ring (approx. weight 8gm) provides a sum equivalent to the salary paid to an average public servant: 500 USD. With a large number of unemployed youths, petty crimes of chain-snatching or burglary are common in society. The role of banks in providing liquidity to gold is encouraging the import of gold on a massive scale, hoarding of gold and flourishing unaccounted money transactions. The role can be reasonably construed as the same as that played by money lenders in the past.

---

[3] http://www.rbi.org.in/scripts/FAQView.aspx?Id=87

End use of loan funds

Money lenders usually lend against land, house or ornaments. As long as the interest is paid, they are not too concerned about the end use of funds. Lending against gold has been discussed earlier. The next most popular way of lending is by accepting property as security. Although ensuring end use of funds is a condition of loans, it is impractical to do so for most of the agricultural and small scale loans because of the sheer number of such borrowers each branch has to supervise. Thus the lack of concern about end use continues.

Preference for collateral security for loans

Commercial banks look to hold the title deeds of land and properties that are owned by the applicant (or his close relative) as collateral security for loans – be it business or personal loans. For loans given to corporate, properties in the name of its directors or the company are sought as collateral for fixing the loan amount although it is not required for it to cover the requested loan amount fully. This makes bank loans for commercial enterprises inaccessible for people who do not own land or properties. This limitation is addressed by the Government's directions to cover loans up to Rs.10 Million (0.15USD) under a credit guarantee scheme and to earmark a certain proportion of loans to priority sectors such as agriculture, small business and small scale industries. However, such loans with precarious economic viability and scale often end up with the borrower becoming a defaulter and the loan no longer an asset for the bank. Money lenders deploy various methods of harassment that are socially unacceptable in a civilised society. They somehow get the documents transferred to them and then sell them off at their convenience to clear the loans. Banks, on the other hand, cannot deploy any uncivilised means to realise their dues. The only resort available to banks is through litigation. Thanks to Article 226 of the Indian Constitution that provides a constitutional right to the people of the country to use a court of law irrespective of the existence of legislation that is adequate to proceed against debtors, the realisation of bank dues gets prolonged indefinitely. In the process, public money lies unproductively in the form of Non-Performing Assets in the balance sheets of banks.

It is not proper to believe that bad loans are creations of the borrowers alone. Individual bank employees can provide many instances when the "wounded" borrower is nursed back to full health by proper discipline. That only highlights the fact that bank loans must be on the basis of viability and the performance of the entrepreneur. Lending based on the value of property offered as security is a feature that is being continued by bankers, and is a legacy from money lenders.

Usury

Charging an uneconomically high interest rate on bank loans is not an acceptable feature of the banking system in a civilised society. The rate of interest on bank loans is regulated by the Reserve Bank of India and is linked to the bank rate and the rate of interest payable on deposits. While the money market looks for a lower interest rate from the RBI, the majority of savers live on the interest earned on bank deposits in the absence of an alternate avenue to grow their savings and capital. However, when the share of bank loans in the capital funding in a business is high and the interest payable to them becomes a major expenditure to be tackled by the businessmen, this becomes a very common reason for loan defaults. In India the finance portion looms at around 80%. If the businessman chooses to manage the remaining 20% from unknown sources, an especially common practice among small scale entrepreneurs, at a higher rate of interest, the role played by the rate of interest in the business can be visualised. The rate of interest for loans has been around 10% for the last two decades except during 2001-3. Ultimately compound interest will become a key factor while pricing goods and services. The situation is the same as when people used to borrow money from money lenders. Shri Panandikar mentions in his book that interest could go up to 60% in those days. One might think that things have not changed, since the rate of interest levied by credit cards issued by banks' levy on credits can go up to an annual rate of interest of 51 per cent[4].

---

[4]   At 2.5% per month and billed for full duration from transaction date to the payment due date. If the bill date is 6th August and the transaction date is 7th July, the interest billed due on the payment date (28th August) will work out to 51% per annum.

Incomprehensible communication with borrowers

Another prominent feature of loans is the poor communication between banks and customers. People who used to borrow from money lenders were left with the minimum information on the amount periodically they were obliged to return. There will not be any notice ahead of due dates. The feeling of a bank borrower is more or less the same as they fill up lengthy documents full of banking and legal jargon. At the time of taking the loan, most of them do not bother to go through these agreements in detail, especially the fine print. For that matter, these agreements are presumed to be drafted in consultation with the experts in banks and not subjected to change. One wonders whether the bank officials who assist customers to complete the documentation are aware of their contents. The rights and obligations of a borrower are seldom explained in simple and understandable language causing a breach of transparency and leaving sufficient cracks for misinterpretation and misinformation. The legacy of such superiority of the lender over the customer can be attributed to money lending practices.

Banks prefer existing borrowers over new ones

Banks prefer to grow by extending loans to existing borrowers rather than entertaining new customers. This trust in existing customers is core to money lending too. If not the existing ones, banks in India prefer to draw on customers of other banks rather than unknown, new clients. While new entrepreneurs find it difficult to get an introduction into a bank for finance, those who are already enjoying bank finance easily get additional amounts. For a new entrepreneur, money lenders and banks appear alike; perhaps the former may be easier to work on.

Sanitise banks from this legacy

Even though thousands of years have passed since people started saving and banking institutions have been with us for centuries, the banking system has not been able to keep pace with the major changes happening around us. It is now very important to understand the significance of having a sound banking system relieved of historical catches like money lending. To put it in simple terms, standardisation of processes and bringing changes into the banking system are urgently required to match the developments happening in other 'aids to trade' areas in commerce, such as communication, transport and insurance. For this purpose, opening up banking to major players of developed countries will help Indian banks to benchmark and improve. History and experience are rings in the ears of bankers. But today, what should spur them to change is the probable evolution that is unfolding. There was a lot of trust between farmers and money lenders and as mentioned in the book by Shri Panandikar, money lending became a not-so-appreciated profession in the society 'owing to the loss of the village community and the legal protection given to the borrowers'. The trust that is missing between bankers and customers has to be brought back for the stability of the economy.

2. BANKS IN INDIA SO FAR

- at a snail's pace

World over, banking would have commenced more or less around the same time. But depending upon the economic and political environment in which banks operated, the pace of their evolution differed from country to country. Today banking exists in various stages of refinement. The transparency demanded by the industry, the certainty provided by regulators and the level of interference by the political system pushes banks into an environment of various degrees of competition, and various levels of efficiency. Competition provides motivation to improve the internal systems of banks and to initiate strategic steps for accelerating growth. Innovation becomes a constant function of efficiency in any industry and such is the case with banking. By adopting proven modern marketing techniques, banks can enhance their scale of operation and benefit from the economy of large scale. The different environments in which banks operate thus set the pace for the evolution of banking in each country.

Recent major changes in India's banking environment were brought about in the 1990s by opening up the economy for globalisation, liberalisation (in licensing) and privatisation of India's trade and industry. The government allowed banks to set up with IT as their delivery platform in the private sector. Domestic remittances and international remittances were made easy. Payment and settlement systems started utilising the power of computing and communication networks. State-owned banks, significant with their more than 90 per cent hold in the industry and business till then, also responded to the changing landscape.

Going back to the period after India gained independence in 1947, the main task before the newly-elected government after years of poverty, illiteracy and a complex attitude to work[5] in the population, as well as the struggle for independence, was to bring forth simple strategies to uplift the large and fast-growing population. Those who provided leadership during the struggle for independence, when bestowed with the gargantuan task of building a nation, were groping in the dark looking for a model, whether it be capitalism or socialism, for faster growth. The concept of excluding non-domestic enterprises from participating in the economic growth of the nation continued for many more years. Leaders preferred to rely on home-grown wisdom as opposed to fresh ideas from other countries where poverty was being successfully tackled, supported by the idea that each country is distinct and unique. Since most people in India were involved in agriculture then, the government invested more money, time and energy for supporting cultivation and other allied economic activities. Industry, which provides more employment and faster growth, needed capital. The services sector, which would have catapulted the other two sectors of agriculture and industry ahead, also found want of capital. In the 1990s, the services sector was given the importance it deserved and it thrived after liberalisation. There was a dramatic change in the way systems functioned in transport, communications, banking, insurance and others. People are the fulcrum of the service industry. The growing population that was considered a deterrent to growth in the 1950s turned into an asset to be pressed into service, to accelerate growth. The number of millionaires and billionaires increased and so did the nation's foreign exchange reserve. However, the initial surge in banking did not last. Many daredevil banks, promoted by business and industry houses, and by Indians both in India and abroad, flopped. Many of them were destined to be merged with bigger ones as was the case in the past.

Indian government holds control of banks and the banking system but treads cautiously. Budget speeches by finance ministers over the years reveal that various governments rely on traditional wisdom and turn away from

---

[5]   People had adapted to live for 3-4 decades with the freedom movement founded on non-violence but built on an attitude of disobedience, strike against managements and a mob culture that stops implementation of legislation.

taking far-reaching decisions and stirring up a hornet's nest. Of course the governments under Indira Gandhi and Manmohan Singh were exceptions. Also, the formation of the Imperial Bank of India by the East India Company, via the merger of three presidency banks, might be the biggest historic event in the annals of banking in India.

The Imperial Bank of India, set up by the East India Company in 1921, served the British Government for many years. After independence, the bank was liquidated and the State Bank of India (SBI) was set up. The new bank was required to play a stellar role in the development of banking in free India. In the history of the SBI[6], as the compilation of its history states: 'The concept of banks as mere depositories of the community's savings and lenders to creditworthy parties was soon to give way to the concept of purposeful banking, sub-serving the growing and diversified financial needs of planned economic development. The State Bank of India was destined to act as the pace setter in this respect and lead the Indian banking system into the exciting field of national development'.

Further, the bank management was given a clear blueprint to organise its operation. In the Chapter 10 Epilogue of the compilation, it is stated: 'The mission of the Bank was to offer constituents, every reasonable facility in the transaction of their business so that the best banking services obtainable in India could be rendered to them. Prompt, courteous and helpful attention to constituents and a proper spirit of service among all members of the bank's staff were insisted upon. Efforts were simultaneously directed towards eradication of slackness or inefficiency so that high standard required by the bank was at all times maintained.'

The mandate was clear and concise. Initiatives were comprehensive but as one could infer from the same compilation, there were demands on the leadership to convert the mission into action. In 1969, fourteen years after the SBI was set up, the government felt that the progress made was falling short of expectations and decided to gather together more banks into the state's programme for the development of banking in the country. Accordingly, the ownership of fourteen large banking companies in the

---

[6]   The Evolution of the State Bank of India - volume 3, page 631

country was taken over by the government. The move was initiated by Mrs Indira Gandhi when she was India's Prime Minister. The objective of 'Nationalisation of Banks', according to the preamble to the legislation, was to control the heights of the economy and to meet progressively and serve better the needs of development of the economy in conformity with national policy and for matters connected therewith or incidental thereto.

After nationalisation in 1969, the idea of involving post offices to provide savings bank facilities to the people was introduced in parliament. During her budget speech on 28th February 1970, Prime Minister Mrs Indira Gandhi (holding the additional portfolio of finance) highlighted the important role that the large network of post offices in the country could play in extending banking facilities. "The extension of banking to rural areas will serve the same purpose. Even today, our postal system extends to many areas which cannot be covered by banks in the near future. The postal system, therefore, also needs to be harnessed for greater mobilisation of savings. At present our small savings schemes, including Post Office Savings Bank accounts, offer facilities for savings with a number of tax concessions. These tax concessions, however, are not of much interest to the rural population or to low income groups, which by and large, are not subject to taxation of income. To these groups, a higher rate of interest would be more attractive than a lower rate with corresponding tax concessions. Accordingly, it is proposed to introduce a new series of timed deposits, recurring deposits and savings certificates, which will carry higher rates of interest without any special tax concessions."

The incentive envisaged for saving with post offices was tax benefits. Though these large networks of post offices and nationalised banks could have grown well on their own, the complex taxation system of the country discouraged people to go public with their actual earnings. They avoided banks and were reluctant to settle debts through banks. Their trust of close friends and business partners helped indigenous bankers to prosper while expansion of banking continued to be difficult for banks or post offices.

Therefore, another round of nationalisation was carried out in 1980 to reaffirm the government's commitment to its objectives by transferring ownership of six more banks. The preamble to the legislation[7] stated: 'to control the heights of the economy, to meet progressively, and serve better the needs of the development of the economy and to promote the welfare of the people in conformity with the policy of the State towards securing the principles laid down in clauses (b) and (c) of article 39 of the constitution and for matters therewith or incidental thereto'. Article 39 in the Indian Constitution refers to ownership and control of material resources and concentration of wealth. The objective of nationalising six big banks from the private sector was to prevent them from functioning in such a way that wealth was concentrated among a few people.

According to the RBI report of the working group on restructuring weak public sector banks dated 4th October 1999, 'by the 1990s the public sector banks had 90 per cent share in the country's banking business. By March 1992 all the public sector banks together had a phenomenal branch network of 60,646 branches and held deposits of Rs.110,000 crores'. For a fair understanding of the scenario, it may be mentioned here that the postal department mobilised small savings of Rs.50,279 crores by March 1991. The stage was set, ready for a major shake-up in the hands of Dr Manmohan Singh.

It is worth recognising the contribution of Dr Manmohan Singh who served as India's Finance Minister from 1991-96. He became the Chief Economic Adviser to the Government of India in 1972 at the age of 40 after an illustrious international career in academia. Later on, he was appointed the Governor of the Reserve Bank of India from 1982-85 and the Deputy Chief of the Planning Commission headed by Mr Rajiv Gandhi as Prime Minister during 1985–87. After the 1991 national election, Mr P V Narasimha Rao became Prime Minister and Dr Singh was made Finance Minister in the newly formed government. Dr Singh initiated some meaningful changes in the banking system. Being an experienced economist, Dr Singh became very popular both domestically and internationally as the finance minister who salvaged the country from financial uncertainty during the 1990s.

---

7   The Banking Companies (acquisition and transfer of undertakings) Act 1980 (40 of 1980)

Almost everyone agrees that he did a marvellous job. The Indian National Congress party chose Dr Singh as India's next Prime Minister from 2004-14.

In his 1992 Budget speech as finance minister Dr Manmohan Singh spoke about the banking system as follows:- 'Our banking system and financial institutions are at the very core of the financial infrastructure in the economy. The widening and deepening of our financial system have helped the spread of institutional finance over a vast area and have contributed significantly to the augmentation of our savings rate, particularly financial savings. This has been a most commendable achievement, but our financial system has developed certain rigidities and some weaknesses which we must address now. The objective of reform in the financial sector would be to preserve its basic role as an essential adjunct to economic growth and competitive efficiency, while improving the health of its institutions. In this task, it is essential to ensure capital adequacy, introduce prudential norms and improve profitability of our commercial banks and financial institutions'.

He further informed parliament, 'I propose to appoint a high level committee to consider all relevant aspects of structure, organisation, functions and procedures of the financial system. This committee would advise the Government on appropriate measures that would be needed to enhance the viability and health of our financial sector so that it can better serve the needs of the economy without any sacrifice of the canons and principles of a sound financial system'. Dr M Narasimhan, his predecessor as Governor of RBI, was appointed to head the committee and the report gave a new direction to banks in India[8].

The significant measures suggested were the opening of more banks in the private sector and adopting a liberal approach towards the opening of offices of foreign banks in India. These steps enhanced the scope of a competitive framework for banking. The new private and foreign banks have higher

---

[8]   M Narasimham was the first and so far the only Governor to be appointed from the Reserve Bank cadre, having joined the Bank as a Research Officer in the Economic Department, and served as Additional Secretary, Department of Economic Affairs. He was chairperson of the Committee on the Financial System, 1991 and the Committee of Banking Sector Reforms, 1998.

productivity levels with information technology as their backbone. The increasing share of the private banks during the last few years in the banking business reflects their competitive edge and their potential.

In spite of such major steps, many parts of the country continue to be under-banked or unbanked. When Dr Singh was Prime Minister, during his Budget speech for the financial year 2009-10, President Mr Pranab Kumar Mukherjee, then finance minister, stated:

'Despite the expansion of banking network in the country, there are still some areas that remain under-banked or unbanked. A sub-committee of State Level Bankers Committee (SLBC) will identify such areas and formulate an action plan for providing banking facilities to all these areas in the next 3 years.' In his 2012-13 Budget he announced: 'A central Know Your Customer (KYC) depository will be developed in 2012-13 to avoid multiplicity of registration and data upkeep'.

From the above excerpts from Budget speeches, it can be seen that the need to expand the banking network was well understood and acknowledged by government and so was the importance of involving people at the bottom-most administrative tier of 'blocks'[9] to achieve results. In order to protect the banking system from antisocial elements and criminals, proper identification of those opening bank accounts was intended to be managed through the KYC depository.

In his budget speech on 28th February 2015, Finance Minister Mr Arun Jaitley placed before Parliament the following proposal: "The Government is committed to increasing access of the people to the formal financial system. In this context, Government proposes to utilize the vast Postal network with nearly 154,000 points of presence spread across the villages of the country." His speech informed Parliament: "Pradhan Mantri Jan-Dhan Yojana (PMJDY) was launched on 28th August, 2014 to achieve the objective of financial inclusion by extending financial services to the large hitherto

---

[9]   The country is divided into states and union territories and they are further divided into 'districts'. These districts are further divided into 'blocks' for easy administration.

unserved population of the country and to unlock its growth potential. The Yojana envisages universal access to banking facilities with at least one basic banking account for every household, financial literacy, and access to credit and insurance. The beneficiaries would receive a RuPay Debit Card having inbuilt accident insurance cover of Rs.1 lakh. In addition, there is a life insurance cover of Rs.30,000/- to those who open their bank accounts for the first time between 15th August 2014 and 26th January 2015 and meet other eligibility conditions of the Yojana. As on 28th January 2015, 12.31 crore bank accounts have been opened, out of which 7.36 crore are in rural areas and 4.95 crore in urban areas". As at the end of the financial year 2015-2016[10], the total number of such accounts opened has gone up to 21.42 crores and the top ten banks are opening half of them.

In conclusion, the following objectives of banking at the time of setting up the SBI, continue to be not yet achieved.

- To ascertain the requirements of traders, manufacturers, cultivators
- Knowledge of trade, industries and crops in the districts
- Detailed compilation of instructions
- System of audit and inspection existing to secure accounting efficiency and integrity
- The bank was placed on an exalted pedestal in the areas of business, profitability, internal discipline and above all credibility

---

[10]   http://pmjdy.gov.in/ArchiveFile/2016/3/30.03.2016.pdf

3. BANKS TODAY

'Experiences change our expectations and the expectations demand changes'

While Indian banks struggle to get the required footwork right, banks world over have become accustomed to providing easy banking for the people by the fullest use of Information Technology (IT). It may be interesting to attempt to understand what people expect from banks today.

a) Currency notes and coins

They expect clean notes in convenient denominations and are glad to leave agents for deposit if currency notes are dirty or mutilated.

b) Bank accounts

The public expect a hassle free account opening process. While banks may have to insist on documentary proof of identification, address, tax department registration, etc., as per the rules and regulations, the public would expect that banks provide them with a list of alternate documents in the case of those who might not readily possess some of these documents. They would expect, in today's networked digital world, once a bank account is opened with a bank, opening more accounts with other banks would be easy and need not be subjected to the same processes once again. A bank account opened is expected to serve as a satisfactory testimonial for all utility service providers such as cooking gas, electricity and water and an easy gateway for all types of accounts required for making investments such as fixed deposits, mutual funds, shares and stocks, government bonds, insurance, etc. The account opened also is seen as a stepping stone for obtaining consumer loans or home loans (mortgage loans). They expect banks to provide credit cards for shopping. An all-in-one relationship is something that is expected from a bank. A bank passbook, usually issued with a photograph of the account holder attested by the bank official, still holds considerable value and provides convenience for them.

c) Interest on bank deposits

Bank accounts are opened for keeping savings and the customer would expect reasonable compensation by way of interest to compensate for the loss in value due to inflation. The interest on fixed deposits is expected to provide in order to take care of monthly expenses. Longer term deposits for five to ten years, or even more if permitted, are utilised by people for keeping their retirement benefits safely. Firms and other associations or incorporated bodies keep employees' compulsory savings in long term deposits. Enterprises park liquid surplus in short term fixed deposits for improving their profit. All of them expect that banks would not forfeit full interest in case they have to discontinue the term. At the least interest at savings rate is expected.

d) Personal or Relationship banking

In today's relationship banking culture, a personal account holder would expect to receive an ATM card, credit card and a passbook. They would also expect to collect IDs, passwords, etc., for internet banking and mobile banking on the same day. They expect to receive alerts from their banks whenever certain operations are carried out in their account, when payments to banks are due, or when their deposits mature. They would expect information on the pre-approved overdraft limit, personal insurance cover for them and also various unique codes (used for clearing, interbank payments, international payments, etc.) for receiving remittances into the account. They would also expect to have the contact details (email, mobile phone, etc.), of the relationship manager or bank officials for one-to-one contact in case of necessity.

e) Advisory services

They expect their banker to advise them correctly on investments they can make within their bank and outside their bank as wealth management solutions. They would also like to be advised on the foreign exchange they earn or receive once in a while. Banks are expected to provide information on good home loan projects and other value added services which banks provide, such as locker facility, safe custody, loyalty programs, and tie-ups for entertainment like cinema, air travel, hotels, etc.

f) Finance for business

Entrepreneurs including all those professional firms, traders, manufacturers, service providers, farmers and others who are dedicated to production, expect their banks to provide capital in easy repayable terms without putting many restrictions on their day-to-day conduct of business. Instead of multiple need-based limits, they would be happy to have a single line of credit for operations. They expect their banks to provide this facility after properly taking into consideration their business plan. They expect their banks to understand the risk fully and advise them on the choice of insurance, refinance, various methods of bank finance, market borrowing, multiple banking, credit guarantee schemes, etc. Ultimately they will be happy if their banker provides a one-stop solution for all their fund requirements at the most economic rates. A relationship or accounts manager who can do the shopping will enable entrepreneurs to concentrate on production processes.

g) Financial consulting

The expectations discussed above give rise to the need for financial consulting. Whether banks perform this function under their umbrella or run a separate division for this service is just a formality. Eagerness to save on overheads, mainly by better management of taxes, and technical knowhow from other countries through merchant banking, work towards achieving professional excellence. The public expects their bank to help them redesign their products and processes. The banking process must be more transparent with increased certainty. Banks are expected to provide instant support that can help the customer shop easily without any worry about funds or liquidity.

Basically, banks should be trustworthy, the bank staff reliable and the safety of savings assured. The customer has to feel comfortable to approach a bank for finance - be it for an emergency loan, regular line of credit or even a long term repayment loan. Banks are looked upon by government as support for converting the enterprising ideas of people into economic development of the nation. Banks world over were all set to make changes to reorient their products and services to match customer expectations during the last two or three decades, with computers taking centre stage of the revolution.

4. CHANGES IN BANKING

'Adapting to changes is evolution'

"The change is the only constant." "No man ever steps in the same river twice, for it is not the same river and he is not the same man." These quotes on 'Changes' are understood to be from the Greek philosopher Heraclitus. In the context of discussion of banks, one can say that banks truly are not the same. The changes that take place in banks are from every corner. Changes come from their customers, development, and process enablers like IT cause a paradigm shift in the real sense.

What matters here is the speed at which banks can notice the changes happening around them and the speed at which they can adapt to those changes. During the last two to three decades, a lot of changes have taken place in the way banks operate all over the world. These were not just limited to banking but to other sectors as well where banks are important for development, such as industries, farming, trade and services.

Most of the changes were based on the need for sharing knowledge, the growth of science, especially in electronics, and the prevalence of peaceful relationships with neighbouring countries. These developments resulted in

a) Globalisation
b) The IT Revolution
c) New management ideas
d) New selling ideas

Globalisation

After the two World Wars, leaders of nations engaged in fixing their economies for the welfare of their people. Better understanding prevailed between them and paved the way for international cooperation and globalisation. However, for fear of exploitation by other countries, various Indian governments tried to live within their means and indigenous knowledge. Neither radical changes were envisaged nor plans for capital flow conceived. The need to import a large volume of defence equipment in view of hostile neighbour nations, neutralised benefits from the income received from Indians working abroad. The payment obligations to outside nations exceeded and weakened the Indian currency against the currencies of other nations. This phenomenon kept the nation inflationary throughout.

By 1990, the government found it would be difficult to honour international commitments. This paved the way for the government to take certain radical decisions that lead to liberalisation, privatisation and globalisation. As a result, economic policies changed and hope emerged. India's image as an attractive destination for investments improved. The fear of exploitation by richer nations that lingered among leaders at the time of independence proved unfounded. The nation derived further strength with other large countries like China, Brazil and Russia and accelerated their growth plans.

As far as banks in India are concerned the main impact of globalisation came from the way the forex business was handled. The government replaced the Foreign Exchange Regulation Act with a 'friendly' Foreign Exchange Management Act 2000. The change augmented the surge of trade with other nations. There was an increase in imports, exports, travel abroad and visits by tourists from other countries. People were allowed to keep with them a reasonable amount of foreign currency legally. Earlier even this was punishable. Foreign currency inflow in the form of foreign direct investment (FDI) and remittances from Indians resident abroad (NRI) increased. Some of the globally active Foreign Institutional Investors (FIIs) were allowed to invest and thereby well-run companies found easier ways to raise capital. On the other hand, regulations on investment abroad in the form of Overseas Direct Investment were relaxed, to enable companies to sell produce by opening offices abroad. Such offices helped them to market their products abroad better. The process of handling and reporting forex transactions to the RBI was simplified.

As companies such as TCS, Infosys and Sathyam, with large numbers of employees, were popular for sending their employees abroad, remittances from abroad increased. Indians who emigrated in the thirties had by now become rich and welcomed the change in India. Easing in the process of the repatriation of deposits made in India also attracted deposits from Non-Resident Indians and Persons of Indian Origin. Though they are not domiciled in India even now, they can save with banks there. Emigration and immigration increased. Both contributed to the increase in the remittance and forex business for banks in India. Even though there is no source known to ascertain the exact number of Indians and people of Indian origin living abroad, it is estimated that about 28.45 million of Indians, roughly 2% of India's domestic population, live in as many as 175 nations. Two thirds of them live in rich countries like the US, the UK, Australia, the Gulf, Canada and other countries with the potential for big savings and remittances.

While globalisation helped banks in India secure savings from Indians abroad and enabled them to support enterprises with foreign currency loans and global tie-ups, it also provided Indian banks with opportunities to benchmark their processes with banks abroad with the help of internationally famous Management and IT Consultants. Thus the need was felt for implementation of a Core Banking Solution as the standard platform for banks in India.

IT and banking products

Initially there was confusion as to the merits of going for a centralised database management system for Indian banks, considering the vastness of the country, unevenly developed sites, the dubious power supply and communications network. But with the speed at which IT was evolving and providing viable alternative solutions, the core banking solution, featuring a centralised database management system, was found ideal by Indian banks in order to accelerate growth.

Basically, changes were brought about in the way in which banks stored the information of customers, the speed at which managers shared information among themselves and the way banks addressed the need to obtain data uniformly. Existing banks had to deviate from their legacy and systems struggled, while banks that started anew could straight away show progress in cost control, expansion and product differentiation.

As banking processes became interlaced with legalities and a lot of practicalities, bank employees may have felt the hurried onslaught of changes to be detrimental. Employees are sensitive to changes. A few of the changes brought into Indian banking are discussed in the following paragraphs in order to comprehend the sensitivity of the employees.

a) Introduction for opening an account

Bank accounts were opened only for those individuals who were introduced by bank employees, existing customers or even by their existing bankers. This practice was designed to prevent the opening of misnamed accounts. However, currently bank accounts are supposed to be opened for individuals who bring along with them their photo identity and proof of residence. Documents commonly accepted are a driving licence, Indian passport, PAN card issued by tax authorities, election card issued by the Election Commission of India and Aadhar card issued by the government, introduced during Dr Manmohan Singh's premiership. Bank officials are not equipped to verify these documents from the database of the issuing authorities. Hence forged documents might go undetected on an overcrowded day at a bank and misnamed accounts could get opened, except for the due diligence applied by the bank official. Until the database of issuers of these identity documents are accessible to bank officials, there will be doubt as to the adequacy of documentary proof for establishing the identity of the person opening the account.

Moreover, these identity documents are not available for all Indian citizens. Presently hope lies in the Aadhar card issued by the Unique Identification

Authority of India. 75% of India's population has been issued with this card[11].

b) Operating bank accounts

Earlier one had to visit the bank branch where the account was opened for operations. Bank officials had to confirm the customer's identity before proceeding to serve them. This safeguarded banks from impersonation. However, with the core banking system being in place and scanned images being available at all branches, the relevance of the branch has theoretically vanished. Bank officials still find it difficult to handle requests from strangers. The responsibility for identifying the customer used to lie with bank officials rather than with the customer. Seemingly this has not changed. Anomalies in the images, a negligently-indexed picture on the database, or difficulty in communicating with customers from other parts of the country, may result in not-so-smooth customer service. While IT has enabled banks to reduce the number of people visiting branches, a foolproof database is necessary for existing banks to fully benefit from the change. The gargantuan task of setting up an accurate and complete database is the most significant challenge of this change.

c) Operating loan accounts

Officers who used to take care of loans and advances were referred to as 'field officers'. They source loan applications, evaluate them on their technical feasibility and economic viability and thereafter obtain sanction for the loans from senior level officers. Once approval is obtained, the officer will help the customer complete the loan documentation, disburse the loan stage by stage or as appraised, carry out inspection on site to satisfy the safety of the loan asset and remind the customer of the repayment of dues. Banks relied on the statement of the loan requesters regarding loans taken from the same bank or other banks and verified in writing the conduct of these accounts.

---

[11]   788 million 9/3/2015 - https://portal.uidai.gov.in/uidwebportal/dashboard.do

IT revolutionised the way loan applications are sourced, processed and disbursed. Banks are able to deploy 'knowledge workers' to source loan applications, especially in the retail market. Credit Information reports are now available for banks in order to verify the credentials of the proposed borrowers from credit information companies. Banks have developed computer applications that can undertake all the required analysis of information and prepare a loan proposal ready for sanction. There is an according reduction in dependency on field officers. One can browse websites for market information on products or manufacturing processes and industry outlook, unlike in the past when field officers used to scavenge through newspapers for information on industry and market conditions to assess the feasibility of a project.

Another change is the reduction of errors in computing the interest on loans. There are no more disputes. It is easy to fix the repayment schedule. It is now straightforward to share information on customers privately among banks. Ultimately more loans can be handled by an officer than used to be the case. However, the personal touch with the borrower or ownership of loans has been lost. A deteriorating loan may fail to be noticed at the early stages. This issue may overshadow the benefits of changes caused by IT on loan banking until the concept of 'relationship banking' stabilises.

d) Issue and payment of bank drafts and other remittances

Other than for operating their bank accounts, people visited banks for obtaining or encashing bank drafts (DD). There are credit instruments similar to DD, such as Pay Order, Banker's Cheque and Manager's Cheque, etc. They are paid at the bank's same office of issue, compared to DDs which are payable at any other office of issue. Other transactions similar to DDs are mail (MT)/telegraphic transfer (TT). In the case of MT/TT, no instrument is handed over to the applicant but arrangements exist within banks for depositing the sum into the account of the beneficiary mentioned in the application.

Before the IT revolution, considerable labour was deployed into this not-so-remunerative business. It was not so remunerative because of the rigorous paperwork to safeguard against fraud and reliance on national telecommunication systems. Even though details of the applicant's name, address and signature have to be obtained for future reference in case of any need to reissue or cancel the instruments, since tax officials found it easy to source details of tax defaulters from bank records, applications were often submitted incompletely or incorrectly. In most cases, bank officials used to rely on signatures to establish identity, or production of the counterfoil of the application for reissue. Banks used to send advices to paying offices promptly to confirm the issue of the draft. Receipt of this advice depended upon the postal system. Legally payment was not allowed to be delayed for want of receipt of this advice as these instruments are payable on demand. A few large scale bank frauds occurred in connection with payment of DDs which were later found to be forged.

The time between issue and payment of a cheque was earlier fixed at a maximum of six months; later this period was reduced to three months. Some traders, who usually restrict their business operation among a trustworthy few, utilised this duration of three months for exchanging DDs among themselves like a large value currency note for their payments without encashing them. On the last date of validity, the beneficiary named on the DD (the payee) encashes it. There was another common practice of purchasing a DD with cash. Tax authorities have restricted the issue of DDs against cash up to Rs.50,000. This was overcome by taking multiple drafts, by applying with different names or by applying for DDs from different banks. These practices were adopted for the continuation of business with unaccounted money and avoidance of payment of tax to the government.

The revolution brought about by IT changed these processes entirely. Since everyone knows that the details of applicants can now be picked up by the core banking system (CBS) itself, utilising the banking system for doing business with unaccounted money would have been minimised. Since the details of the purchaser and beneficiary of DDs are viewable at the paying branch instantly, forgery-related loss is alleviated. The cost of operations and fund settlement between banks would have been reduced and banks can now offer these services affordably at low remuneration. Real Time Gross Settlement systems have replaced the MT/TT business. The revolution has helped banks considerably to eliminate antisocial elements from using banking systems for their activities. Bank officials are happier with a reduction in reconciliation work relating to the large number of credit instruments. CBS and other computer applications in banks have taken care of the issues arising out of delay in all related processes, enquiries from tax departments, the labour related to despatch of advices, issue of identification of beneficiaries, payment of cash beyond the prescribed limit over the counter, etc.

e) Collection of payment of cheques or discounting them

Cheques and DDs are similar except that DDs are issued and paid by banks. To that extent beneficiaries are assured of payment. Banks thus handle cheques in two different ways - one way is to send the cheque to the paying bank for payment and pay the customer on realisation. Alternately, to advance the cheque amount to the beneficiary by discounting and then send the cheque for realisation. When a cheque is discounted, the discounting bank has faith in the paying bank to remit the cheque amount in due course. The process includes accepting cheques, scrutinising for error, despatching to the paying bank, receiving payment through a common bank and marking off the payments in the case of discounting or depositing into the beneficiary's account in the case of collection.

Troubles that used to be faced by bankers were the delay in receipt of funds from the paying banks, compensation payable to customers for the period of delay, loss of instruments in transit, loss on account of forgery when discounted and other issues arising from improper work flow.

With electronic banking in place, such interpersonal payments using cheques have been reduced. Documents sent through the post can now be tracked and the date of delivery can be confirmed. Banks holding cheques and delaying the processing deliberately can be fixed. Thanks to CBS in place among banks, collection of cheques takes place more through clearing centre branches of banks than between bank branches where customers hold accounts.

f) Clearing cheques

Collection of cheques through clearing did not face the difficulties of delayed realisation and loss of instruments in transit. Customers were able to utilise the funds on the third day after depositing cheques with their bank. The problem faced by banks was that all branches could not be made part of the clearing system. With CBS in place, the number of instruments has increased. Bank branches sent instruments to their own clearing centre branches for quick realisation. Now they are experiencing a different set of problems, such as error in data entry, increased volume of transactions and reduced time for organising funds for intra-day settlement with other banks. The three days have now been reduced to instant transfers by electronic transfers, same day speed clearing and Real Time Gross Settlement Systems. Instruments presented for payment through usual clearing are given three days for realisation.

People used to wait indefinitely for information from their banks regarding the fate of cheques handed over to them. This has become a thing of the past as the IT revolution increases the speed of processing bank transactions accurately.

g) Daily checking of transactions and balancing

The accuracy of balances in each of the millions of individual accounts depended upon the numerical aptitude of bank employees. (Banks started using desk-top calculators from the eighties.) There used to be a system of jotting down balances in all individual accounts and then the sum of the outstanding balances was tallied with the total of the branch General Ledger. A Trial Balance was prepared from all General Ledger account balances and ensured that the numbers were correct. It used to be laborious work. This system of confirmation of individual bank account balances periodically (weekly or monthly) gave an authenticity to the passbook or statements of account issued to customers. Fraudulent transactions put through either erroneously or deliberately were detected at the earliest instance. The computerisation of banks relieved bank employees of this arduous job.

h) Reconciliation between bank branches

Each bank branch was treated legally as a separate entity as far as a customer was concerned. Therefore, for all payments and settlements between the banks' offices, a system of manual reconciliation used to be in place. The most common inter-bank transactions include: issue and payment of demand drafts, MT/TT, payments of cheques received for collection, travellers cheques, international payments, etc. Reconciliation depended upon the accuracy of the identifying number of the instrument for which the payment was sought or made. It also depended on the quickest time to mark off the original entries. Outstanding entries were treated as receivables or payables and aged outstanding receivables were like bad debts and were subject to provisioning in the profit and loss account. This accounting requirement demanded deployment of a large labour force to detect errors and initiate steps to mark off, entry by entry. Commonly in Indian banks, this responsibility is assumed by the organisation even though the outstanding entries in the real sense represent omissions in processing committed by individual employees, and poor follow-up.

With CBS in place, the whole job ceases to exist and the large number of employees engaged in the unproductive task is saved for utilisation elsewhere. Thus IT has helped banks to improve the productivity of employees in a significant way.

New management ideas

Changes do not happen in isolation. They bring about changes in other areas as well. Ultimately all the changes will result in a revolution. Many new management ideas too emerged as a result of the IT revolution. Some of them were in the areas of selling and marketing techniques. Some of those management ideas that brought about changes in the banking industry are discussed below:

a) Business Process Reengineering (BPR)

Process improvement is a continuous job. Banking processes are refined and modified from time to time to suit changing needs. However, such modifications preclude a simple alternative revamp of the whole process. The BPR process was to rewrite the processes fully from the start to the end. The expected result after implementation of BPR was to reduce the 'turnaround time' for providing service. Challenges were the rigid conventions meticulously followed by banks for a long time and the vast network of branches operating different vernaculars of people, multiple layers of management levels, demand for the same information in different formats, etc. The way IT was evolving, finding solutions to such complex issues became simpler, easier and less costly.

b) Centralised processing

Computers became less costly, communication networks became stable and faster, and the processors in the computer became faster. In this scenario, centralised data storage and retrieval systems became ideal for banking solutions. These lead banks to adopt standardised processes across all branches. Further, centralised data management systems helped their MIS and developed Decision Support Systems based on data warehousing and data mining tools. Managements established centralised processing of account opening, processing of retail loans, clearing, discounting, etc. Centralised despatch of account statements, ATM cards, and passbooks become possible. This centralisation enabled banks to handle large transactions with routine staff and thus increase their productivity. However, a feeling in the minds of employees sank in, of distance from customers.

c) Risk Management systems

Risk management is on the agenda of all management, but the focus on risk was looked at in general. With special tools for measurement of risk available from IT, risk management germinated in the minds of bank managements as a system to be set up. Historically, loans were approved on the basis of safety margins and the security available. The probability of loss was not ascertained by logical systems. There was no risk assessment, risk mitigation or risk compensation. Other non-banking losses were not properly ascertained and analysed. The changes in the risk management systems made operational risk of equal importance to credit and investment risk.

d) Human Resources Management Systems (HRMS)

Even though employees are the most important and significant resources of banks, being service organisations, adequate efforts to improve their productivity were not undertaken. This may be due to the inadequacy of systems for collecting data for analysis. Usually employees are given regular routine training. Placements were centred on the government regulations on mandatory services and the opinion of their seniors. Most of them progressed in their career by virtue of their keenness to learn on the job and the experience gained by working under a good supervisor. As a result of the IT revolution, Enterprises Resources Planning (ERP) solutions became popular and investment was found rewarding. Similar software solutions were also developed in house by banks or outsourced. Thus HRMS found a place among the many management systems in banks. As a result management can now obtain information on the number of employees, their individual experience, skills and even contact details from their desktop. Indian banks, often having a large number of employees, found HRMS an important tool to enhance employee productivity.

New selling ideas

Banks used to function like a library where a visitor can choose books from whatever is available. It is the borrower of books who takes the initiative to find books in a library. But banks cannot function profitably, if they function like a library. Changes in IT and management ideas paved the way for changes in selling products and services in banking too. With the centralised database management systems in place, people could visit any bank branch for their banking requirements. ATMs and bank kiosks made banking operations 24 x 7 possible. The changes brought about in processes threw out surplus employees available for deployment. It was in this scenario that new selling ideas cropped up.

It was debatable whether government-owned banks could go for class banking instead of mass banking. However within the available framework, some banks used to set up specialised branches and thus became competitive with better ambiance. They proved successful and proved that it was not difficult for government-owned banks to adopt the new popular selling ideas. Separating retail and wholesale banking was one such idea. While in retail, banks designed suitable schemes to cater to a particular group of people; for wholesale customers, consultative selling or customised products were adopted.

Other concepts that brought changes include loan repayment under Equated Monthly Instalment (EMI), separation of loan processing charges from interest rates, pre-approved loans on the basis of minimum information, etc. Some innovative products such as flexi-deposits, multi-option deposits, loans on phones, etc., became easily possible in the computerised environment. Banks were able to do cross-selling and up-selling to their existing customers utilising the large volume of data available from the CBS.

Conclusion

Globalisation, the IT revolution, and new ideas in management and selling changed many aspects of India's banking system. A lot of labour was saved and the speed of service to customers improved. Antisocial elements too benefitted from these changes. Cheques, currency notes, bank guarantees, etc., became riskier products to handle than in the past. Employees needed more vigilant supervision.

Different verticals within the same management could be established to provide specialised service at the most economic rates. A single line of credit could be approved to customers, instead of multiple loans with varying terms and conditions. There was improvement in the consistency and transparency of the banks' dealings. Errors were reduced and time saved thereby. Banks managed new offices with existing employees. Despite managing these changes, Indian banks still continue to be at the receiving end of criticism of their efficiency.

5. THE UNDERWHELMING SCENARIO

'Not even a perfect market'

Something would have befallen the banks in India for they were not able to progress as much as their western counterparts. This is in spite of steps being taken in banking from the nineties for globalisation, privatisation and the IT revolution. The banks appeared "dodgy" as they continued to accumulate non-performing loans year after year. Woe betides these banks as they regularly expand without being able to provide basic banking facilities properly to the people of India.

Scenario

According to the census carried out in 2011, out of 1.05 billion people, only 764 million are literate and capable of independently operating bank accounts. The total population has been represented as 247 million households and 168 million live in rural surroundings. Approximately 100 million households are found to be not used to banking. Therefore, potential exists for banks to accelerate the economic development of the nation.

From the recent penetration of mobile phones, cable television, and broadband connectivity to territories deep inside India, the excuses provided hitherto for their failure to get banking to people in the remote areas because of the difficult terrain, may now be taken with a pinch of salt.

The census provides the following information:

Table: Improving the conditions of living among 247 million households

Amenities	Total	Rural	Urban	Gap (out of 247 million)
Telephone/mobile	141	86	55	106
Banking	145	91	54	102
Television	117	56	61	130
LPG fuel	70	19	51	177
Car/jeep/van	12	4	8	235
Bicycle	110	77	33	136

It is interesting to notice from press releases that between September 2011 and September 2016, the telephone/mobile subscriptions have grown by 47 per cent in rural areas compared to 4 per cent in urban centres. There is no doubt that people have shed their inhibitions in accepting new conveniences.

According to data available at the RBI website, as of December 2014, commercial banks have 123,184 branches, reflecting an annual growth of 10% over 2011. This rate of growth is not comparable to the growth of mobile phones or cars, etc.

Perhaps managers may not have a free hand to organise their affairs and to proceed in order to achieve the mission of extending banking services to the people of the country. The reins are in the hands of the following:

    I.   Department of Financial Services - Ministry of Finance, Government of India

    II.   Reserve Bank of India - as the bankers' bank and regulator

    III.   State governments - the responsibility for social development is entrusted with them

    IV.   Foreign Exchange Dealers Association of India - the RBI's extended arm for forex regulation

    V.   Indian Banks Association - the voice of Indian banks' management

    VI.   Judiciary - that protects the constitutional rights of citizens

    VII.   Central Vigilance Commission - for safeguarding the nation from miscreant public servants

I. Department of Financial Services of the Government of India

The Department of Finance functions to control almost every aspect of banks, as can be seen from roles stated in the Annual Report of the Ministry of Finance (2015-16). Even though the report dwells mainly on government-owned banks called public sector banks (PSB), any bank in the private sector can be directed to be merged with a PSB or taken over by government on the basis of recommendation by the RBI. The inspection carried out by the RBI on private banks plays a critical role in preserving their position in the private sector. This only gives an indirect message that their freedom to operate is more or less akin to a PSB. They have the privilege of selection of a board of directors and management personnel. The following are a select few of them to provide a glimpse of the role of the government in controlling Indian banks' operations.

Sl. No.	Section	Functions
	Banking Operation-I (BO-I)	1. Appointment of Governor/Deputy Governor of RBI
		2. Chairman & MDs of SBI, CMDs and EDs of Nationalised Banks
		3. CMDs of NABARD and NHB
		4. Appointments of Whole Time Director in EXIM BANK, SIDBI and IDBI
	Banking Operation-II (BO-II)	1. All Policy matters related to Banking Operation
		2. Administration of legislation such as Banking Regulation Act, 1949 and Payment and Settlement System Act, 2007, The Negotiable Instruments Act, 1881, the Chit Funds Act, 1982
		3. International Relations (Banking, Insurance and Pensions Reforms)
		4. Opening of currency chests; Local Area Banks
	Banking Operation-III (BO-III)	Customer Service in Banks/FI/Ins

Banking Operations and Accounts	1.	Annual consolidated review of public sector banks (PSB)
	2.	Appointment and fixing remuneration of auditors of PSB
	3.	Taxation matters of PSB
	4.	Scrutiny of reports of inspection of PSB conducted by RBI
	5.	Operation of guarantee schemes of PSB
	6.	Government contribution to share capital
	7.	Release of external aids under USAID
	8.	Arbitration between PSB, Government departments/undertakings, etc.
	9.	Opening and shifting of administrative office of banks
	10.	Licensing, amalgamation, reconstruction, acquisition of private sector banks, overseas banks of Indian and foreign banks, banking sector reforms
Agricultural Credit	1.	Agricultural Credit
	2.	Debt Waiver schemes
	3.	Matters relating to NABARD
	4.	Bank credit to KVIC, handloom and handicraft sector
	5.	Cooperative banks
	6.	Others
Credit Policy (CP)	1.	Priority Sector Lending
	2.	Lending to weaker sections of Priority Sector including SC/ST
	3.	PM's New 15 Point Programme for the Welfare of Minorities
	4.	DRI Scheme; Government Sponsored Schemes -PMEGP, education, employment
	5.	Generation scheme of SJSRY, SGSY, etc.
	6.	Educational loans
Regional Rural Banks (RRB)	1.	Legislative matters relating to RRBs
	2.	Appointment of chairman and directors
	3.	Review of performance
	4.	Employees service regulations, etc.

Financial Inclusion (FI)	1. Branch expansion
	2. Lead Bank Scheme and Service Area Approach
	3. District and State Level Bankers' Committee (SLBC)
	4. Business Correspondents/Facilitators, Mobile Banking, etc.
	5. Matters relating to e-Governance
Industrial Relations (IR)	1. Service matters of PSBs
	2. HR matters relating to PSBs and RBI Unions
	3. Pay and Allowances of bank employees in overseas branches
Industrial Finance-I (IF-I)	1. The Export-Import Bank Act, 1981
	2. Scheme for financing Viable Infrastructure Projects (SIFTI) of IIFCL
	3. Exim Bank, IIFCL, IWRFC and IIBL Ltd
	4. IFCI Ltd, IDFC Ltd
Industrial Finance-II (IF-II)	1. NHB and Housing Policy
	2. BIFR
	3. Small and Medium Enterprises (SMEs), SIDBI, SFCs
Vigilance	1. Nomination of CVOs for PSBs/FIs
	2. Correspondence with CBI
	3. Anti-corruption measures
	4. Investigation of cases of fraud by CBI & RBI
	5. Complaints against GMs/EDs and CMDs of PSBs/FIs
	6. Major frauds in PSBs (in India and abroad)
	7. Bank security
	8. Robberies and loss prevention in banks
Debt Recovery Tribunals (DRT)	1. Establishment of DRTs/DRATs
	2. Posts in DRTs/DRATs
Recovery Section	1. Banks and Financial Institutions (RDDBFI) Act, 1993
	2. Securitization and Reconstruction of Financial Assets and Enforcement of Security Interest (SARFAESI) Act, 2002
	3. Central Registry
	4. Credit Information Companies
	5. One Time Settlement/Compromise of loan accounts, etc.
Micro Finance	1. Self Help Groups, NABARD's Micro Finance

From the above it can be observed that critical aspects of banking such as customer service, credit policy, expansion of banking operations, and appointment of chairmen of banks, are controlled by the government.

II. Reserve Bank of India

The Government of India appoints the Governor, Deputy Governors and other Board members of the Reserve Bank of India (RBI). Therefore an independently functioning RBI is in the hands of the political leaders running the government. As the preamble to the establishment of the RBI states, the function of the RBI is "to regulate the issues of bank notes and the keeping of reserves with a view to securing monetary stability in India and generally to operate the currency and credit system of the country to its advantage".

The RBI controls the operation of banks mainly in the following ways, either by the power derived from the Act itself or from powers delegated to it by the government.

   a) Currency notes: issue of bank notes, circulation, exchange, counterfeit and keeping account of it
   b) Credit and monetary policy: operation of CRR/SLR/other open market operations with a view to regulate the supply of money and credit, engage in open market operations, control credit by interest rate operation
   c) Control of forex movement by administration of FEMA

Derived functions are

   a) Inspection of banks and reporting to Government: the inspection under section 35 of the Banking Regulation Act, 1949 gives ample power to officials of the RBI to carry out inspections of records maintained at the banks' offices and make recommendations, even for the liquidation of banks that have failed to comply with RBI regulations or have the potential to affect the banking system adversely. By this, the freedom of operation of banks both in the private and public sector stand at the same level.

b) Regulation and supervision of the Payment and Settlement Systems: the RBI regulates the clearing system, sets the clearing house rules and engages other banks to supervise the clearing houses at centres where the RBI has no presence.

c) Banker to the government: with the assistance of its large network of banks, the RBI obtains government revenues by way of taxes, levies, etc., and disburses payments approved by various offices of the government.

d) Operation of public debt office: the RBI manages the issue of government bonds, holds custody and sells to banks to fulfil the requirement of statutory liquidity ratio.

e) Issuing licences for new banks in India and abroad: the licensing system of banks relies on balancing the profitability of banks and expansion to remote areas. A lopsided expansion of banks is not envisaged and hence, while there is freedom to open branches in rural areas, overcrowding of banks in urban areas with the higher cost of operation impacting profitability, is regulated.

f) Acting as a conduit for transmission of government subsidy and incentives to people in the rural area: policies announced during the annual government budget usually contain favours in the form of subsidies to poor farmers and small scale entrepreneurs, and incentives to exporters and industrialists. The RBI plays an important role in getting these subsidies and incentives to the target people identified by the government.

Banks in India look to the RBI for guidelines on the following routine operations:

a) Credit including interest rates on loans and advances

b) Foreign exchange - remittance for capital and current account transactions, investment, etc.

c) Operational areas like maintenance of capital, licensing for banks, reporting of fraud, customer identification norms popularly known as KYC norms, etc.

d) Rural development which includes the welfare of select communities of the population.

The following table illustrates master circulars issued by the RBI during 2014-15. It may be worth looking at them in order to have an impression of the type of control the RBI exercises on banks. RBI Master Circulars are issued annually for reference on various subject areas as on 1st July. From January 2016, the RBI has started issuing master directions. As usual, changes in instructions will be advised through circulars or press releases and master directions get updated simultaneously. These master directions are expected to replace master circulars over a period.

Sl. No.	Subject	Operational area
1	Bank Finance to Non-Banking Financial Companies (NBFCs)	Credit
2	Exposure Norms	Credit
3	Exposure Norms for Financial Institutions	Credit
4	Guarantees and Co-acceptances	Credit
5	Interest Rates on Advances	Credit
6	Lending to Micro, Small & Medium Enterprises (MSME) Sector	Credit
7	Loans and Advances - Statutory and Other Restrictions	Credit
8	Prudential Norms for Classification, Valuation and Operation of Investment Portfolio by FIs	Credit
9	Prudential Norms on Income Recognition, Asset Classification and Provisioning pertaining to Advances	Credit
10	Export Credit Refinance Facility	Forex
11	Guidelines issued under Section 36(1)(a) of the Banking Regulation Act, 1949 - Implementation of the provisions of Foreign Contribution (Regulation) Act, 2010	Forex
12	Instructions Relating to Deposits held in FCNR(B) Accounts	Forex
13	Interest Rates on Rupee Deposits held in Domestic, Ordinary Non-Resident (NRO) and Non-Resident (External) (NRE) Accounts	Forex
14	Rupee/Foreign Currency Export Credit and Customer Service To Exporters	Forex
15	Basel III Capital Regulations	Operations
16	Branch Authorisation	Operations
17	Cash Reserve Ratio (CRR) and Statutory Liquidity Ratio (SLR)	Operations
18	Credit Card, Debit Card and Rupee Denominated Cobranded Prepaid Card operations of banks	Operations

19	Customer Service in Banks	Operations
20	Disclosure in Financial Statements - Notes to Accounts	Operations
21	Disclosure Norms for Financial Institutions	Operations
22	Frauds - Classification and Reporting	Operations
23	Know Your Customer (KYC) norms/Anti-Money Laundering (AML) standards/Combating of Financing of Terrorism (CFT)/Obligation of banks under PMLA, 2002	Operations
24	Para-banking Activities	Operations
25	Prudential Guidelines on Capital Adequacy and Market Discipline - New Capital Adequacy Framework (NCAF)	Operations
26	Prudential Norms for Classification, Valuation and Operation of Investment Portfolio by Banks	Operations
27	Prudential Norms on Capital Adequacy - Basel I Framework	Operations
28	Resource Raising Norms for Financial Institutions	Operations
29	Credit Facilities to Minority Communities	Rural
30	Credit facilities to Scheduled Castes (SCs) & Scheduled Tribes (STs)	Rural
31	Guidelines for Relief Measures by Banks in Areas Affected by Natural Calamities	Rural
32	Housing Finance	Rural
33	Lead Bank Scheme	Rural
34	Priority Sector Lending - Targets and Classification	Rural
35	Self Help Group - Bank Linkage Programme	Rural

One has to appreciate the respectability RBI holds among Central Banks world over despite the multifaceted role assigned to it in India's banking system. The RBI is the single source for comprehensive data on the Indian economy. There have not been many changes in the role or function of the RBI in the past, unlike in banking in general, where several experiments were tried to promote banking to remote areas. With so many levers to be handled by this one entity in India's banking system, changes in the structure and function of the RBI may perhaps trigger changes in banking in India. The role of the RBI in sharing information with the public about customers came up for discussion and it was ruled that since the RBI was not having a fiduciary relationship with the financial institutions, the public is entitled to information on the operation of banks.

III. Judiciary

The judiciary of India consists currently of the Supreme Court of India, eighteen High Courts and 14,249 district and subordinate courts, which recognise the importance of the institution of banking. Roughly there are more than 30 million court cases pending in various courts. Many of them involve banks as one of the parties. Property disputes may involve banks as witness for the payment of a sum to the seller or for the buyer for having made payment. Banks file suits against the public for recovery of loans. Banks go to court for cases relating to fraud, forgery, etc. Numerous cases exist where the parties seek an injunction preventing the banks' payments of deposited sums, Bank Guarantees, Letters of Credit or from release of documents in respect of land and property pledged with banks. Banks will have to be present in these court proceedings until matters are finally settled.

The functioning of the judiciary affects the banking system in two ways. The foremost is the supportive role of the judiciary in realising bank dues and the second is the time lost by banks while deputising their employees when their physical presence is insisted on, in cases where banks have nothing to gain. One can add to these two, an additional loss caused to banks due to lack of clever advocates in their legal department to defend causes.

Judges are found to be lenient to defaulters of loans. The relief provided to the public in allowing the litigation process to continue, in the guise of providing the fundamental right guaranteed by the Constitution of India to go to court for any of its citizens, delays final settlement with banks. In India cases are not disposed of as quickly as one would expect and both the public and the banks suffer loss of time and earning opportunities from the assets involved.

The number of cases pending in various courts of law only aggravates the case and creates a vicious circle where an increase in pending cases increases the delay and delayed cases increase the overall number of cases. There is legislation enacted to speed up the banks' recovery process, reducing the documentation for deceased accounts, etc. Institutional support is provided by setting up Lok Adalats (meaning people's court), debt recovery tribunals, consumer forum, Banking Ombudsman, etc. Lok Adalats are voluntary agencies monitored by state legal aid and Advice Boards as an alternative forum for the resolution of disputes through reconciliation. Every award of the Lok Adalat is considered as the equivalent of a civil court order. In a situation when a lot of bank assets are lying unrealised due to court injunctions, Lok Adalats are considered as an opportunity by banks to save time and money. The Ombudsman is under the supervision of the RBI.

Indian courts often deliver high quality judgements, even if these are delayed. But for a bank, any delay in closing a money case is harmful or damaging.

IV. Indian Banks Association (IBA)

The Indian Banks Association presently has a membership of 131 banks and associate membership of 56 other entities. The IBA is managed by the chairmen of banks and often functions as consultant to the government and the RBI on policy and regulatory issues. They provide a common database on matters relevant to the day to day operations of banks. They provide a database of creditable road transport operators, whose transport receipts can be treated as documents of title to goods. They finalise and circulate the quarterly dearness allowance payable for employees of those banks linked to the IBA for wage settlement.

The fact that the senior members are from large sized public sector banks, gives the IBA the image of a government body. The IBA negotiates wage settlements for almost two million employees of banks of different efficiency levels uniformly. In the process, bank managements are disarmed from adopting a "carrot and stick" approach to employees and therefore are left with only persuasive measures to improve employee performance.

V. Foreign Exchange Dealers Association of India (FEDAI)

The Foreign Exchange Dealers Association of India is similar to the IBA in supporting member banks. However membership of FEDAI is limited to Authorised Dealers in Foreign Exchange. FEDAI has more than 100 members. They undertake liaison with the RBI on matters relating to forex business of member institutions and issue guidelines on handling foreign exchange business. These guidelines are known as FEDAI rules. These rules, along with codes issued by the International Chamber of Commerce, help bank officials handle forex transactions uniformly. The role of FEDAI needs to be evaluated in the light of developing a competitive forex market in India.

VI. State/Local governments/SLBC

The concept of uplifting the rural population finds a prominent place among the various operations of the RBI. The Rural Planning and Credits Department and Urban Banks Department supervise these activities with the help of the State Level Bankers Committee[12] constituted at each state and Union Territory. The SLBC has members from banks operating in the state, local government and representatives from the RBI and NABARD, an organisation set up for refinancing agriculture loans of banks and rural development. As of now, the country is divided politically into 671 districts and implementation of various government welfare schemes in all these districts is monitored by the SLBC as is also the expansion of banking. An individual bank's performance in the state/UT is monitored by their Credit Deposit Ratio which reflects the ratio of loans outstanding to the local population as against the savings mobilised from them. Ideally 60% is the least expected from a commercial bank. A lower ratio in respect of a particular state reflects the flight of capital from the state to elsewhere. It also reflects the lack of infrastructure for industrial development.

---

[12]   http://www.rbi.org.in/SCRIPTs/NotificationUser.aspx?Id=9077&Mode=0#CT19

VII. Central Vigilance Commission

This is an apex body that looks after the conduct of public servants who are in a position to jeopardise public property. With the majority of bank business falling under the public sector, the role of the Central Vigilance Commission in the operation of banks cannot be stymied. Banks' employees work in a fiduciary situation and are vulnerable to illegal gratification. While the government or banks cannot refuse an enquiry against any official, senior level officers appointed as the Central Vigilance Officer (CVO) at all state-owned banks help in completing the process quickly so that innocent officials do not face hardship for long periods of time. It is difficult to separate negligence, intentional deceit and fake reports of fraudulence on colleagues.

Banks in India operate in an underwhelming scenario with regards to the institutional support they require for smooth operations. These disruptions may be positive or negative, hijacking the banks' time and constricting their freedom to operate. These add insult to injury for the bank and its officials who have to manage a juggernaut of processes.

SECTION 2

6. JUGGERNAUT OF PROCESSES

'Knotty'

As seen from the previous chapter, the reins of Indian banking are held not by the bank managements but by other parties. In order to live up to the expectations of those controllers, banking processes were modified year after year. The underlying feature of banking is the trust between the parties and the basic process is to crystallise the trust between the banker and the customer. Such basic processes, having outlived their time, became traditional and a characteristic of Indian banks. These brought certain rigidities and banks which adhered to such processes above relevance to changing times, lagged behind.

After the changes that were enforced on banks from the 1990s by way of liberalisation, globalisation and privatisation by government, banks improved their processes but did not switch over to the change demanded in the modern fast-paced environment brought about by IT. The new banks that came onto the scene did not have the traditional wisdom while the old banks did not have the boldness to bring about revolutionary changes in their traditional processes. As a result, some of the new banks failed due to their inability to adapt to the prevailing circumstances, while others merged traditional wisdom into their business processes. Old banks adopted some new business processes after witnessing new methodologies evidently working well for the new banks.

It is important to understand the processes adopted to run the day to day business of banks to comprehend the quality of service provided to the public. Therefore, some major processes currently adopted by Indian banks are discussed in this chapter.

In order to make them intelligible, these processes have been grouped as Business, Operational, Ancillary and Capital management. The Business processes portion covers core banking functions such as taking deposits and offering loans. The Operations portion discusses regulatory processes such as obtaining licenses, managing premises, employees, systems and procedures, auditing and customer service. It also covers functions handled by some banks like government business, clearing houses, foreign exchange business, investor management, etc. The processes involved in rendering services such as safe custody services, safety deposit boxes/lockers, etc., are covered in the Ancillary services portion. The Capital management portion discusses the thorny issues related to capital adequacy and profitability enhancing processes such as risk management, interest rates management, non-performing loans, and statutory investments such as CRR and SLR.

Section 1 - Business Processes

The relationship of people with banks begins with a visit to a bank branch and the holding of discussions with officials there. This process will ultimately culminate in the opening of one or more bank accounts that will serve the purpose of the relationship intended. While the visit crystallises in submitting an application in writing for the services intended, the discussion takes place as an interview with the intention of imparting understanding of the pertinent rules and regulations. Normally a copy of the banks' rules containing the applicable terms and conditions is made available to the public or at the least handed over on demand. Thus, before operating the account, all aspects are completed in respect of a simple contract such as identity of the parties, understanding the purpose of the relationship, communicating the offer, acceptance and the circumstances under which the contract gets terminated, etc.

Over time, the processes have undergone changes. In this section, the processes of opening a bank account, operating it, accepting deposits and the processes for approving loans and monitoring those loans are discussed very briefly to enable the reader to understand whether current systems procedures have become more feeble than in the past.

1. Opening a bank account is the beginning of a relationship

Today, banks cannot refuse to open a bank account if an application in the prescribed format is presented to a bank along with the following documents in original:

a) Photo identity - any of these issued by the appropriate authority, namely, a passport, an identity card indicating the Permanent Account Number issued by the Income Tax Department of the Government of India (PAN), a valid driving licence, an identity card issued by the Election Commission of India or an Aadhar card issued by government

b) Proof of address - utility bills or one of the above with current address

c) Photograph of the person requesting the opening of the bank account

d) PAN Number

The above documentation is known and comes within the purview of Know Your Customer norms. The processes of interview and understanding the purpose of opening bank accounts are non-existent. But bank officials are expected to make sufficient enquiries and verification under a process called a due diligence exercise. While intending to increase the number of accounts opened, activities such as organised identity thefts get overlooked.

Once an account is opened, the bank provides the following to the customer:

a) Passbook in the case of a savings account with photo affixed and signed by bank official

b) Cheque book (mailed or handed over)

c) ATM card & PIN (handed over or mailed separately)

d) E banking ID and password (mailed separately)

Though nowadays the necessity of carrying a passbook for withdrawal is not as significant as alternate means are available for withdrawal of deposits, the issue of a passbook to savings bank account holders has not been dispensed with as it still serves as evidence of deposits and a proof of identity convenient for illiterate and poor customers. There are instances when passbooks are lodged with local money lenders as security for taking loans. Cheque books allow customers to draw on funds without producing the passbook and thus serve an important role in the banking business. Signing cheques uniformly is important. Since stolen books and forgery have not yet fully exited from banks' day-to-day experiences, cheque books have to be kept safely and securely by customers.

Keeping the following information in respect of bank accounts will be handy for smooth operation in future.

a) Customer ID number - Each bank will have a unique ID for each customer
b) Account number - For each and every account
c) Branch code - Banks provide to their branches a unique identification number
d) MICR[13] code - An identification number, printed on the cheque, which is linked to the place where a branch is located. It is allotted by the RBI to help banks sort their cheques so that clearing cheques can be presented to the correct branch. Whenever a cheque is received or issued, it is worth ensuring that the code is clearly visible on the cheque.
e) IFSC code - This code identifies a bank branch, is used for on line remittances and is very handy for RTGS and other similar payments.
f) SWIFT code - All branches are not allowed to handle forex remittances in India. Therefore it is necessary that branches which are not authorised are linked to an authorised branch. Banks use an internationally popular financial telecommunication system known as SWIFT for handling forex transactions. Knowing the unique ID commonly referred to as the SWIFT code therefore becomes essential for sending and receiving remittances correctly with an overseas client.

There is no uniform practice among banks in general to provide this information to customers unless they ask for it. When an account is opened,

---

13   MICR – magnetic ink character recognition that helps machine sorting of cheques when presented for clearing

banks could provide all this information in a uniform format for all banks as documentary evidence. Perhaps an authority to voice such concerns of the public may be doing this in future.

2. Operating bank accounts

The most important purpose of opening a bank account is to save money by the deposit of cash or cheques received from others and from which money can be withdrawn by using a cheque or by various other means such as ATMs, transfers, etc. The account number and home branch where the primary account is opened are the key information required while operating a bank account.

The account number and the name of the account holder have to be clearly printed on the deposit slip. The personal details of the person making the deposit are important. This information, along with details of the denomination of currency notes and the number of pieces, needs to be mentioned in the pay in slip or cash deposit slip provided at the branch. Earlier, one has to confirm the details with the clerk before proceeding to the cashier to deposit. The cashier provides the counterfoil, perforated portion of the pay in slip, checking the cash deposited. The pay slip with cashier's stamp affixed reaches the clerk for suitably updating the accounts maintained in ledgers. Only after this process can the depositor get the passbook updated for the cash deposited. Later the teller system allowed small amount transactions to be done by a single person in one stroke. With computers taking over, passbooks are updated by bank cashiers using passbook machines and the need to verify the correctness of the details of the account by the bank clerk no longer exists. Further, deposits can be made through ATMs facilitated to accept cash, and complete the paperless transaction.

Drawing amounts from bank accounts involved either presenting cheques or using withdrawal slips along with a passbook. One had to go to the clerk who issued tokens against receiving the cheques or withdrawal slips. The account number, name of the account holder, etc., are verified from the ledger and other records. If the balance outstanding is sufficient, the amount is entered and the balance reduced to that extent. The same entry is copied in the passbook if presented together. This is referred to as 'posting'. An officer designated will then verify the signature from the records, check the entry made by the clerk, and put his or her signature with an instruction to the cashier to make payment. This is called 'passing' and passed cheques are then handed over through a book called a 'transit book', where passing officers enter the serial number of the cheque or slip. This ensured that all cheques reached the cashier promptly. The token number is shouted and those who present the token are given the amount of the cheque where the token number is written. Anyone was allowed to take cash with a token and the only condition was that the cashier will insist on the signature of the person accepting cash. Later, token display machines halted the shouting process. In the teller system, cash was paid directly to the customer without issue of a token. ATMs later got rid of all these cheques, slips, passbooks, etc. However for large amounts the process is the same even now. Use of the individual transit book by each passing official ensured proper accountability and countered forgery in instruments in transit. The lost token procedure was important and the customer was accountable for the loss. The signature obtained by the cashier before handing over cash provided assistance to the police to establish the identity of miscreants.

A transfer transaction means there is no receipt or payment of cash involved. Transfer of amounts to other accounts, may be to an account opened at the same branch or another branch or to another bank. Transfer transactions also cover the transfer of amounts to banks for obtaining credit instruments such as demand drafts, pay orders, etc. Similar transfer transactions such as mail transfers and telegraphic transfers have become historical. Currently, online transfers initiated by customers sitting in front of a home computer and transfers put through by bank employees at the requests of customers, exist. Other than home computers, transfers can be carried out by customers using mobile phones or ATMs. For transferring money to a beneficiary living abroad additional information is needed, such as the purpose of the remittance, the beneficiary's bank details, including the sort code, etc.

There are some more interesting things about bank accounts in India.

There used to be a compulsory minimum **initial deposit** by way of cash. In order to open a bank account there was a requirement of an introductory reference from employees of the bank or their account holders. This procedure is no longer followed. Most of the accounts opened as part of **'financial inclusion'**[14] do not hold any deposit. Even though in the short term, the financial inclusion campaign may not be a sound commercial proposition, as employees have to be disengaged from their routines for mobilising any large amount of deposits, it might benefit banks in the long term, as a large number of people in India keep their savings in the form of cash and gold.

In addition to people who are residents of India, both people who are born in India but living abroad, referred to as Non Resident Indians (NRI), and people whose parents or grandparents were born in India, referred to as Persons of Indian Origin (PIO), are also eligible to open and operate a bank account in India. Their bank accounts are referred to as NRI accounts.

Indian banks are allowed to open accounts for minors who are below eighteen years of age. For those minors above ten, individual accounts can be opened independently but with limited operation. For those below ten years, operation is allowed by their parents or guardians. Thus, there is hardly any reason for rejecting a request for opening a bank account except for not producing complete testimonials. **Date of birth** in the application form for opening accounts is very important as it distinguishes the accounts of minors or senior citizens from others.

In case of death, banks are allowed to settle by payment of funds lying in the accounts of the deceased, with the person nominated by the account holder. **Nomination** is a convenient way for bankers to hand over the sum outstanding to the nominee, on production of documentary proof of death and identification of the nominee. Wherever there is no nominee, banks have to be guided by RBI instructions. If bank accounts have to be closed for other reasons, the request to close should specify the reason.

---

[14]   Financial inclusion is a campaign to bring more people into the habit of banking. India has a large population without a bank account.

While there are no restrictions on the **deposit of cash** into deposit accounts, a combination of regulations will result in the scrutiny of accounts by the tax department if cash deposited into a savings account annually exceeds Rs.1million. Or if a demand draft, fixed deposit or foreign currency, etc., is obtained by making payment in cash for more than Rs.50,000. Crossed cheques are not paid in cash across the counter.

The concept of **deposit insurance** may not be relevant in India as in other countries because of the fact that the majority of the banks are owned by the government and history provides very few instances when any bank in India is allowed to be liquidated. Perhaps one remedy cited for the poor performance of Indian banks is for healthy banks to take over sick banks.

People who have lived abroad might find, while operating bank accounts in India, that they are missing a regulatory body other than the central bank in the country, which can ensure a uniform standard of service from banks to people, while safely protecting the institution of banking.

3. Deposits

Even though deposits or advances are common throughout the world, banks emerging from similar situations are expected to offer similar products and services by name. However, this is not so in the case of Indian banking. Neither the savings accounts restrict withdrawals nor are the fixed deposits locked for the contracted period. Therefore it may be interesting to discuss the products and services offered by banks in India.

Basically, banks accept deposits in three categories, namely: savings, current and fixed.

a) **Savings** accounts can be opened without any minimum deposit to be maintained. Currently banks offer 2% interest every half year which works out to an annual yield of 4.04%. It may be interesting to know that there used to be restrictions on the number of withdrawals. The account holder was allowed to draw cash from the bank by presenting 'withdrawal slips' along with the **passbook**. Those who are provided with a cheque book, can obtain cash through their representative or use cheques for the transfer of funds to others. Nowadays ATMs and internet banking facilities have reduced usage of withdrawal slips. Accounts can be opened by individuals alone or jointly.

The interest on savings does not compensate for the fall in value due to inflation. For savings deposits, even whilst paying 4% interest on a deposit payable on demand it is a profitable preposition for the bank since sizeable savings account balances stay for a long period.

The procedural simplicity of savings account operation along with the tax relief on interest earned from savings deposits encourages people to lodge their capital funds in savings. Knowing this public stance on savings accounts, banks conduct campaigns to stockpile their savings portfolio, keeping the interest rate below the rate of fixed deposits. Leaving aside some smaller private banks offering annual interest rates around 6%, after adding their own red lines, most Indian banks are probably profiting by mobilising long term deposits at a 2 to 3% cheaper rate of interest.

b) **Current** account: Features of current accounts offered by Indian banks are more or less similar to those offered by banks abroad. Cheque books are freely issued and there are no restrictions on the number of transactions in a current account including currency deposits and cash drawing. However, folio charges are being levied. Interest is not paid on current accounts. Current accounts are ideally suited to enterprises. Individuals can also maintain a personal current account. Another attractive feature of a current account is the facility of overdrafts, which is unlikely in the case of savings accounts. Therefore a combination of a current account, multiple fixed deposits and a pre-approved overdraft limit against the fixed deposits, provides convenience and earnings.

Perhaps due to the opportunity current accounts and savings accounts offer for a long term relationship, and for holding funds at no interest cost, banks in India run Current Account and Savings Accounts (CASA) campaigns, for increasing their current account and savings portfolio. Ironically a larger portion of these CASA accounts stay for long periods undrawn while fixed deposits are encashed before completion of the terms.

c) **Fixed** deposits are commonly referred to as term deposits in India and if the deposit involves compounding of interest, it is referred to as a special term deposit. Though literally it means the depositor has a claim to get back the amount deposited after the contracted period, banks in India allow the depositor to take back the sum by cancellation. They may have to forgo interest fully or marginally less than the contracted rate. So long as the reduced rate is more than the interest paid on the savings account, this method of keeping fixed deposits and cancelling earns better.

As different banks follow different rules and banks do not communicate fully and properly, customers will have to check and verify the sum paid on cancellation. Banks change their rules independently. Reliable or authentic information is not provided at the website of all banks. Under these conditions, an authority to protect the interests of the public to take care of such information exchange may be convenient.

There are some variants to fixed deposits such as recurring deposits, multi option deposits, etc. **Recurring deposits** are fixed for a period and a fixed amount is accepted as a deposit every month regularly until the full term. The entire sum of deposit together with interest is returned to the depositor on maturity. It is basically a thrift scheme. The maturity amount is linked to the interest rate for fixed deposits applicable to the term.

Multi option deposits are based on a mandate from depositors to keep a fixed balance in the savings or current account and to transfer excess funds to fixed deposits. In case of need of cash, the bank breaks these deposits one by one and provides funds in their savings or current account. While the fixed portion earns the higher interest rate, the savings portion continues as payable on demand. This product used to be time consuming before computerisation.

Inoperative, unclaimed deposits, dormant accounts, etc. According to RBI guidelines[15], accounts where there are no operations by customers for more than two years, are to be treated as inoperative accounts. If no operations have been noticed for more than ten years, they are called

---

[15]   http://rbi.org.in/Scripts/NotificationUser.aspx?Mode=0&Id=9199

unclaimed deposits and the sum of balances lying in such accounts is to be transferred to an account with the RBI under a scheme called the Depositor Education and Awareness Fund Scheme 2014 – under Section 26A of the Banking Regulation Act, 1949[16]. The arrangement is that the public can view if any such account is in their name from each bank website and contact the bank for a refund. Banks are advised to pay the customers after proper identification and obtain the refund from the RBI once a month. The documents relating to such customers have to be maintained at banks and the responsibility of tracing the customer also lies with banks. Thus banks are not relieved of any responsibility but deprived of the gains from such funds.

People used to operate accounts in the past in various banks simultaneously to evade tax. This is no easier as accounts have been linked to the tax department registration number called PAN. Another cause of inoperative accounts lying with banks is the absence of the habit of writing a will before death. Banks find difficulty in tracing many depositors for want of details in the bank records. Since banks are utilising these funds, it may be worth thinking about converting these funds to the respective bank's capital reserves and boosting their capital. For the future too, banks must have a system of obtaining balance confirmation from all customers for all deposit accounts at least once a year, since there are possibilities for embezzlement of funds from such accounts.

4. Loans

The sum of deposits and outstanding loans is usually referred to as the total business of a bank. The business of lending is very important from that point of view as is also the potential to make the profit the bank strives for ultimately. The loans processes are evolved according to traditional practices, regulations and views from the government, judiciary and bureaucracy. Depending upon the terms and conditions of a loan, it is denoted as a particular facility such as an overdraft facility, cash credit facility, demand loan, term loan, letter of credit, etc. These facilities can

---

[16] http://rbi.org.in/Scripts/NotificationUser.aspx?Mode=0&Id=9532

be grouped by their nature such as funding, terms of repayment, purpose, customer group, customer type, etc.

a) Repayment On the basis of the nature of repayment, loans are denoted as overdrafts and cash credit facilities. They are repayable on demand. Banks allow operation of these accounts by means of cheques and periodic interest is collected as and when due. In the case of demand loans and term loans, disbursement is done in phases and no disbursement is allowed against deposit. Banks often design their own products. But in all cases the regulators would expect that the due amount of interest be collected systematically and promptly.

b) Funding Banks offer credit in the form of funded and non-funded facilities. In the case of funded facilities, the loan amount is disbursed as agreed. While in the case of non-funded facilities, the bank stays as a surety and offers to release funds in case of contingencies. Banks need not have to earmark deposit money for such non-funded facilities. Common non-funded facilities are Bank Guarantees and Letters of Credit. Even though the risk and exposure are the same for both funded and non-funded, the remuneration collected for funded facilities is in the form of interest and for non-funded, as commission and service charge.

c) Purpose of loans The Indian economy is classified into three sectors. The primary sector is Agriculture, the second is Industries and the third is the Services sector. The purpose of bank loans depends on the scope, performance, infrastructure and potential of these sectors. However, the government has identified a few areas known as priority sectors where a certain percentage of bank loans have to be directed. This includes agriculture, SMEs and some other selected beneficiaries. Therefore, the purpose of the loan is important in order to determine to which sector banks' funds are deployed, for the government to strategise the growth of the economy. Ultimately, the characteristics of loans change with the purpose for which they are going to be utilised.

d) Customer group Banks offer finance to government-owned enterprises and also others. Loans given to government-owned enterprises are grouped as credit facilities to the Public Sector. Some of them provide a government guarantee as security. The risk profile of these customers differs from the private sector.

e) Customer types Banks finance all types of customers which include individuals, professional firms, proprietary enterprises, partnership firms and companies in the corporate sector. Then there are others such as trusts, societies, autonomous bodies set up by government, government departments and undertakings, and offices of international organisations. Bank finance depends upon the mandate given in the charter. Conveniently, loans given to individuals are denoted as retail or consumer loans, small and medium enterprises (SME) and corporates.

The loan business of banks is often stifled by regulatory restrictions arising from the credit control mechanism of the RBI, such as fixing the ceiling for individual limits, or limiting it to a particular industry or activity, etc. These also include guidelines to go slow on financing certain activities temporarily. Interest rates on loans are regulated by the RBI through direct measures, allowing banks to fix their own interest rate for various categories of loans or indirectly as a result of 'open market operations' it undertakes that impact the liquidity position of banks. Banks have to have a loan policy prepared on the basis of their business plan, accommodating all guidelines issued by the government and the RBI. The efficacy of the loan policy depends upon the level of delegation the bank management is comfortable with.

4.1. Loan Policy

The loan policies of banks are approved by their board of directors. It collates decisions taken hitherto in respect of loans and guidelines issued by regulatory authorities and helps banks to ensure that processes relating to sourcing, sanctions, documentation, risk mitigation and follow up in respect of loans are carried out. These are handled by various offices across the bank in the light of the banks' standards and direction from regulators and government, chambers of commerce and local bodies. Briefly, the loan policies provide information to employees on the type of loans banks would prefer to mobilise, the type of securities their officials look for while considering loan proposals, and views on take-over from other banks.

4.2 Interest rates on loans

Interest on loans is the most important of earnings from banks' operations and the smarter the bank management, the higher the yield. Efficiency and providing value-added services helps banks to retain good customers, generating a higher yield. The average yield on advances is worked out by dividing the interest received on loans by the average outstanding for total loans.

In the past, interest rates were dictated by the RBI but it has now been deregulated. Banks are now free to fix their rates subject to conditions[17] and on the basis of the interest rate they offer for deposits and the REPO rate. This is the rate at which banks can obtain funds from the RBI for managing their liquidity to meet obligations to other banks. The REPO rate is revised by the RBI periodically.

Banks used to finalise their 'base rate' of interest to which interest for all loans in general is linked. Since the base rate of banks and the REPO rate of the RBI are not linked, delay and discretion by bank managements in effecting change in their base rate, in response to the revision in the REPO rate, often fails the mechanism of controlling money in circulation and inflation. Therefore, the RBI introduced MCLR from April 2016, replacing the base rate method. MCLR is more transparent and responsive to RBI rates.

As discussed earlier, in India the interest rate offered on bank deposits and the rate of inflation are higher than in many developed countries. Naturally, the lending rates of banks are also high. Since the cost of funds borrowed from banks is higher and forms a major component of the cost, the selling price of goods and services increases with an increase in banks' lending rates. Thus, everything by nature becomes inflationary in the economy.

Compounding the rate of interest adds to difficulties for enterprises who struggle to achieve the sales and profit envisaged at the time of approaching banks for loans. The entrepreneur who finds it difficult to manage a 15% annual rate of interest is greeted by rates of 17%, 20% and 23% in subsequent years. No wonder then that they land among the pile of bad loans banks

---

[17]   https://rbi.org.in/scripts/NotificationUser.aspx?Mode=0&Id=9499

carry over year after year, publicly or unrecognised. There is one measure to ascertain whether to continue a relationship with business at this rate. That is referred to as the interest coverage ratio, which is worked out as a ratio of profit before deducting depreciation, interest and tax to interest. If it is below one, it is worth quitting unless cheaper funds can be arranged or the proportion of loans to own funds can be reduced. This accumulation of bad loans dents banks' yield and profitability. With no clear cut strategy to break out of this vicious circle, the net worth of impacted small size banks gets eroded while large government-owned banks look towards government for pumping funds into their equity. Banks with a share price above book value can look up to the share market for raising funds.

4.3 Margin money for a loan

The term 'margin money' refers to the owners' contribution to the project - be it for business or the purchase of a vehicle. Depending upon the type of loan, the concept works differently. To illustrate:

a) When a private car is financed, the down payment insisted on by the financier is the margin money. This down payment amount will absorb the interest, and the cost of recovery in case of default. The rate of margin thus is linked to the duration of the time before recovery is commenced, so that, for example, the vehicle can be sold at the value of the loan and the cost of recovery. If sales do not take place at the appropriate time, the bank will have to bear the loss, as well as additional loss for the delay and the resulting fall in value. Therefore it is a policy matter to fix the appropriate margin for the loan and the latest time to initiate recovery.

b) In another case, if a company is looking for bank loans for their working capital, the financing bank would, at first, work out the funds available with the company out of its equity. This is done by earmarking funds for acquiring fixed assets such as machinery, infrastructure, etc., and arriving at the left-over sum available as the working capital of the company. The next task would be to estimate the cost of the proposed current asset. In India, banks use their experience to help customers to ascertain this sum after taking into consideration the supplies available, usually on credit terms. The funds required at first will be met from the working capital available with the company.

In effect, current assets net of creditors can be contributed to by the company's own equity and bank finance. However, banks distribute the loan amount into those assets that can be monitored such as stock, receivables, etc. Therefore, they individually fix a margin on each one of those current assets in such a way that the bank loan needs to be disbursed only to finance those assets. A full value of the other assets is expected to be borne by the equity, in this context, stated as cent per cent margin. Generally, banks in India set their own minimum margin on various types of assets and this varies from one industry to another.

Since margin money has an important role to play on the performance of banks in India, the system of arriving at bank finance discussed above is illustrated below:

For example: Let us assume-

Total capital of a company	- Rs.1,000
Cost of fixed assets own funds	- Rs.400
Funds available for working capital	- Rs.600
Total current assets	- Rs.2,320
Current liabilities	- Rs.400
Working capital required	- Rs.1,920
Working capital deficit	- Rs.1,320
Bank finance	- Rs.1,320

Break up of current asset and margin, loan portion will be as follows:

For	of Rs.	Margin at	Will amount to Rs.	The loan portion will be Rs.
Bank balance	50	100%	50	Nil
Paid Inventories Rs.1600-400	1200	20%	240	960
Receivables	600	40%	240	360
Prepaid expenses	70	100%	70	Nil
Total			600	1320

The financing banks are not bound to increase their exposure proportionate to the level of stocks or receivables, beyond the projections made at the time of loan processing. The drawing power, depending upon the level of assets declared in periodical statements minus the margin, will be fixed as the maximum allowed to be drawn by the company, if that is less than the loan amount approved. It can be discerned that this system of financing discourages overstocking, excess selling on credit and results in reduction in the loan outstanding with banks, as the level of operation of activity at the company falls. This system is known as 'cash credit', a design of the Scottish banking system and according to Chas Northcote Cooke[18], the Scottish banking system tends to 'the cultivation of industrial habits and sobriety of conduct'.

The intensity of supervision for such types of lending process is indeed very significant. It needs constant monitoring by bank officials to enforce discipline. Therefore, the manpower management in banks has a major say in the performance of enterprises in the country. The placement of employees at bank offices where loans are processed, training those officials regularly, and in turn, the ability of those bank employees to develop a culture of credit discipline among the entrepreneurs, are important factors for successful implementation of this financing model. The shortcomings might cause over-financing or under-financing, resulting in the piling up of non-performing loans. It could also lead to diversion of funds by borrowers for other purposes harmful to society or to the economy.

4.4 Loan approval process

After opening deposit accounts, the loan approval process forms the selling part of the job. The process is linked to booking regular income, safety of funds, easy administration and risk transmission. The process involves an interaction with the applicant, to know the purpose of the loan. From the interactions and documents presented to the bank, the bank provides approval to the proposed if the loan request conforms to the loan policy and the commitment of the applicant is evident. The approval or sanction, as it is usually referred to, is reported for control to the next higher level authority,

---

[18]   The Rise and Present Condition of Banking in India by Chas Northcote Cooke

who may be an individual, an official or a committee. The controlling authority is expected to make an overview of the sanctioned proposals and any aspect overlooked or not considered at the time of sanction is pointed out to the sanctioning authority for future guidance. Thus the response is an important part of the loan process.

In the case of retail loans or consumer loans, assessment and appraisal are not so complicated. Some of the loans are personal loans, linked to personal income, and appraisal is based on the cost of the item to be purchased out of the loan amount. The loan officials need to be satisfied that the applicant is trustworthy and that documents presented are genuine. Thus decisions in respect of such loans start from the stage of recommendation to sanction and control.

In the case of other loans, all the steps such as assessment, appraisal and recommendation, hold a strong bearing on the future course of the loan. If the assessment goes wrong, it can result in under-financing that gags the enterprise or in over-financing that can make a dent in the profit. If the appraisal is not properly conducted, the real risk will be more than anticipated and covered for. Going further, if the recommending authority has not applied his or her mind to ensure that the proposal is technically feasible and financially viable, the bank's loan basket will be filled with rotten eggs over time.

Loan appraisal standards are different from bank to bank. In order to accommodate a good customer from other banks, the loan policy of banks often provides for deviations. Such practices slightly dilute the main objective of the loan policy. The loan process is entirely dependant upon the attitude of the bank official and whether it is in their nature to take risks, for example arising from misinformation and ignorance of regulatory guidelines.

There is a lacuna in the whole system of loan processing by banks. There is no authority or establishment regulator to ensure that loan proposals reaching banks have reasonable standards. Many of the loans are pushed through by heavyweights and many poor customers are pushed around. Therefore, the introduction of something like a panel of professionals who can vet proposals before they reach banks can be tried to improve the quality of loans, and from a periodic review of loans vetted by them and their subsequent performance, their role can be stabilised.

4.5. Loan documentation

Loan documentation has a profound impact at the time of recovery. Mainly the legal risk arises from imperfect documentation. Therefore, all initial discussions and exchange of communications between the bank officials and the loan seeker have to be brought in to perfect the documentation. It may be easy for banks to add conditions in the agreements or obtain additional documents to make the contracts safer and safer. But the inconsistencies that creep into the documents come to light when multiple documents belonging to the same borrower are read together, usually when suits are filed.

Ultimately, it is the quality of documentation that decides whether the loan amount is to be written off without going to court immediately or subsequently. In their eagerness to obtain the loan from banks, loan applicants may overlook the terms and conditions spelt out in the agreements. They sign the loan documents but may not be so keen to obtain a copy of those documents from the bank. Usually bank officials fill in these documents at convenient times, but omissions do occur. However, all banks use a standard document format approved by the management. The Indian Institute of Bankers' publication on legal decisions affecting bankers provides a number of cases when omissions and commissions have jeopardised the banks.

Some of the common features of bank loan documents are as follows:

i. They are usually prepared by a panel of legal experts and thus contain a lot of **legal jargon and complex sentences** and this makes them very difficult to comprehend - they have to be simple and in easily understandable language.

ii. Mostly the **language** used is English though neither bank officials nor the loan applicants are conversant with the legal jargon in these agreements - they need to be in the local language that parties understand or at least need to be translated and explained.

iii.   One can come across **references** to other legislation or other documents - the effect of such legislation on the contract needs to be explained to the loan applicant.

iv.   Illiterate borrowers are significant in number. Banks have a system of obtaining a statement from an interpreter for having explained the documents in respect of **illiterate** borrowers. With IT solutions potentially available, the process can be carried out in better alternate ways if legally approved.

v.   The documents **run into pages** and may be time-consuming to read within a limited time provided at the time of loan documentation - 'By this condition what it means to you...' can be highlighted for easy reading at a glance. Thereafter, important information regarding the loan such as the interest rate, margin money, disbursement dates, obligations, timelines, etc., can be handed over separately for ready reference.

vi.   Various **banks use different types** of documents prepared by their experts but many of them might not have been tried and tested - it may be advisable to share documents' format among banks to save from pitfalls arising out of faulty documentation. The IBA can play a pivotal role on this matter.

vii.   The use of **arbitration** is not common in bank documents. Arbitration is worth exploring, for example the possibility to involve officials of the Indian Bank Association, FEDAI, Chamber of Commerce, government or RBI, as arbitrators. It could save the parties from going to court and also save time.

viii.   Some of the loans sanctioned initially for a year or so are subjected to renewal but documents are kept for a continuous period - proper loan management has to ensure that **documents go in tandem** with the loan. It may be advisable to obtain a fresh set every time a loan is renewed so that the implication of tenor is understood. The maximum period in which a borrower can be away from the bank is limited to the minimum tenor (for the most common working capital finance it may be one year). It helps banks not to keep old documents for any number of years and fix the problem of time-barred documents. Stamp duty on loan documents is one of the important aspects where banks and the public avoid documentation. An alternate system of remitting an annual fee, recovered along with interest, to government, can be examined to replace the hassle of stamp duty on bank loans.

In conclusion, the loan documentation of banks offers considerable room for improvement, which would benefit both the loan applicant and bank officials. Such improvement in documentation should not leave room for manoeuvre for either party or for the involvement of parties such as the judiciary.

4.6 Operation of loans - conduct

Once the sanction letter containing the terms and conditions of the loan is handed over to the customer against acknowledgement, the loan amount is released in the way agreed upon. If the operation of the loan account is understood to be a running account, as in the case of cash credit or an overdraft account, drawing is allowed within the permitted level. Generally the limit is linked to the level of inventory or current assets of the company or the value of other securities such as mortgages, fixed deposits, etc. Cash credit accounts are allowed for working capital finance which requires deposit of sales and drawing for purchases and other payments. They are usually approved for a year but renewed thereafter.

In case the repayment of the loan is agreed upon in instalments, by paying in instalments the loan is denoted as a demand loan or term loan. In the term loan accounts, banks generally expect deposits into the account, once the loan limit is disbursed completely. However one should not misunderstand that by renewal, banks in India would rework the whole proposal afresh to reduce or retain the same level of risk. The renewal process is a default exercise, if no serious violation of terms and conditions are noticed, no major changes in the circumstances prevailing at the time of the previous sanction noticed, or the loan account has not shown any symptoms of non-performance.

The successful conduct of such loan systems depends on the availability of time with bank officials to monitor the borrowers, case by case.

Their knowledge and skill should be employed to ensure that customers comply with the conditions of loans, without hampering the progress of the enterprises. Implementation of an alternate system depends upon the customer type/size, banking awareness, retail vs. wholesale, etc.

4.7 Loan recovery process

Term loans are recovered in regular instalments, usually monthly instalments, along with interest. It can be in equated monthly instalments (EMI). Failure to repay three instalments makes the account a non-performing asset (NPA), in which case the borrower loses the regard and respect of the banks.

In the case of loans taken under cash credit or overdraft, borrowers will have to pay the monthly interest promptly even though the outstanding amount is within the outer limit of the loan facility agreed by the bank. If they fail to pay the interest for three months, the account is denoted as an NPA. Such accounts can also be declared an NPA, if the outstanding loan amount continuously exceeds the permitted drawing limit for more than three months.

Once an account becomes an NPA, the loan recovery processes commence. The bank serves a notice indicating the exact amount payable to the bank, which includes interest up to the date of the communication. This is followed by bank officers calling on the defaulted borrower to gauge the probability of repayment. If the borrower can be contacted, discussion between the bank officials and the borrower will be on the repayment of arrears to regularise the account, extension of repayment time for the defaulted instalments, a compromise structure to rework, taking into consideration changes in the assumptions made at the time of loan approval. These revised terms may sometimes include: the waiver of some portion of interest, a longer repayment period, or even separate finance to help the borrower over the difficult situation. In cases where the borrower honours the revised obligations perfectly, the recovery process will not be initiated but the account will still be called an NPA until the irregular portion is fully repaid. In case of compromise when the bank allows the borrower to forgo some portion of interest, in order to help the borrower tide over their financial difficulty, banks have the right to recoup such losses once the unit is back to normal healthy operation.

If the compromise terms cannot be honoured by the borrowers or in case the borrower cannot be contacted, the bank's advocate issues a legal notice. If that is not responded to, the bank begins the process of filing a suit for the amount against the borrower, guarantor, etc.

The government has facilitated two major routes for banks to take up the journey of recovery of bad loans. One is Debt Recovery Tribunals and the other is action under the SARFAESI Act. A Debt Recovery Tribunal is a government establishment to help banks obtain the order to recover and sell the assets to adjust against loan dues. The latter is a recovery mechanism without involving a court. The process is to issue a public notice and conduct an auction for which the government has approved the appointment of resolution agents for professional support. However the set-up is not so favourable to banks or gracious to bank officials as in numerous instances, banks have been dragged to infamy by the media and judiciary.

Loans require delicate handling. In general, there is a culture of carrying out banking imperfectly and on an ad hoc basis. Drawings allowed in excess of what is required, leads to diversion of funds to non-banking activity - maybe for other personal financial commitments or for investing in other sister concerns. Preventing such diversion requires daily monitoring of individual accounts. Since interest rates in India for loans of a general nature hover around 12 to 16%, the outstanding amount in loan accounts doubles within no time. The growing debt, though it might initially look manageable for a borrower, soon becomes something impossible in the normal course. The borrowers' mind-set changes from 'willing to pay back' to 'finding reasons to avoid repayment'. Therefore, the quicker the action, the better it is for the borrower.

The absence of bankruptcy law is cited as a reason for the accumulation of a large amount of non-performing loans and the large number of entrepreneurs who live their life between the court and the bank. More and more borrowers resort to the judiciary to save their property which has been given as security for loans. Initially they seek time for managing funds on which courts normally take a lenient view. Banks suffer from prolonged bank recovery suits that deplete the value of the security they hold in custody before sale. Expenditure in the form of payments made for services to advocates is in the form of an investment for the borrowers. However, for banks, it is an additional loss.

Investment

Banks have to invest a proportion of their deposits in government bonds. This ratio is known as Statutory Liquidity Ratio and these bonds are known as SLR securities. Currently the ratio fixed by the RBI is 21.5% of total demand and time deposits. The choice of securities is up to the bank. Therefore, investment in a good decision support system improves the return on investment. The RBI publishes the list of bonds eligible as SLR securities. All banks are expected to operate an account at the office where the bank has its headquarters. It is basically a current account used for maintaining a cash balance. The same account is also used for crediting the sale proceeds of securities. The public debt office manages the buying and selling of securities falling under both SLR and non-SLR. This is a government function and the RBI discharges it as an agency on a commission basis.

This current account as such does not provide any interest. However, it is used for maintaining the Cash Reserve Ratio (CRR). The daily balance in the account is verified with the fortnightly statement of deposits submitted by individual banks. The RBI penalises banks for failure to keep the minimum prescribed. Currently the ratio is 4% of total deposits in India compared to 0.18% of the Bank of England in the UK, or the highest slab of 10% of balances in transaction accounts (comparable to the sum of current and savings deposits in India, popularly known as CASA deposits[19]) in the USA. There was some debate on the significant loss of profit because of the holding of such funds by the RBI. A statement found in the Bank of England annual report sounds interesting - earnings out of these funds from banks

---

[19]   In India CASA form 50 to 60% of total deposits which means the US CRR at 10% is comparable to India's 4%.

are utilised for central banks' policy functions. Surely the RBI too provides commercial banks with a lot of valuable service for free.

It may be interesting to note that in the case of government-owned banks, the government has invested in the equity of banks. Simultaneously, they have taken funds from them in the form of investment in government bonds. In the case of the State Bank of India, as of 31st March 2016, the share of capital including the general reserve from government adds up to Rs.1.08 trillion rupees, compared to the bank's investment in government securities of Rs.5.36 trillion on a deposit base of Rs.22.53 trillion. A debate on reduction of SLR or reduction of capital invested by the government may provide a better solution to improve public sector banks, and the need for creating a high yielding bond market where banks can invest.

Section 2 - Banking Operations

Other processes relating to the operational function of banks are obtaining licences, upkeep of operations, employee management, handling complaints and control functions such as audit.

The RBI issues licenses for opening of branches, ATMs and administrative offices, not only to banks, but to money changers and non-banking finance companies. The terms and conditions for such licences depend upon the functions envisaged to be handled at the site. The licence is a notice to the public, stating approval for carrying out the functions listed therein or unambiguously inferred from what is stated therein, and cautions those who approach banks for any service. These licences used to be displayed prominently in the main banking hall in the past as information for the public.

1. Opening of banks and offices - licensing

As regards branch licensing procedure, the master circular issued by the RBI provides the information required for opening a branch of a bank. The licence used to be the first item in the process of opening a branch. Once the licence is obtained, banks look for premises and other logistics to open the branch. This has since been simplified. Banks can now declare the proposed centres for opening their offices in the ensuing financial year and inform the RBI of the exact date of opening for their record. The RBI maintains and publishes the statistics of bank branches and local government offices maintain the details as part of their planning programme.

Before commencement of operation, the following are some of the important pieces of information the bank must have:

- Details of premises
- Officer identified to be the branch manager
- Status of core banking system
- Branch code
- Indian financial system code (IFSC) essential for payment systems such as RTGS/NEFT, etc.
- Name of the clearing centre to which the branch is attached
- MICR code required for cheques
- Currency chest branch linked for cash replenishment and depositing surplus cash
- Category for handling forex business and the link AD branch with its SWIFT code
- Villages under the village adoption scheme
- Name of the lead bank for the centre

2. Process of manpower management - human resources

As on 31st March 2015, there were 1.29 million people directly employed by banks. Since the way the performance of these many people is managed impacts the performance of the banking system, Human Resource Management is the most important function of bank management. Therefore, leadership matters overall and management matters when it comes to recruitment, training, placement, career planning, preserving good conduct, and retirement or termination.

2.1 Recruitment

The Institute of Banking Personnel Selection[20] (IBPM), a society made up of banks and including representatives from the government and the RBI, takes care of recruitment and is now enhancing its activities to include promotion as well. However, some of the private banks and foreign banks are not covered by the IBPM. A large number of students in India complete their graduation from universities and try for job opportunities in banks. Employment in commercial banks, particularly in public sector banks, is considered to be a safe, secure and respectable vocation. The IBPM offers great convenience in the process of recruitment. Other methods followed by private sector banks are by references from existing employers, the services of placement agencies or by posting vacancies at their website under 'careers', etc.

Recruitment is based on tests of the numerical ability and communication skill of the candidates. Thus the selected candidates happen to be fit for all types of office work and the banks are left with the major task of training them. Recruited employees constantly endeavour to be near their home town, or use time and opportunity to prepare for selection to higher level positions elsewhere including in the Indian Civil Service. Consequent labour turnover often cannot be considered as insignificant as banks spend two or three years on these recruits. There is no practice of a system of bonds for a minimum period of service. Thus banks do incur losses on this count too. However one has to agree that in general the candidates selected on the basis of competitive examinations from the large pool of fresh university graduates, often show higher capabilities, ethics and levels of integrity.

Managing the adequacy of employees, at least at the front office, is not regulated by any controllers even though demand for expansion of the branch network comes from the government. It is for the management to have a long term strategy for their human resource management. The strategy should focus on increasing the productivity of labour within a safe and respectable working environment.

---

[20]　http://www.ibps.in/html/background.htm

2.2 Pay and emoluments

The pay and allowances in respect of employees of banks that are members of the Indian Banks Association, go for wage settlement through the Indian Bank Association. Their pay and allowances differ from certain other banks, mainly a few new banks in the private sector and foreign banks that stay away from the IBA settlement. The IBA package provides for pay and allowances including the composition of allowances for inflation adjustment, by way of the Dearness Allowance (DA). This allowance changes quarterly, dependant upon the inflation indices across the industry. The package finalised between representatives of the labour unions and officials from the Indian Banks Association is usually valid for four to five years. Since the DA is linked to the inflation rate, the cost on staff expenses in those banks increases annually by 10-15%.

As most of the bank employees come under the IBA settlement, control on staff expenses is limited to reduction in the number of employees, which may be counterproductive. Interestingly, a senior employee in a lower cadre and a junior employee in a higher cadre are often paid similarly. Thus an aspiring employee and frustrated employee are remunerated more or less at par. This feature in the pay and allowance system fails to motivate employees for higher responsibilities. Similarly, discontented employees did not often leave banks, in the absence of alternate opportunities for employment, until the IT revolution and opening up of the Indian economy in the nineties. As a result, banks in India had to remunerate senior employees with two or three times the payment made to a fresher, for handling the same jobs. Statistically too, the situation reflected that a larger share of employees were drawing median salary. Socially, it gave the impression that bank employees were affluent, as lower cadre employees took home handsome pay and could take staff loans adding to their comfort.

In the absence of a tamper-proof human resource management system, the issue arises of the prevalence of a culture of favouritism by senior managers shown to juniors belonging to the same community or language, when a decision on promotion, placement or reward is undertaken. The system provides for the use of discretion. Instances can be observed in many biographies irrespective of the nature of the organisation - be it a government department, private-owned or a corporate in the public and private sector. A common adage is: love your work and not the organisation, because the organisation can ditch you and your career pursuits at any moment.

The scope of bringing improvement to PSBs in India by reforming HR is quite large. As regards bringing changes to HRM in PSB, the scope is very large. It is necessary to reform on the basis of how human psychology works and the importance of physical and mental fitness at different ages. One can find people from two distinct generations doing the same job. The net impact on profitability and productivity can be imagined. Regular voluntary retirement or similar retrenchment schemes may be worth experimenting with to reduce costs as well improving productivity.

Banks outside the bilateral negotiation usually go for finalising pay privately and individually with each employee. These banks are attractive to the employment market by higher start-up and incentives for individual performance and for teams. Employment in such banks emanates a culture of inherent insecurity and a factory-like working environment. Therefore, genetically intelligent but financially poor jobseekers overlook such banks for employment. The employees of these banks work keenly for the incentives and often quit at short notice to take up better offers. Integration within the organisation seemingly will be lower unless it is tied up with employee stock option schemes or similar loyalty schemes. The employees need much more supervision than those aiming for a long term career. This aspect is very important when shocks arise out of fraud, or complaints arising out of conduct damage the image of banks. A highly standardised operating environment with little discretion to employees takes care of such limitations. While multinational banks succeed with systems, indigenous small private banks often fall victim to the conduct of unscrupulous employees. These issues will increase as offices spread and the number of employees rises.

2.3 Placement

There are too many layers of employees, without clear division between worker, supervisor, controller or strategist. Commercial banks, other than the new set of private banks and foreign banks, have as many or more than eight or nine grades of officers. Very rarely does any fresh injection at middle level take place. All employees proceed from the bottom to the top. Due to certain regulations on placements and assignments before promotion, it is difficult to provide equal opportunities to employees while nurturing them in any particular stream of business like credit, IT, branch operations, treasury, foreign exchange, accounts and audit, etc. Thus a person reaching the top may not be experienced in all fields or any one in particular.

Grades: Officers in grade I are referred to as junior management. Those in grades II and III are referred to as middle management. These three are basically in operation as supervisors, credit officers, branch managers, currency officers, etc. Depending on the size of banks, comparable grade officers will be posted. Officers in grades IV and V are called senior management. They usually head departments in administrative offices or regions. Some of them can be seen as branch managers too, in the case of large banks. Thus we find grades I to V working as branch managers and between them the experience can be a minimum of fifteen years or so. Senior managers can be branch managers, heading controlling offices and can be heading single departments in a controlling office. Officers in grades VI, VII and VIII are referred to as top executives. They generally head controlling offices or head single departments in the corporate office and report to the board. Ultimately what may be found is that even though the salary and allowances are more or less the same, the responsibilities are different, causing a huge loss of manpower costs. This scenario goes with Parkinson's Law of 'work expands to fill the time available'. There is ample scope to rationalise, especially in the present IT scenario in which huge branches are no longer necessary.

Public servants One more aspect that impacts the selection process is the special privilege of public sector bank employees who are brought within the definition of a 'public servant'[21]. These employees are subjected to greater scrutiny, for misuse of government funds or of their position for personal ends. The Central Vigilance Commission is the outfit set up by the Indian government that manages the surveillance, reporting and taking

---

[21]   Section 21 of IPC

of appropriate action against public servants who display doubtful personal integrity or whose actions are not in the interests of the nation. Bringing them on a par with government servants, they are advised to be familiar but not friendly with customers. This hampers public sector bank employees in their performance, for example while engaging in conversation with customers to collect market information and in providing smart solutions to customers, compared to their counterparts in private sector banks.

2.4 Leave, transfers and absence management

In general, bank employees are allowed to take twelve days leave annually on short notice, called 'casual leave' or 'CL'; one month of leave on a month's advance notice, referred to as 'Privilege leave' or 'PL'; and one more month of 'sick leave' on medical grounds with half pay. Employees can save and accumulate leave, subject to a ceiling fixed for accumulation. This practice of accumulation brings up certain operational issues. For example, one employee may have got leave approved with a month's notice, another may have some emergencies requiring immediate leave and a third may have been hospitalised. Secondly, in keeping the leave accumulated against each employee, banks are bound to pay the enhanced pay and emoluments at the time of encashment.

The Leave Fare concession is another employee benefit offered by banks that affects their productivity. Public sector banks allow their employees to avail Leave Fare concession or Leave Travel concession once in two years for visiting their home town, and once in four years for travelling to any destination in India from their place of employment. Banks can save the cost of labour by reducing the number of employees who are placed away from their home town. The cost aspect to be considered in this respect is the average size of the family of an employee travelling along with them, and the impact of cost once applied to a million PSB bank employees. On the employee productivity side, the facility has an impact when the sanctioning authority has to yield to requests for leave applied just before they elapse. Allowing employees to encash the balance by year end or avail themselves of it during the year will be more accurate as regards the costing of labour and tax payable to government, as the tax rates vary year after year too. Banks also need not to have to provide for these expenses.

The transfer or shifting of employees from one office to another is regularly done for various reasons. Some of the reasons are: as part of relief arrangements for those who are promoted and taking up a new assignment; another is the bank's own policy that ensures that no employee is retained at the same centre or same job for a specific period. It is worth examining the relevance of continuing this practice in a core banking and mobile communications scenario. Yet another reason is for the opportunity to be given to employees to complete their mandatory assignments to qualify for career advancement. This is more mandatory in nature on the part of the human resources department. In addition to all these, transfer happens when employees are found redundant or wanting in a particular position, or even when they are unable to see eye-to-eye with superiors. Since there is no limit as to how many times an employee can be transferred in his or her career, some of them end up with 20 to 30 assignments in 30 to 35 years of service. Whatever be their grade, all employees are subjected to transfers at very short notice. Such transfers are commonly inferred as punishment transfers, even though it may or may not be the real reason behind the move. Such transfers show the interference of seniors rather than a well functioning human resources management system. The impact of cost on this account is significant, especially in the case of officers who are reimbursed for the cost of transfer and at least a week's time off work. Banks in the private sector, particularly the new ones, have limited incidence of this, although they are sometimes affected by the sudden exit of employees performing exceedingly well. In this case, they have to move senior employees among the existing staff to fill the resulting vacancies.

There are a few aspects that affect the performance of banks in India because of their practice of shifting employees. The first and the most important is the avoidable cost incurred by them, the second one is the impact on the morale of the employee who has been shifted away from their family and the third one is the cost of handling their requests for cancellation of such shifting. The requests for cancellation are either taken up directly by employees or by involving labour unions, government officials, political activists or even court injunctions, usually taken up on medical grounds. Even though these appeals can be few in number, the cost of managing the requests and the working time lost until the matter is settled can be reduced by better management practices.

The cost of transferring employees can be reduced. While clerical employees as part of their service conditions can live at home and serve at the same centre without getting shifted to far-off places, employees in the officers' cadre are bound to live away from their home town for the major part of their career. Taking into consideration the geography of India and banks having operations at remote and under-developed areas, shifting is often found to be troublesome by employees. The personal touch being important, placement of officers can be productively handled on merit, case by case.

One of the most important problems faced by banks in India is the absence of employees in their offices and establishments, even though the number of employees based on productivity gives a different picture. The reason is poor absence management. The adequate number of permitted leave days combined with the privilege of accumulation of leave days and the right to avail these at the employees' convenience, also working days interspersed with holidays, all contribute to poor management. The management are often more compassionate to employees than to the requirements of their organisation. Recent features of leave include maternity leave, available to employees who are permitted absence with pay for childbirth. Though the intention can be seen positively, the practice turns out to be mismanagement. Recently recruited employees taking such leave with salary are left with the opportunity to return from absence after childbirth and leave the organisation for good. Inadequate manning at offices causes collateral loss such as the loss of business and tarnishing of the banks' image.

In the past, bank employees rarely had the privilege of taking leave of office frequently. The leave rules were followed rigidly and requests were refused if sufficient hands were not available to man the office. There was a system of keeping employees as leave reserve to take care of absence. Mostly they would be senior employees having sufficient experience to handle work relating to any desk at a particular office. The focus of attending to customers who visit banks was never lost. Organising meetings during opening times, allowing employees to leave customer windows during business hours, and assigning more than one heterogeneous set of jobs to a single employee are commonly observed nowadays in banks. All of these affect harmony among employees adversely and result in chaotic management of labour resources.

Therefore one can find ample scope for improvement to streamline absence management and enhance the productivity of banks.

2.5 Training

The process and the platform on which banks operate change frequently. Therefore, the importance of training comes from the scope of labour time and processing time saved. Inappropriately trained or untrained employees not only take longer to complete the job but also waste the time of other employees. As soon as changes in the form of innovations are available in the market, banks have to re-skill their employees.

Usually, orientation and induction training is imparted to fresh recruits. Further opportunities for periodical training to brush up skills rarely occur. In effect, employees carry on their work drawing resources from what they learned in the universities, from induction and by seeking guidance from colleagues and superiors who may not be professionally skilled in doing that job. This results in a reduced number of smart employees.

Guest lectures are arranged for specific subject areas. It is necessary that every employee visits a training centre to take a break from the routine, to refresh existing skills and gain the opportunity to mingle with other employees. Due to poor absence management, only employees who can be spared are frequently sent for training. By imparting training properly before taking up an assignment, with customised course designs and course materials for future ready reference, the productivity of banks is improved. However, due to the lack of skilled trainers in banks, training is not available on-tap for employees who need it at some point. There is enough scope to look towards training centres run by retired bank employees. Perhaps regulators can recognise these centres and certify their quality.

3. The process of managing banks' premises

Like human resources, banks have a large amount of premises to be managed. Premises management in banks has two objectives. One is to project banks' image impressively and the other is to cut down the overheads relating to owning and maintaining premises. Prime locations, attractive frontage, spacious forecourts, de-cluttered and spacious ambience with welcoming interiors all definitely enhance the image of banks. In addition to these, it is necessary to provide sufficient parking space for visitors' vehicles.

The choice of better premises depends upon the potential to attract additional business, so that the increased overheads are compensated for by additional tangible and intangible benefits. Therefore a realistic study of the surrounding environment is necessary when looking for premises suitable for banks. Foreign banks used to maintain premises far better than Indian banks until new private banks came onto the scene. Since then branches of other banks also improved their ambience and some of them relocated their branches to better premises.

However, their ability to de-clutter the work area continued to be poor, perhaps as a result of insufficient knowledge to decide on the relevance of papers they hold. Even disposal of the old furniture is not easy since an inventory of fixed assets is an important item in the audit of a bank. Formalities and accountability weigh against taking the major decision of 'to do or not to do' during employees' tenure. The sale and buying of fixed assets is also a common area of favouritism and corruption alleged against employees. The rules of tender have adequate limitations.

Since old items are not removed, new ones cannot be brought in. Employees thus continue to work in stressful cluttered environments. The importance of providing adequately lit, cool, dust-free space to employees at work is borne out by improved productivity. Finally, those superiors who were convinced of the need for keeping their office neat and tidy, carried out the change, while others delayed the change, meanwhile piling up the back yard or closets. With digitalisation sweeping across organisations, banks too may look for ways that enable them to get rid of paper and manage space neatly.

4. Own versus rented premises

Is it better to have one's own premises or manage in leased premises? In earlier days, banks were not interested in increasing their non-banking assets and therefore opted for leased premises rather than to own premises. However, some old banks do hold certain prime property in major cities thanks to their inheritance. Today, acquiring property for offices is considered by management to be an investment. This is because of the consistently increasing trend in property prices for the past three decades.

Buying a new property is a cumbersome process in India. There is a lot "between the cup and the lip". There are issues ranging from the genuineness of ownership to environmental issues. Banks owning heritage buildings face a different set of problems. The maintenance of such buildings is often expensive. Such issues often encourage bankers to go in for leased buildings. Banks, after taking on a lease, create suitable interiors. The leased premises offer fewer legal issues but often end up lacking space for expansion.

Rental expenditure increases not only due to rising rates but due to the opening of new offices, and increases in manpower strength by the creation of more senior level positions. The increasing staff component results in banks paying more for their accommodation. From the data on the staff complement of 81,750 branches of government-owned banks as of March 2014, it may be found that the average number of front office staff (clerks, assistants, associates, etc.) per branch is 5.8 persons while that of supervisory staff is 4.32 persons. Since four clerical grade employees are not usually reimbursed for the cost of accommodation, banks may not incur rental costs for 475,527 employees. However, most of the 353,280 officers would be claiming rental expenses.

It is not difficult to conclude that banks in India have a lot of opportunities to control costs and increase profitability by better policies and systems for management of their premises.

5. Core banking and IT

Banks in India were run on manual ledgers till the middle of the nineties. There was a fear of losing job opportunities and the labour union opposed such change until then. There was another fear of the inability to revert to ledgers once banks switched over to computers for running day-to-day functions. Another factor of diffidence was the lack of confidence on the ability of computer companies to supply the required number of computers and the capability of computers to process huge numbers of transactions. Banks also found the cost as against their annual profit generation favourable to proceed. Having said that, there was no alternative in order to stay competitive but to proceed towards computerisation, as new generation private banks and foreign banks were run on computers from early 1992. Unions were appeased with higher wage compensation and the opening of new branches offered absorption of redundant employees.

Progress from independent computerised branches to networked branches would have helped. The focus therefore shifted to networking which duly depended upon the satellite availability and the cost. Soon the situation improved and earth-bound, very small aperture terminals (V SAT) became popular and ATMs became a possibility. Banks now changed their direction of expansion towards installation of ATMs and networking their offices. The issue of having a centralised database was not considered feasible at that point of time for large banks having a huge volume of data traffic. Many consultants then advised that centralised database management systems were working successfully elsewhere for large banks. By 2000, there was acceptance for this set up and Core Banking Solutions (CBS) were implemented by banks in India one by one. Later, by 2007, looking at the benefits of having banks for customers rather than as hitherto customers relying on their local branch, the RBI persuaded banks to go for CBS and by 2012, even cooperative banks were encouraged to have CBS to be part of the clearing systems. The real time gross settlement systems (RTGS) became very successful and were well received by large value customers.

Thus Indian banks became on a par with international banks as far as IT systems went. However, banks in general faced issues relating to legacy data such as incomplete data, inaccurate data, untraceable customers and non-availability of scanned images of signatures, etc. Complying with Know Your Customer norms in the absence of valid identity and home address became difficult as the system adopted in the past was only by introduction by employees or existing customers. For many customers, especially those holding government accounts, as well as government officials and important customers, these basic matters were overlooked. On the one hand a lot of time during the latter part of 2000 was spent on improving databases. This reduced the focus on business. Serious impact was made on the follow up of loans and non-performing loans increased considerably. The public found the rigid implementation of sanction terms by banks a bit irritating and many accounts were classified by the system as non-performing on the basis of strictly followed norms. In reality, for the bank officials, many of them were not really non-performing, but were judged callously or for reasons beyond their control, including unduly delayed settlement from government. The situation worsened when cleansing exercises of bank balance sheets were directed. When the common database of all bank borrowers maintained by the RBI (CRILC) linked customers on the basis of their Tax ID, many undisclosed non-performing accounts of customers maintained with other banks came to light. If any one account of a borrower is non-performing, all other accounts are expected to be classified as non-performing. The CBS facilitated implementation of this and for banks, the financial year of 2015-16 in general was a poor show.

The CBS implemented in most of the banks provided capabilities for developing data warehouses and other Decision Supporting Systems. Because of issues relating to the accuracy of data, they could not be fully developed and move forward from there. Appreciable development in the phenomenal growth in the number of ATMs, the volume of transactions using RTGS and same day clearing by other payment systems, are benefits of the CBS. Going forward, banks will have the task of elimination of accounts in multiple names for a single person, linking accounts to common identification such as tax identity or the newly introduced AADHAR. Once this task is completed, one can expect a lot of improved decisions from bank managements and better use of labour resources that are grappling with correction of data in systems. Moving unclaimed money to the RBI also clears the bank balance sheet.

The problem will be far from over for the banks. The modern technological competition from mobile phone companies and social network companies such as Facebook, Google, etc., in banking needs to be tackled. If someone can provide loans for a purchase at a shop in a jiffy, where does the retail banking job go? The retail segment is the profitable segment for banks in India. Another major issue that needs to be handled will be the cost of upgrading the present CBS to migrate to banking solutions using new generation mobile telecommunication (3G, 4G and 5G, etc.), cloud computing technology and so on. The immediate challenge will be providing for such expenditure which is on their doorstep. But there can be good development too. With almost all banks uniformly moving to compatible systems, customers can expect portability of accounts from one bank to another soon.

6. Audit

The importance of audit in an organisation where computerisation has become successful is drastically reduced as hardly any leeway exists for committing errors or intentional manipulation of the accounting records. Most of the rules are centrally applied by the system. However, as far as banks in India are concerned, due to legacy issues relating to missing basic data, one cannot conclude that they are fully digital in that sense. Older generation seniors who were nurtured on authority, discretion and not listening to the practical issues of juniors, still prefer a system that can be manipulated to make decisions more just and realistic than by being technically correct towards the customers. On the other side, customers too are not accustomed to such strict following of rules without the application of thought and understanding of the circumstances. Over a period, the number of such customers may thin down. Since such customers continue to exist and bank officials continue to serve, manipulating the systems in banks in India, one cannot conclude that bank audit has lost its significance.

Audit function is a combination of inspection of books, verification of transactions and records, examining the adequacy of checks and balances embedded in the system, issuing certifications required to be submitted to the RBI and summarising the performance of the bank for the period under consideration to the regulators, shareholders and the management. The benefits of the audit function are the opportunities it provides to unearth embezzlement or fraud, plug leakage of income, comply with regulations and save the bank from penalties. However, there are limitations under which auditors complete the task in the short time allowed to them. The ability to standardise the processes and reduce the discretions and deviations by proper automation is one way to harness the cost incurred for audit. Banks have a lot of opportunity for improving the efficiency of audits.

Most banks have their audit committee at board level to review and improve the efficiency of their audit system. Various types of audit carried out by banks in India are discussed below:

Transaction verification or checking Before computerisation of banks, daily transactions were verified and correctness ensured manually. Only the values input and standards of checks and balances embedded in the system need verification. Therefore the benefit of verification audit or checking is in improving the quality of data in the system from which a sound MIS for various functionaries can be set up. Unless the auditors do a professional job and the management at board level take audit observations seriously, the inherent opportunity for manipulating data at operational level will stay and banks will not be able to move towards decision taking based on strong MIS. It all depends upon the efficiency of the audit committee in banks.

Statutory audit Statutory auditors are guided by instructions from regulators and guidelines for interpretation issued to members by the Institute of Chartered Accountants. Interpretation by banks' officials and regulators may cause some confusion during audit. Generally less exposed to banking, the individual or small firm of chartered accountants does not contribute much. Inadequacy of time to complete an audit and lack of a strong concurrent audit system at branches make this audit a ritual. There are exceptional and experienced auditors who point out irregularities of a serious nature. This sort of audit is carried out simultaneously at a large number of bank branches in a computerised environment soon after the financial year ends. Statutory auditors confirm the risk weights of assets, provisioning made for non-performing loans, classification of assets as per RBI norms, and accounting of receivables in the form of subsidies from government, etc.

RBI inspection This is another important audit usually known as an RBI section 35 inspection. The Banking Regulation Act, 1949 empowers the RBI to conduct inspection of banks and report to the government. The inspections focus on compliance of bank branches to licensing terms and to ensure that their functioning is not detrimental to the interests of the depositors. They also have a look at the overall quality of assets of the banks, and systems and procedures followed that contribute to the stability of the banking system. Unlike the statutory auditors, RBI inspectors offer better interpretation of RBI instructions. Their reporting of instances of serious violations can lead to cancellation of the licence of a branch or even liquidation of a bank. The on-site inspection is complementary to off-site inspection, primarily based on reports known as DSB returns submitted by banks and by holding discussions with the chairman and other senior executives of banks quarterly.

Common topics for such informal discussion used to be the following:

- Wrong classification of accounts detected during inspections as performing assets
- Inadequate provision made for bad loans
- Computation errors in claiming subsidy from the government
- Performance of the branch opening vis a vis the target performance
- Application of correct risk weights for assets while computing capital adequacy
- Frauds and media coverage of scams
- Functioning of management, mainly transmission of RBI instructions to their operating units for implementation
- Profitability of branches
- Omissions, if any, in the maintenance of funds with the RBI for CRR and investments for SLR requirements
- Compliance-related issues

One has to give credit to the regulators for a stable banking scenario in India by timely interventions and removing unethical banks from the scene. While bank officials may view there to be a lack of pragmatism in RBI inspectors, RBI officials see the inadequacy of training among bank officials in implementing RBI instructions.

Currency audit Other than the section 35 audit as a central banker, the RBI coordinates a few other banking operations that need closer supervision, such as the supply of currencies and custody of foreign exchange. For the purpose of managing the supply of currency notes across banks in India adequately, the RBI has established currency chests. These chests are managed through selected bank branches and these branches have to follow the prescribed rules of the RBI from time to time. In order to verify that the branches comply with the rules, the RBI deputises its officers and reports on the omissions in a constant effort to improve the housekeeping of these chests. If poor upkeep of chests is reported, the officers advise that they be closed. This may not be in the interests of a bank, as there are some inherent advantages of hosting a currency chest.

Usually, shortage of currencies, untidy maintenance of the chest, mixing up bank articles inside a chest, unauthorised access allowed inside the chest, inadequacy of security equipment, etc., are common shortcomings pointed out in such reports.

Forex Audit With liberalisation of handling forex under the Foreign Exchange Management Act 2000, and "anywhere banking" facilitated by the core banking solution in commercial banks, the importance of forex audit at the operational level has been reduced. Therefore, forex audit is being carried out along with RBI section 35 inspection. The focus of the audit, among other factors, is to detect any remittance made handled by the bank exceeding the limit, failure to report capital account transactions promptly and the involvement of bank officials in any money laundering transactions.

Government audit Another external auditor who has access to banks' books are the inspectors deputised from government to those branches handling government business. Many banks referred to as 'accredited banks' are appointed to handle banking expenditure for certain allocated departments of the Indian government. In addition, banks also handle pension payments to retired government employees and maintain a savings account called the public provident fund.

Officials from the respective government departments visit branches to verify that settlement of funds received is prompt, statements are submitted properly, payments to pensioners are made after obtaining life certificates annually, deposits are accounted for in the PPF accounts, claims made for commission for handling government business are error-free, etc.

Other common Internal Audits There are many other audits carried out on banks' books such as credit audit, spot audit, management audit, forensic audit, etc., carried out internally by banks.

Credit audit While credit approvals and documentation are guided by the same regulations across a particular bank, variations do happen, perhaps due to the scope for misinterpretation or individual excesses. The usual internal audit brings out individual excesses, and variation due to interpretation may not surface. A credit audit is intended to plug this loophole so that across the bank, loan requests are handled uniformly. This audit is carried out by officials who have considerable exposure to credit. They focus on assessing the quality of loan appraisal, follow up, documents held as security, etc. The success of this audit depends purely upon the professionalism of the auditor.

Spot audit Banks receive communication directly from the public on certain accounts, officers or customers. Sometimes, the press also provides information which may have the scope to result in a bank scam or a bank fraud in the future. Acting on the first information to hand, the management deploys officers to inspect records, submit a report on the situation and check the veracity of the information. Even the RBI also conducts such audits under similar circumstances. Early action or dismissal of hearsay will hold bank managements in good stead.

Forensic audit The objective of this audit is to gather credible evidence or financial information to be presented in a court of law against a member of the public or employee who has committed financial crimes such as embezzlement, forgery, impersonation, acceptance of a bribe, etc. Personnel from criminal intelligence departments, senior auditors and former employees of regulators discharge this service.

Management audit Banks, in the course of making improvements, create many positions with certain objectives. Later, due to various internal reasons, the purpose of many of these positions gets diluted as they are combined with other positions or vacancies are not filled up. Thus the intended purpose is not served. Therefore banks carry out a management audit to evaluate the performance of personnel in various management positions vis-a-vis their role as envisaged. This helps to restore the merits of the thoughts behind the creation of each position in a bank.

Even though there are so many audits and inspection processes carried out by banks in India, they throw up surprises or shocks year after year, by increases in their non-performing assets, loan loss provisions, violations of anti-money laundering guidelines, etc. Managements will have to point their fingers at audit personnel. The merit of personnel is the key to achieving better results. Other reasons for such poor returns on investment for the audit process are the misuse of authority of inspecting officers, poorly drafted or edited inspection reports, etc.

The audit system can be improved by bench-marking their audit process against that of better banks. Some banks carry out corrections simultaneously during the audit rather than setting aside rectification as a task for the future.

While cent per cent checking of daily transactions is advisable, an audit can be effective by detailed analysis of sample data followed by the required policy level changes, organisational changes and countermeasures to thwart operational risk.

Two core issues still remain among banks. One of them is to prefer internal officials to chartered accountants on contract terms, for internal audits. The second issue is whether statutory auditors are representatives of the management or of shareholders. Their enthusiasm to conduct an audit and report fearlessly is dampened by the fact that the renewal of the audit contract depends largely upon their trouble-free consummation of the audit work.

7. Foreign exchange (forex) business

A lot of money transactions happen in currencies other than the Indian Rupee (INR) which is the home currency in India. All such transactions handled or invoiced in foreign currency involve foreign exchange (Forex) and are subject to the rules circulated under The Foreign Exchange Management Act, 1999 (Act 42 of 1999), commonly referred to as FEMA. The RBI is the custodian of foreign exchange in India. It manages with the help of commercial banks and authorised money changers spread far and wide throughout the country. Issuing guidelines and obtaining periodic reports enables the RBI to manage the forex of the nation.

There are two types of commercial bank branches which are permitted to handle forex. One of them is permitted to open independent bank accounts abroad with other banks and can also open bank accounts for banks in foreign countries. They are usually referred to as Category A branches. They buy and sell and their net position reveals how much forex they have. For the accounts they operate abroad, they maintain the mirror account called a Nostro account and for accounts operated by foreign banks from their country, they maintain accounts called Vostro accounts. Now, with online facilities available, issues relating to reconciliation are not as important as in the past.

The other categories of banks that are allowed to operate forex are referred to as category B banks. Customers can obtain forex and they handle all remittances and export and import business through them. These banks complete their foreign exchange transactions through their linked category A banks. They are also authorised to recommend proposals to the RBI for foreign direct investment (FDI) arranged by local companies, or overseas investment by Indians. A consolidated report on forex handled by their category A and B branches will enable the RBI to understand forex movement during a period. Current forex regulations do not permit any banks to allow current accounts in forex for the public.

A Foreign Currency Non Resident (FCNR) account allows the customer to keep deposits in forex in the form of short term deposits. There are some accounts which allow international traders to hold forex in accounts under the Exchange Earners Foreign Entitlement Scheme known as EEFC accounts or Returning Indians Foreign Exchange Entitlement accounts (RIFEE). Indians are now allowed to hold forex up to a small sum (USD 2,000) instead of the earlier regulations to deposit all forex with a bank within 7 days.

A lot of Indians work abroad and a lot of trade takes place with other countries. Therefore, forex transactions are plenty and the inflow and outflow of forex depends also upon the fiscal measures of other countries, such as interest rates and taxation. There is a need to preserve foreign exchange especially to meet obligations to acquire essential imports of oil and defence equipment, hence forex is considered to be precious for the nation. However, it may not be prudent to hold too much foreign currency against the Indian rupee which is consistently falling against hard currencies. In order to maintain a near optimum balance, just sufficient to meet forex obligations in the near future, the RBI relaxes norms for allowing repatriation of remittances.

The change in norms impacts Indians living in India (Residents) with connections abroad, Indians living abroad (Non Residents and Persons of Indian Origin), Indians doing business abroad (exporters and importers of goods and services), recognised Foreign Institutional Investors, etc. Privileges are different for them for obtaining forex, holding it for the future or repatriating it. All forex operations are channelled through category A or B banks. Banks' auditors verify the transactions and certify correct compliance to regulations and reporting.

One report submitted by banks is on currency transactions and another is on goods and services exported. Goods and services exported need to be followed up in order to obtain a fair price for them within a reasonable time. Auditors, by verifying customs department documents, certify the landing of goods imported into the country for all remittances made earlier. The amount of forex released to the public is monitored by examining the due diligence observed by the exchange, both on the purpose stated by the person requesting forex and on their personal identity.

FEMA classifies all transactions into Capital and Current accounts. While regulations on current account transactions are relaxed, transactions falling under capital accounts require approvals before making remittances from the RBI and the government, above the delegated levels of banks. RBI guidelines are available in the form of master circulars, updated annually. The delegated powers for banks in respect of capital account transactions are intended to save time in processing and therefore, banks have to complete the process of approval and report to the RBI regularly on such approvals and remittances.

Inadequate data on the number of Indians abroad and their earning capacity is an important gap in information that leaves scope for improving forex management. Lack of knowledge and inability to get rid of transactions in unaccounted money (money laundering) are other problems faced by the RBI in controlling banks' forex operations. There are also issues faced by the Indian government regarding Indian entrepreneurs who operate from other countries because of the better hospitality offered to them with better tax saving, labour laws and recognition.

8. Payment systems – clearing, etc.

Almost the entire banking system has been brought under core banking except for a few cooperative banks. Therefore, the payment and settlement system uses state-of-the-art technology. The attitude of the public regarding the adoption of an electronic system is visible as paper based systems like cheques, drafts, etc., are falling consistently by 9% annually in volume while electronic transactions are growing by 30%. Though there are more than a thousand clearing houses, the large volume is handled by the RBI. The entire system of payment and settlement functions under the supervision of the RBI which has been mandated by the legislation - The Payment and Settlement Systems Act, 2007(Act 51 of 2007). The preamble to the Act states 'to provide for the regulation and supervision of payment systems in India and to designate the Reserve Bank of India as the authority for that purpose', etc. Clearing houses managed by other banks do so on the basis of the RBI's clearing house rules[22]. The last lap is to move large volume cash transactions into bank transactions. The issues faced are the high tax rate, low profitability in business and the illusion that 'tax is complex and hassles follow thereafter in life'.

With the core banking solution implemented in almost all banks, the concept of linking a customer to a branch has changed to that of linking to a bank.

---

[22]   http://rbidocs.rbi.org.in/rdocs/Publications/PDFs/73100.pdf

The various payment and settlement systems such as Real Time Gross Settlement, retail electronic clearing, usage of debit cards and credit cards, ATMs and Points of Sale of various banks, enable the public to remit funds without much fuss. With internet banking becoming more popular day by day, a visit to a bank branch is no longer required. Mobile banking offers further scope for making banking a pleasant experience. As at the end of March 2016, according to the RBI,[23] there are 199,099 ATMs and 661.82 million debit cards in usage. There are also 24.50 million credit cards in use. The ease of obtaining currency at odd hours, the proximity of ATMs and the facility to draw cash from any bank's ATMs, all provide ample scope for people turning more towards banking and settlement through banks. Electronic systems also save a large amount of time for bank personnel that used to spend their time on daily settlement between bank branches, and between banks. Further, proliferation of payment banks, which can convert mobile phones into a bank, to remote areas, will make the transfer of funds between banks very easy and comfortable for the public.

Section 3 - Ancillary functions

Other prominent functions that banks in India undertake for their customers are the safe custody of articles, providing safety lockers/deposit boxes, discounting bills against foreign and inland LCs, maintaining tax-saving government accounts and currency management.

1.(a) Safe custody

Banks utilise their vaults for keeping packets deposited by customers for safe custody. Banks will not open them except in emergencies or in the event of customers not turning up for abnormally long periods and not responding to their communications. The bank levies an annual fee. The public uses them for keeping land documents and other such important documents. Banks also provide a nomination facility as in the case of deposit accounts.

---

23   https://rbi.org.in/Scripts/ATMView.aspx

2.(b) Safe lockers

Banks provide the key for the cubicles and allow them to be operated independently at the customer's convenience during banking hours. The facility suits the public as gold and jewels are pinned or otherwise adorned onto female members' bodies during family functions such as marriages, etc. Customers usually deposit such items back before the closing time of the bank and avoid keeping the ornaments overnight at home. Banks levy locker fees on the basis of the capacity of the cubicle. Even though for banks, the investment per se for offering this service may be high, it is mostly continued because of its low maintenance cost and the opportunity to offer value-added service to high value customers. Difficulties which arise in pursuing this business are litigation on account of breaking open the locker in case of customers not responding to their communications, and difficulty in recovering locker fees. People, once they have lodged their things in the locker, often go away and are uncontactable for a long time, as many Indians work at locations far away from their home in India. Looking to the future, the locker business will get a boost once banks are able to provide this service as a special service.

2. Currency management

96% of currency chests are held with government banks and two thirds are with the SBI group. A commercial bank branch maintaining a currency chest is under a regulatory and reporting relationship with the RBI directly. All banks linked to currency chest branches form part of the currency distribution system. The objective is to provide good notes in convenient denominations. It involves adequate storage with appropriate denominations. Exchanging fresh notes against soiled notes, cut notes, etc., and confiscation of counterfeit notes, are also functions of the system. The rupee being a low value currency, the number of pieces of currency changing hands is large. Value-wise, roughly 85% of the currency notes in circulation are in denominations of Rs.1,000 and 500. Quantity wise, these two denominations share 22 % of the total notes in circulation. The number will further increase as the number of ATMs rises in future.

The popularity of ATMs has major importance in currency management., as does the demand for higher denominations such as 500 and 1,000. Also, the practice of stapling currency notes has been disallowed. Therefore currency counting machines become more necessary at counters and sorting machines at branches. The number of ATMs has mushroomed.

Banks maintaining currency chests have a portion of their human resources dedicated to currency chest-related activity. Apparently banks that want to hold currency chests have to balance the benefits of having a comfortable position as regards currency notes for their customers, and obligations that are not so economical from other associated work such as collection of soiled notes, sending them to the RBI periodically, daily reporting of balances, maintaining sorting machines, dedicated staff, etc. They are also subject to periodical inspection from the RBI.

The system of passing on the cost of handling currencies by chest branches is not practiced perfectly. They should be in a position to pass this on to other banks who should in turn pass it to the traders and other customers who deposit large amounts of currency notes into their bank accounts. Traders and merchants handling currency may be encouraged to pass the savings in cost of handling currencies to customers who use electronic payments. In this respect, it is also necessary that banks are strongly discouraged from offering concessions to customers for continuing with large amounts of cash deposits into bank accounts.

3. Discounting bills

Banks in India advance funds against bills of exchange of customers. Though this discounting is done on the strength of the person on whom the bill is drawn, the banks usually do this for their regular customers who have separate credit lines for discounting. The risk of such discounting is mitigated by obtaining letters of credit from the bank or banks of the customer drawing (or drawee) and the documents are drawn up according to the procedure accepted under International Chamber of Commerce guidelines. The system is followed for bills payable both in India and abroad. Banks also do discounting without the letter of credit provided, the security from collaterals and indemnities being sufficient. The success of the discounting business depends upon the employees' skill in selection of borrowers, scrutiny of documents and a proper follow-up mechanism that ensures prompt realisation of sums advanced. Operational risks involved are undetected forgery in documents, impersonation of any of the parties, the drawing customer remitting directly to customers instead of the bank that has discounted bills, etc. Quite a lot of disputes lead to litigation and the resultant addition to banks' non-performing loans.

Issuing letters of credit and discounting bills is necessary for traders to manage their cash flow. Importers or buyers will have to look for support from their financiers, by issuing letters of credit whenever suppliers do not sell them goods on credit terms. Similarly, whenever buyers demand credit terms for their purchases, the exporters require their bills of exchange to be discounted. Therefore traders, irrespective of the volume of their business, expect an efficient discounting set-up to be in place. The efficiency of the discounting business depends upon the knowledge and experience gained by employees over a period and the vast database of counterparties coupled with a reliable intelligence network. From the scenario of banking in India, the scope for developing this business is quite large, as most banks do discounting for small and medium borrowers against their personal indemnity or mortgage of security rather than on the strength of the buyer. One option could be to organise the discounting business in India by way of exclusive institutions in the form of factors, discount houses, etc., or by setting up separate verticals in banks.

Banks in India also carry on the business of discounting cheques. This is a bit more common among individuals and SMEs than the discounting of bills. However, the volume of business is getting reduced as almost all banks are under the centralised core banking solution by which there is no delay in getting payment. While some bank cheques are paid instantly on presentation, cheques drawn on other banks get cleared in two to three days' time. However, discounting of cheques continues, especially in the case of dividend warrants not drawn as 'payable at all branches' or cheques issued by government departments, etc. However these have moved to a direct credit to the bank accounts of shareholders.

In the absence of banks not offering the facility of discounting bills or cheques separately, traders use their working capital finance in the form of a running account facility. In this case bills and cheques are sent for collection direct to the buyer or drawee and on realisation, the fund is made available. Thus, traders suffer from higher interest cost, increased cost of sales and add-on cost, on account of taxes thereon. Ultimately, the profit is affected if traders are not able to pass on the cost to consumers.

4. Issue of Bank Guarantees

Bank guarantees were considered as financial guarantees earlier, since the obligation of the guarantee-issuing bank was to make payment unconditionally on receipt of a notice from the beneficiary. Banks were not expected to verify the veracity of the alleged failure of obligation from the applicant of the guarantee. However, there has been a distinction drawn between financial guarantee and performance guarantee according to the RBI[24]. According to them, financial guarantees are seen as a direct substitute for credit, while performance guarantees are for transaction-related contingencies such as bid bonds, performance bonds, etc.

Though it is easy for bank employees to issue bank guarantees and book remuneration upfront without much work, they are occasionally drawn into litigation challenging the procedure followed by them while honouring the obligation. A notice from the beneficiary along with the original bank guarantee is necessary for them to process payment of the guaranteed sum. If an injunction is issued by a court of law and is received by a bank before actually making payment, the whole process of making payment is put on hold.

The guarantee agreement needs to specify the date of expiry of the guarantee and the last date of receipt of the notice. If a guarantee is to be renewed for a further period, it is expected to be done before the expiry date. Government departments may delay in returning the expired guarantee and may hold it

---

[24]   RBI/2012-13/467DBOD.No.BP.BC.89.21.04.009/2012-13 dated April 2nd 2013

for an indefinite period. However, in the absence of any alternative, bank guarantees are issued for all requirements within the country.

In spite of awareness of the issues that could possibly emerge any time during the currency of the bank guarantee, customers like their banks to issue guarantees in order to save cash outflow. If the bank guarantee business is kept out of the purview of court interventions, and government departments return expired guarantees, there is some commercial sense in continuing with this business or banks may have to offer standby letters of credit that lapse after the expiry date automatically, in place of guarantees. Except in cases where bank guarantees are issued against the full cash margin, the remuneration levied while issuing guarantees may not offset the cost of litigation and other collateral expenditure.

5. Handling complaints from customers

Complaints from customers are quite common against banks in India. Many of them go unrecorded and are settled mutually. After an initial outburst, the customer may leave aside the issue and not pursue it with the bank. Bank employees mostly settle the issues by compromise and by resolving any misunderstanding. Those that are left unresolved become complaints. Therefore, it may be difficult for banks to have a record of customers lost on this count or of the cost incurred on such compromise settlements. Perhaps regular market research by independent agencies or monitoring authorities can take care of this, thereby improving the standard of service of banks in India.

Most of the complaints originate from the banks' own advertised features of products and services. Some of these announcements arise on account of the government, or other practical problems. There is no watchdog to check or vet all communications and fix compensation from banks for complaints due to misunderstanding emanating from websites, communications, publicity brochures, etc.

However, banks follow certain accepted practices of handling complaints. A written complaint submitted to their office will have to be acknowledged at branch level and will be followed up by higher level management. The service of the Banking Ombudsman is available for customers who are not satisfied with the banks' handling of the case. The Ombudsman, after listening to both the bank official and the customer, issues an order and settles the matter. If the complaint is about a case of deficiency of service, customers have the option to pursue the complaint through the Consumer Redressal forum.

There is a system of reporting and monitoring the number of complaints received and disposed of periodically in all banks. The banks have a Customer Service Committee at all levels to monitor this and the committee is vested with the power to inflict punishment on employees. If the committee, whose members are eventually responsible for providing service, pay the required attention to training, miscommunication may be prevented and customer education improved.

Insights one can derive from the illustrative cases of complaints handled by the RBI Ombudsman, taken from their annual reports, are as follows:

i)   Failure of banks to set up an authority and decide on a process to settle grievances. Bank officials are hesitant to compensate customers voluntarily for the loss incurred by an action to which the customer has not contributed. This may have happened due to some system misuse or impersonation. They wait for orders from the ombudsman or a consumer court as an authority for determining the compensation, if any.

ii) Once a fraud is detected the subsequent process is delayed causing the aggrieved to visit the ombudsman.

iii) When two or more banks are involved in a case, in case of cheque collection, interbank remittance, etc., both banks do not always put in earnest efforts to resolve the issue jointly.

iv) The process of handling an 'alert' is not complete negating any effective use of alerts for customers. Banks do not provide a separate channel to reply to alerts and fraud may have happened by the time the alerted customer is able to contact the bank.

v)   The system of returning all telephone calls and attending to all emails from customers is not done as an obligation to customers.

Most of the complaints were related to ATMs, internet banking, credit cards, imperfect communications, uncoordinated system set-up by banks (tax deductions, etc.), lack of job knowledge on the part of bank employees, etc. There were also cases where miscreants try to gain by false complaints.

In order to improve the standards of service in banks, another initiative was the setting up of The Banking Codes and Standards Board of India[25] in 2006 by the RBI. The Board provides a comprehensive code of conduct to be adhered to by its members for the fair treatment of customers. Membership of BCSBI is voluntary and open to scheduled banks, Regional Rural Banks and Urban Co-operative Banks. As of March 2014, 127 members are committed to this code and a paltry number of 512 complaints were handled during the year 2013-14. Perhaps the low number reflects that the Board is just another outfit not so popular with the masses.

A set up like a 'watchdog' to represent customer issues with the appropriate authority and advise on course correction in processing is necessary. They should also take the initiative to conduct surveys among customers and advise banks on any shortcomings in their systems and procedures. This may help banks to improve the quality of service rendered and to save on overheads incurred to manage complaints. It is also necessary that any recourse available to a customer for unsatisfactory service is spelt out clearly and the process of taking it up with the appropriate authority is safe and easy. There is a long way to go before Indian banks consider their customer as an asset or as described by the father of the nation, Mahatma Gandhi, during a speech in South Africa in 1890:

"A customer is the most important visitor on our premises. He is not dependent on us. We are dependent on him. He is not an interruption of our work. He is the purpose of it. He is not an outsider of our business. He is part of it. We are not doing him a favour by serving him. He is doing us a favour by giving us the opportunity to do so."

It all depends upon the management as to how they have disciplined their employees to take care of their customers, how each and every system helps

---

[25]   http://www.bcsbi.org.in/

their employees to work better in rendering better service to customers and when lapses are come across, the opportunity is provided to improve in that instance.

6. Vigilance over public servants

All employees of banks owned by the government are brought under the term 'public servants' and they are within the ambit of the Central Vigilance Commission Act, 2003, so that employees causing loss by acting negligently or for personal consideration are proceeded against. However, delays in processing accusations need to be quickly resolved. Therefore, all public sector banks have the services of a Vigilance Officer, mainly to track any instance falling under the Prevention of Corruption Act, 1988.

Most banks have a separate vertical system for vigilance so that employees are cleared of accusations quickly. Even though the processes are designed to be fair, the circumstances provide ample opportunity for the disciplinary authority to take arbitrary decisions. Word-of-mouth opinions vitiate the decisions. In the end the employee loses his career and banks lose promising employees. In fact, employees hurt by these decisions often become unproductive or less productive. The number of employees who have lost their initiative and languish in banks may be significant. There is ample scope for transparency and standardisation of processes and less discretionary decision-making. A suitable mechanism may be necessary to save banks from such accountability, as an exercise to save time and apply appropriate punishment in the event of the rarest of rare cases which are proved beyond doubt.

7. Fraud management

Banks, by the nature of their business of handling public money, offer a fertile place for evil minds to try their luck, either as an employee or as a customer. From bank to bank the situation will be different depending upon their level of rigidity in enforcing systems and procedures. Once a fraud comes to light, the objective of fraud management is to recover the money lost and save innocent employees who are caught in the process from harassment by the police. The idiom 'prevention is better than cure' is appropriate here, as recovery will not close the matter. Therefore, it is necessary for management to plug loopholes in the systems.

There is a need for analysis of information collected from various formal and informal sources for continuous improvement in the systems, as technology can only take care of the changing attitude of employees and customers towards wealth accumulation.

The 'intent to deceit' for gaining wealth implied in a usual transaction makes a fraudulent transaction appear different from a normal transaction. Mere deviation from the banks' policy per se need not be construed as fraud but the intention alters the character of the transaction. Perhaps the number of instances relating to deviations from the banks' policies and a disproportionate increase in the wealth of employees are the main areas where intelligence is required. For a fraudster, opportunities are everywhere. Cheques are an opportunity presented by the banking system to fraudsters. The 2002 Steven Spielberg film 'Catch me if you can' is about a person who found opportunities beckoning everywhere. Starting with forging his own father's cheque, he could impersonate a doctor, airline pilot, etc., on the basis of opportunities presented to him. Fraudsters are likely to go after every opportunity that comes to them until they are caught. Once they are caught, they offer a lot of information that lays bare the loopholes in the banks' systems and procedures. Since banks follow different systems and procedures, the nature of frauds reported also differs. Crowded places offer less opportunity to people for fraud. As the number of employees per branch reduces, the potential for employee-related fraud may perhaps increase, unless control systems are cent per cent implemented and no room for allowance is given or excuse for exceptions encouraged.

It is mentioned in a report by the RBI[26], that government-owned banks' share of frauds using the traditional methods of impersonation and forgery is higher, while new private banks and foreign banks are more prone to technology-related frauds.

---

[26] http://www.rbi.org.in/scripts/BS SpeechesView.aspx?id=826

Commonly occurring frauds in Indian banks are as follows:

- Forgery of cheques used for discounting
- Forgery of land documents offered as security for loans
- Forgery of identity cards and proofs of address used for opening accounts to encash stolen cheques
- Impersonation for opening benami (misnamed) accounts
- Impersonation while declaring ownership of land and other assets offered as security
- Theft of personal details for using others e-banking facility
- Setting up entities such as
  - o Non-government organisations for availing government aids
  - o Hospitals, colleges, etc., with fake qualifications
  - o Building projects on land in respect of which the owners are not known, abroad or even on government-owned land
- Staff involvement in
  - o Pilferage of cash and valuables from vaults
  - o Embezzlement of customers accounts
  - o Putting through inter-office transactions that are not genuine
  - o Sending out wrong confirmation of credit
  - o Employees sharing passwords

Banks submit reports periodically on frauds detected and the progress of investigation to the RBI. The process adopted for instances of fraud is circulated to banks so they can take the necessary preventive measures. There are vigilance and whistle-blower systems in vogue in Indian banks. There is room for improving the intelligence systems of banks for preventing loss on account of fraud.

8. Handling the media of publicity – less sharing

Banks incur expenditure for advertising and publicity, mostly for statutory requirements such as declaration of quarterly results, information regarding the opening of new branches, shifting of offices and notices inviting tenders; and not for creating a market for their products and services. Of course, one finds some publicity for awards and recognitions conferred to banks' executives by others.

Banks have to move to targeted advertisements and publicity methods with the help of professional firms engaged in the business, like other consumer companies do. For banks, there is scope for new customers, wherever there are people. Prominent hoardings can be used to stimulate thoughts of banks or banking services. Regular distribution of pamphlets at social gatherings will bring people to the bank office. On their first visit, brochures on various products and services should be in vernacular that is designed to provide answers reasonably to all questions and enable them to judge their eligibility, and need to be made freely available. It is necessary that they are up-to-date. All of these require meticulous planning and form part of the overall design of productive marketing.

There is a need to handle media requirements professionally. Most of the communications have to be presented from the point of view of answers to an information seeker. Bank websites need to be benchmarked to the best in the world.

9. Brand management

Most common banks are government-owned and they are outside the momentum of stock price movement. Similarly, government ownership provides much wanted trust to the public regarding safety of funds. In India it also provides the right to complain which can be used even in parliament. However banks in the private sector enjoy a local market and brand value created by them during the period of their existence. Real brand value is to charge a little more for services, which a customer won't mind paying. Among banks in the vast geography of India it is the regional strength, government ownership, stock market index and familiarity of employees that matter.

There are certain other interesting factors that affect the bank brands. Common-sounding names make it difficult to derive a unique value for a bank's service. Banks have used words such as India and national in their names quite often, e.g. Punjab National Bank, Central Bank of India, Union Bank of India, City Union Bank, United Bank of India, South Indian Bank, Indian Bank, Bank of India, State Bank of India, etc. There are a few banks with distinctive names linked to places in India such as Canara Bank, Dena Bank, Bank of Baroda, Andhra Bank, Allahabad Bank, Karur Vysya Bank, etc. New private banks have unique distinguishable names. Many banks also have slogans or tag lines. Popularity is proportionate to their publicity and frequency of exposure.

Beyond this, whether any individual bank has unique features other than those that are service related, such as names, emblems, tag lines or slogans, and whether these have had any major impact in promoting the brand value of a bank, needs to be ascertained after conducting a thorough independent market survey through the length and breadth of the country. A proper brand-building exercise is also necessary as brands are an important tool for word-of-mouth marketing that helps to penetrate into unbanked areas.

Ultimately, only after a company is known for its efficient systems and procedures and sound financials, can brand promotion become successful and provide an edge to increase its margin of profit.

Section 4 - Capital Management

Banks do not have to depend on their own funds to do business, in the real sense. They grow with deposits received from account holders. The role of the regulator is very important for having a sound banking system. Since the size of the bank and its hold on the economy by its network are important factors in order to estimate the devastation a bank can cause upon liquidation, regulators in India have prescribed a ratio of Capital to Assets to be maintained by each bank. This ratio is popularly known as the Capital Adequacy Ratio (CAR). Periodically a statement is submitted to the RBI with details of the type of assets and their risk value and capital reserves, etc. The risk value of assets is worked out on the basis of the risk weight of assets prescribed by the RBI. A loan against the banks' own fixed deposits for example, carries lower risk than a consumer loan. As a result of these norms, banks need to have a risk management system, credit rating system, and loan approval system based on risk rating.

Banks have to engineer to pack their loan portfolio with low risk-weighted borrowers, better credit rated borrowers or borrowers with easily realisable collaterals. They also need to invest their funds in better investment-rated securities and higher rates of return. Ultimately, over and above the capital reserve accumulated over the long period of their existence, banks in India depend upon the professionalism of their present employees and the capability of their systems to extract up-to-date information accurately in order to manage their capital.

1. Managing Assets

Banking depends on its professionals and the risk management system when it comes to managing assets. There is no dearth of good human resources but training is required to make the best of their potential for the job. The risk management system depends upon collection of data and accurate analysis of data to forecast probable loss, and management systems and policies to prevent risk getting converted into loss.

Data management is an issue and many banks are bogged down with a legacy of data. Audit systems depend upon the sincerity of the auditors and the seriousness with which the management makes any policy-level changes, on the basis of deviations reported by auditors and the regular analysis of assets, so that accurate rating will ensure the good quality of assets.

Finally, it is from the market that banks have to pick and choose their loans and investments. Government banks have to offer loans under schemes and assist the government in its development programme. In addition to the loans, the labour diverted to manage them takes resources from the banks. The bank leadership should be able to devise such mechanisms in consultation with government, so that their overall banking services still remain competitive. Banks like the SBI with 450 billion USD assets, go to the same market where local money lenders, finance companies or rural cooperative banks operate. Foreign banks with limited funds and under more regulatory restrictions often are choosy in selecting assets. New private banks focus on improving shareholder value, and have their own method of picking customers.

Since the country is under-banked, there is a large market lying untapped. Banks need to have a prospective look at the opportunity and devise schemes to spread their network and grow assets to gain dominance.

2. Managing profit

Banks operate in a highly regulated environment that provides little leeway for independent decision-making to boost profit. The leadership in government-owned banks is influenced by government. And the activities of government banks influence the market and thereby the operation of private banks as well. Some of the major areas of influence on profit are related to interest rates, the Cash Reserve Ratio (CRR), the Statutory Liquidity Ratio (SLR), banks' policy on buying and carrying non-banking assets, the recruitment of employees, etc.

High interest rates A major segment of customers of banks includes the pensioners and salary earners who depend upon the interest on bank deposits for their living. They form a sizeable vote bank during elections. Therefore any policy towards the abnormal reduction of interest will not connect the government favourably with that segment of electorates. Therefore, the interest rate offered by banks on deposits will have to match the high inflation rate prevailing in the country.

Another factor that influences the bank deposit rate is the interest rate offered on public deposits by the government through National Savings Certificate and Postal Saving Schemes, even though they are not as flexible as bank deposits. An investment made by a person in the highest tax bracket of 30% will see a big gap. NSC VIII series offers 151.62 after five years for Rs.100 which means a total return of 51.62 in five years. An investment of Rs.100 in effect being only Rs.70 after netting saving on account of tax rebate, the average annual return works out to 14.75%. On the other hand, the bank deposit at 8 per cent per annum, after deducting the tax deducted at source, earns just 7.20 per cent which is a mere half of what someone gains from investing in NSC. Another investment that influences the interest rate is the Public Provident Fund for which deposits can be made and withdrawn at identified commercial bank branches.

The strategy to reduce the impact of the high interest rate on deposits is to mobilise more of current account deposits with no interest, and savings accounts with 4% interest. These two deposits are referred as CASA and most banks have a 40-50% share of CASA deposits. The sanctity of the ratio of CASA is not great as Indian banks freely allow premature closure of fixed deposits. Precisely, deposits can more or less be taken out on demand. Secondly, savings accounts balances usually stay longer and may lie unattended, as these accounts are simple to operate and earn tax free interest. This is a positive option for people who are not so conscious about their wealth management requirements. In the end, the interest rate on deposits is high and so is the interest rate of loans. The high interest on loans makes a serious dent in the profitability of enterprise and easily becomes a non-performing asset.

Provisions for NPA Non-performing loans trouble banks in two ways. One of them is the inability for banks to book interest on such loans and thereby reduce the net interest margin[27]. Secondly, it requires provisions to be made from operating profit. The loans go bad because of the recessionary phase in the economy. Encouraging withdrawal of more funds would perhaps lead to an increase in the interest expense and can cause further loss to the borrower.

Cash Reserve Ratio Other significant factors that adversely affect growth of capital in Indian banks are non interest-yielding Cash Reserve Ratio, high employment, the low-yielding investment market and the low-yielding government-mandated loans.

---

[27] Net Interest Margin is the ratio of interest income less interest expenses over interest earning assets, while interest spread is net of average cost of deposit reduced from average yield on advances.

The current cash reserve ratio in India is 4% of their net demand and time liabilities (current savings and fixed deposits). Commercial banks with eligible deposits of 97 trillion rupees (1,465 billion USD), had kept a balance of 4.75 trillion rupees (72 billion USD) with the RBI without any earnings as at 31st March 2016. Even at 8.5 per cent annual yield, the opportunity lost can be around 403 billion rupees or 6 billion USD. When the top three banks make just 5 billion USD net profit in 2015-16, the argument for reducing the rate of CRR may look reasonable.

Employee Cost The banking industry is primarily employee-oriented and the quality and skill level of employees affect the ultimate profitability of banks. Even though employee strength can be reduced by the deployment of IT systems such as core banking systems, the expansion of the branch network demands more employees. Another aspect of employee cost is the delayering of management levels with development of available management information systems and decision support systems.

While new private banks have the advantage to move to these systems and reduce employees, they still have demand for employees to expand their network. Traditional banks and government banks are not able to do delayering as these banks continue to have nine to ten layers or levels when they could have managed with four or five. At operational level, even if there are two or three, the middle level and strategic level can comprise one or two each. There is large scope for reduction of strength in these two top layers. In addition, the average age of officials at the level of middle and top management hovers around 50-55 years since there is no middle level injection of fresh blood. At this age, usually human cognitive senses start becoming less efficient. They also tend to be like-minded as they climb up the management level simultaneously. There is scope for rejuvenating bank boards.

As regards employee payment, most banks other than the new private banks are under the wage settlement with the Indian Bank Association. There is hardly any way to introduce an efficiency-linked pay structure. Benchmarking with other banks as per employee cost will not be helpful as logistic support and control levels are vastly different from bank to bank. There is one more aspect to this matter of employee cost. In the case of IBA member banks, the difference between the highest pay and pay and allowances in general, of an official who forsakes promotion and continues in the same grade and another official who gains all promotions, can be double. If the additional tax payable is deducted from the gross, the difference can be narrower. The situation is different from that of new private banks in which pay and allowances include incentives, profit share or stock options and in such cases, there can be control on the employee cost.

<u>Government Mandated Loans</u> The third aspect that is often debated is the loss on account of handling government-mandated loans. The loss accrues from the accounts becoming non-performing, loss of man hours for campaigns and recovery. Though such loans are of small denominations, the number of loans is large and is approved under some form of coercion from government to hesitant bank officials. However, better handling of the loan may perhaps change the impact.

3. Capital adequacy and banks

Capital adequacy, Tier 1 capital, provisioning, etc., are now popular among people compared to earlier days, when banks' accounts did not even reveal the details of income. That was to preserve creditability and a bank failure was supposed to have a domino effect on other banks as public trust in the institution of banking will wane.

The capital requirement according to guidelines issued by the RBI is determined by the following:

- **Exposure** The exposure which means the higher of the approved loan limit or amount outstanding in the accounts. This includes both fund based and non-fund based exposures taken on a customer. However, in case the loan agreement confers a right to the bank to cancel the limit unutilised, then the gap between the approved limit and what is outstanding can be taken out of reckoning from the exposure.

- **Type of borrowers** They can be government companies, companies where the government holds more than 50%, usually described as public sector.
- **Security** offered for loans - loans against gold, letters of credit from first class banks, banks' own fixed deposits, government securities, etc., carry low risk.
- **Rating** by external rating agencies - AAA rated units carry 20% risk weight, a rating below BBB warrants capital to the extent of 150% of the exposure (150% risk weight).
- **Investment** in subsidiaries.

Banks have to get their database correct especially on the above factors. Overseas branches of Indian banks need to follow whichever are the tighter norms between the host country regulators and the RBI. Provision made for non-performing loans can be included as Tier 2 capital. Banks in India are advised to switch over to Basel III norms of 9% total capital from 1st April 2013 which can be in the form of:

- Common Equity - Tier 1: share capital, premium and general reserves representing gains from sale of assets and profit
- Other Tier 1: preference shares, its premium and debt instruments; Tier 2: provisions and other reserves kept for meeting future loss

The RBI has advised banks on the transitional arrangements so that by March 2018 banks will have 5.5% Common Equity - Tier 1 and a total of 11.5% of their risk-weighted assets.

Conclusion

The processes discussed in this chapter would provide a fair view of operations. The scope for change in processes is apparent. There is a practice of relying on internationally popular consultants to initiate a process change in Banks. But what is undermined is the superiority of Indian banks which is a blend of Indian banking which is much older than the western banking, as stated by Mr Panandikar, the superior Scottish banking that has not failed many banks in the past as stated by Mr. Chas Northcote Cooke in their books, and that has produced immensely large banks like the State Bank of

India. Reliance on good quality employees and consistency of policies and practices has produced better results than quick flash in the pan tricks. There is no doubt, banks will have to go far inside the villages and sell banking there. Meanwhile, weeding out bad practices and keeping the integrity of the organisation at a very high level are matters of the utmost import. Strong internal processes wither external factors that pose hindrances for growth. In the history of Indian banks, once can find at some point in time many banks that have been in a strong position, "on top", but could not sustain this position. From the juggernaut of processes, we move onto the external factors of uncertainty, competition and age-old legislation after discussing the issues regarding securitisation of assets of banks.

7. SECURING BANK LOANS

- *A process revamp is imminent*

Loans constitute more than sixty per cent of the assets of banks in India and securing the loans adequately is a challenging and difficult job for bank officials. The whole process is governed by the law of the land and local practices followed by competitors. Some compromises also happen due to practical difficulties in taking the custody of securities and problems in fetching a fair market price. Banks cannot push growth and profitability whilst overlooking these issues. Therefore, the following presents a perspective on the situation by looking at the common securities available with banks in India and how banks manage them for securing their loans. The main aspects that banks look at, regarding security, are the realisability, ownership, possession and marketability.

There are some common usages of terms such as 'primary security', 'collateral security', 'third party guarantee', etc. Primary security is an asset procured with bank finance. If any security is offered other than the primary security, those additional securities are referred to as collateral security. This may also include the personal guarantee of the loan applicant or a guarantee offered by some other person who may or may not be directly connected to the business or stand to benefit from the loan. Such a guarantee by a person or persons other than the loan applicant is referred to as a third party guarantee. This third party guarantee becomes useful whenever their property is taken as collateral security. By taking the guarantee of another person or persons, the bank is more secure as the law states: the obligation of the guarantor is co-extensive with that of the debtor.

Some of the most common securities obtained by banks are same-bank deposits, other bank deposits, government securities, gold ornaments, inventories, land and buildings, plant machinery and others such as fixed assets, fixtures, patents, etc.

Features of securities accepted by banks

As mentioned earlier, the difference between securities lies in the realisability, convenience to hold in custody and marketability.

Realisability of securities Securities can be classified as follows:

a) Those that can provide full value and the accrued interest - e.g. bank deposits, government securities, etc.

b) Those that can provide only the face value - e.g. guarantees, letters of credit.

c) Those that can provide value that cannot be ascertained *ab initio*. They could fetch more or less depending on the market value at the time of sale, e.g. inventory, equity, ornaments, vehicles, land and buildings.

Ability to own and hold in the custody of banks The securities for which ownership can be transferred in favour of the bank at the time of loan approval can be grouped as follows:

a) Those that are endorsed in favour of the bank and can be kept in custody - e.g. government securities, share certificates, mortgages registered in favour of the bank, etc.

b) Those that can be under constructive possession but where actual possession is enjoyed by the borrower - e.g. vehicles, plant and machinery, inventory, etc. - under a hypothecation agreement

c) Those securities that can be kept in custody under an agreement of pledge - gold ornaments and other precious metals, etc.

d) Those that can be deemed to be owned but cannot be sold and are not held in the custody of the bank: property under equitable mortgage, also referred to as property under 'mortgage by deposit by title deeds'.

Liquidity and Marketability Securities can be at different stages of their convertibility to cash to liquidate the outstanding loan. They can be grouped as follows:

a) *High liquidity* Those securities that can be appropriated by the bank without the intervention of court or consent of the owner, e.g. the bank's own deposits and government securities endorsed properly in favour of banks.

b) *Medium to high liquidity* Those securities that have a ready market and where there is uncertainty over the price. The probability of fetching a higher or lower price is not predictable at the time of loan approval, e.g. gold ornaments and equity stocks. Banks have to watch the market daily, so that the realisable value of such securities held is always above the loan dues.

c) *Poor liquidity* Those securities that do not have a ready market and where actual sales realisation is affected by the delay due to completion of certain mandatory processes. Securities such as machinery, used cars, mortgages, etc., fall into this group and for these, an adequate safety margin is required to be factored in while processing the loan.

Which is the safest security that a bank can hold in India?

The bank's own deposits Obviously, these are the safest because custody of the instrument is with the bank and it has a mandate to offset too. However, there are certain risks attached, even here. The risk lies in the process of gaining possession and establishing ownership of the security - in this case, the deposit receipt. A bank approaches its own deposits as security in two ways - one is to mark a lien on the deposit account and another is to take custody of the deposit with an undated signature along with a letter consenting to deliver the deposit as security for a loan. The most common problem is imperfect documentation, followed by impersonation and forgery, compounded by omissions on the part of bank employees in taking due care in identifying the depositor.

The mandate given to the bank regarding payment in case of joint ownership also causes problems. The most common mandate is 'either or survivor'. In this case, the bank official can pay to any one of the depositors on maturity and jointly before maturity. It is necessary to confirm the death of the alternate depositor if any one of them presents the instrument with a request. There have been occasions when the alternate beneficiary has fled with the sum without the knowledge of the principal depositor. This often leads to complaints and litigation between banks and depositors. In case of default in repayment of loans, banks use their right to offset the loan amount against the fixed deposit account.

Banks create a charge on the deposit by marking a lien on the deposit. In the past, when deposit receipts were printed on specially designed paper, banks used to prominently mark their lien on the face of it so that payment by oversight is avoided on the due date. In the digital age, bank employees can note the lien on the system and thus the incidence of payment by oversight is prevented. However, there are examples, rare though they are, when employees have failed to note the charge or failed to remove the flag after repayment of loans. The audit and verification systems of banks have to take care to point out such omissions without fail.

Government Securities In this case, the amount representing the security is with the government. The recovery of the full value is therefore assured, providing comfort for banks when they grant loans against government securities. National Savings Certificates issued by the government through post offices is one such security. Banks can get their name endorsed on the certificate before accepting it as security and that ensures repayment. Thus realisability, possession and liquidity are assured. Auditors note that to ensure endorsement is important. Other than losses incurred due to imperfect paperwork, government securities offer a better form of security than many others. Since these securities are payable on demand or on completion of a fixed term, accrued interest on the deposit may be found to be less than the sum of the accrued interest and loan amount. Therefore a higher margin is usually maintained, say 30 to 35%, between the loan amount and the maturity value.

Gold ornaments Among securities, gold ornaments fare well with regard to marketability. Indians have a passion for gold and gold jewellery. In fact this passion for gold is troubling the banks and the government of India. If someone has surplus money to save, the question that arises is not which bank they should invest in, but which jewellery shop has the most favourable rate for gold. People invest in gold and keep their ornaments in a bank locker. They take items out of the locker and gain pledges for their requirement of funds. Banks, including indigenous banks, and non-banking finance companies, are omnipresent. The gold price fluctuates due to the world market for gold, and the forex exchange rate, as India is an importer of gold even though the local market demand and supply is intact. Therefore banks decide the loan value on the basis of the market value of gold, depending on its purity, and tenor of the loan. Banks accept gold ornaments on the basis of a pledge agreement, with the right to sell on default. Banks periodically auction such gold ornaments which had belonged to defaulting borrowers. Problems faced by banks while accepting gold as security are the deceit of the public in handing over poor quality gold, embezzlement by bank custodians, fraud, and borrowers abandoning gold lodged with a bank when there is a steep fall in its market value. In spite of that, gold ornaments are preferred as security for small size loans to customers with acceptable integrity, as they are realisable, marketable, and ownership can be transferred easily.

Guarantees Loans are granted also against the personal security of the borrower or of a third party. Acceptance of such personal security depends upon the assessment of means of the persons offering to stand as surety, by the bank official. Since the guarantor's obligation is co-extensive with the loan outstanding, bank officials have to ensure that communications are sent regularly to inform the guarantor about the borrower, of all relevant facts, particularly the net amount due from the debtor. Guarantees as security on the basis of the factors of realisability, marketability and ownership, may not be the most sought-after. If the person standing as surety enjoys a revered position in society, there will be a moral compulsion to repay loans, otherwise it is difficult to realise dues. Guarantees are prone to litigation and in isolation bank guarantees may not be realisable. Therefore, a guarantee is preferred when landed property and other real assets are also offered as security.

Letters of credit Letters of credit are accepted by banks, and issued by member banks of the International Chamber of Commerce. There is realisability and marketability of the security. In India, letters of credit are common but not standby letters of credit. Standby letters of credit do not require the bank to present documents evidencing default. Letters of credit derive their credibility from the International Chamber of Commerce and are guided by their approved trade practices.

Stocks equity, debentures, etc. Granting loans against the security of shares of joint stock companies depends on the type of stock, the issuing company, the rating of the company and the market value of the shares. Even though in general the market price goes up above the average price, the occasional fall cannot be ruled out. Therefore, banks prefer a high margin on the market price of the share while arriving at the loan amount. Ownership is easily possible by transfer. Private company shares are not accepted as they are not transferable by nature. Bank loan policy and instructions are very important.

Inventory Even though bank officials accept different types of inventory, they are not specialists in assessing the value but deal in papers only. Realisability depends on the slow-moving or fast-moving nature of the inventory. Marketability depends upon the 'time' taken up for sales. Bankers in India, as common practice, do not proceed to sell inventory promptly from the day of default. The delay in selling causes fall in value.

Banks create a charge on the inventory by way of an agreement of hypothecation, which means possession is left with the borrower. Therefore, from taking custody of the security onwards until actual sale takes place, banks require the support of courts of law and law-enforcing agencies such as the police. If more than one bank has financed and the banks are not under a consortium arrangement, the threat of double financing exists. The information sharing culture among banks in India is not sufficient to avoid double financing. In the case of smaller enterprises, double financing practically goes unnoticed. This also causes diversion of funds to non-viable banking or non-banking activities. Sometimes, goods already bought under letters of credit or unpaid stocks are included as goods in transit due to the ignorance of the borrower, or otherwise in the periodical statement of inventory to inflate the value of stock submitted to banks. This statement is the basis for fixing the limit for drawing funds. All of these are part of financing working capital under the cash credit system. The system intends to keep a tab on the level of the inventory and end use of bank funds. The system works successfully however selection of the borrower is critical. Banks make loans easily available, and compromise of credit quality over a period may provide a reason to criticise Indian banks.

Of late, inventory financing schemes of banks have become common and that takes care of some of the pitfalls of the cash credit system. However, there is a need to change the way the cash credit system is utilised for financing working capital.

Movable assets like vehicles In a very similar fashion to accepting inventory as security, banks accept vehicles, machines, etc., on the basis of a hypothecation agreement. While the borrower can use the vehicle or machines, the bank holds the right to seize and sell them after legal formalities. Therefore these securities do not provide possession. As regards realisability, it depends upon the ability to take custody of the security (machinery, vehicles, etc.) and find a buyer for it, whatever condition it is in. Since the asset provided as security is left in the custody of the borrower, banks insist that the bank's name is prominently displayed on the body of the machine or vehicle, to avoid double financing. In the case of vehicles that have to be registered with the government transport authority, noting of the hypothecation charge is possible. This system prevents the owner from selling without the knowledge of the financier. However, banks face problems from thieves. They steal cars and machinery and sell them with forged documents in other parts of the country. Therefore, insurance of such hypothecated assets and availability of support from the police department are critically important for these loans.

Immovable properties The agreement for securing assets changes on the basis of possession. For example, in the case of ornaments, when the security is physically handed over, the agreement is called a pledge. When it is in the custody of the borrower, as in the case of vehicles or inventory, etc., it is referred to as a hypothecation agreement. Now in the case of immovable property, the agreement to secure an asset is called a mortgage. Banks have to take possession before auctioning them. Landed property is attractive due to the aspects of safety from theft, probability of appreciation in value, and the positive side of the emotional attachment of owners to their property, which often makes them keen to repay the loan. For the same reason, owners are motivated to resort to legal measures to delay or thwart any attempt to sell the land and building by banks.

Banks have a liking for land and buildings as security and India[28] has 1.57 million square kilometres of arable land and 1.17 million square kilometres of non-agricultural land. Land legislation is difficult and in addition, land records are not convenient for commerce. Bankers probably derive comfort from taking land as security, to protect themselves from the general poverty faced by Indians and the uncertainties faced by entrepreneurs in India.

Realisability, possession and marketability of securities are very much related to the economic conditions and business culture of the country. Centuries-old methods of securing assets by banks have to change in order to make banks have genuine control of credit decisions. And, instead of banks, the borrower should have the responsibility and control to manage the loan. Any reformation of banking in India therefore shall also have to revamp the practises of securing assets by banks.

---

[28] http://data.worldbank.org/indicator/AG.LND.TOTL.K2/countries

8. LEGISLATION

- The power of democracy

Indian law is based on English law. Thus, there are numerous old examples of legislation enacted during British rule which are still followed by banks in India. Some of them have become irrelevant with the passage of time. The government has since taken up the task of repealing some of that legislation relating to day-to-day banking.

Democracy and banking

India is a country where democracy is happening. The voices of the people are heard. A majority decision is part of democracy. The country is divided into so many factors such as regions, language, Hindi speaking and non-Hindi speaking, caste, political ideology, etc. Yet, when it comes to electing their government, the people of India have shown exemplary wisdom in overthrowing a government that took the law into their own hands. There are so many regionally strong political parties that one would expect a fractured mandate to the government. But when a coalition government was found to be wanting, the electorate voted a national party to power with a full majority, displaying their power to decide wisely.

However, democratically-elected governments, for the last six decades, have not been able to accelerate growth towards the full potential of the economy. Often there is an absence of the right leadership from a management perspective. Democratic government depends on the bureaucracy which is regulated by the judiciary. The fundamental rights guaranteed to all citizens are the cornerstone of the judiciary. When the importance of individuals scores above the importance of respect towards development institutions like banks, employees become less sensitive to the purpose of their organisation. Perhaps that is how democracy failed to bolster banking and slowed down economic growth. Hopefully, democratic institutions will change their line of thinking when a revolution becomes inevitable.

Trade unionism and banking

Banks used to face problems in the past from labour unions, before computers were put to use and bank employees were paid overtime allowances. Trade unions in banks are usually led by the banks' own employees. There are different unions for different banks and for different cadres of employees. The main legislation connected to employees is the Trade Union Act, 1926, Industrial Disputes Act, 1947, and the Constitution of India. Issues related to pay and allowances are based on industry-level agreements which are denoted as bipartite settlements. The Sasthri award, a comprehensive industry-level award dated 28th March 1954, is the precursor which the present bipartite agreement is built upon. Supervisory grade officers are under separate bank-level service conditions. Although service conditions of employees in public sector banks are guided by these agreements, some of the banks in the private sector are outside these. While these award and service conditions take care of issues relating to the provisions of the trade union act and industrial disputes act, article 226 of the Constitution of India comes into play at the time of termination of an employee from service.

Banking Laws

There is various legislation that facilitates the operation of banks in India. Some laws are old, and/or complex, yet others have stood the test of time. The introduction of new legislation has been related to the expansion of banking operations, improving the services rendered by banks such as reduction of the delay in realisation of cheques and other instruments, improving the recovery of dues in respect of loans, etc. In order to suggest further changes to improve banking, the Indian Banks Association has set up a working group.

Working group to suggest changes

The working group set up in 2003 by the Indian Banks Association to review and suggest changes in the laws relating to creation, enforcement and registration of Security Interest submitted its report in 2004.

The studies conducted by the committee on the commercial laws of India suggested changes by plugging legal loopholes in order to protect banks from exploitation by the public. The following are some interesting observations[29]

- The current Transfer of Property Act, 1882, does not recognise the rights of the owner of a portion of a multi-storeyed building and enforcement of a mortgage, without the intervention of a court of law, was not feasible against an individual
- The Registration Act, 1908, does not provide for issuing title certificates
- There is no uniform system for the grant of a certificate to the heirs
- There are multiple stamp duty laws as the right to levy these has been given to states
- The prevailing practice has been to give priority rights to tax authorities over secured creditors
- The income tax department allows depreciation over leased assets to the leaser, while auditors allow it for the lessee
- The validity of a bank guarantee issued in favour of the government is for 30 years
- The Hire Purchase Act, 1972, has not been brought into force[30]

The report comments on many significant issues faced by banks in their operation. These suggestions may be at various stages of implementation or under consideration by the government. The following comprise some of the legislation significant for banking in India.

---

[29]   http://www.iba.org.in/securities.asp
[30]   This act was repealed in 2005

THE BANKING REGULATION ACT, 1949 (10 OF 1949)

The banking system is regulated by means of this legislation by the government of India. The Act empowers the RBI to exercise effective control over all banking operations. It covers commercial banks as well as state cooperative banks. The licensing of banks is undertaken by the RBI. Other than that, supervision of banking operations, and collection of data relating to activities undertaken by banks, is also carried out on the basis of regulations issued under this act. The act also enables the RBI to advise the government on monetary and credit policies. It is important to note that the act gives powers to the RBI to regulate or deregulate the interest rates applied by banks on loans and advances. Banks have to follow the RBI directives. Courts of law hardly entertain cases regarding the appropriateness of interest rates for a loan. The BR Act, 1949 is the principal act on which other Banking Laws (amendment) Acts are enacted whenever there is a major insertion. For example, the **Nomination** facility for depositors was included in the Banking Laws (amendment) Act, 1983. Further, the 2013 amendment act provided the establishment of a 'Depositor Education and Awareness Fund' with the RBI where **balances of accounts not operated for more than ten years** have to be transferred by banks, without forfeiting the claims of the depositors.

THE RESERVE BANK OF INDIA ACT, 1934 (2 OF 1934)

The Reserve Bank of India is the central bank of India, holding both supervisory and regulatory roles and established under this Act. The government of India, vested with the powers to develop the banking system in the country, delegates to the RBI through the RBI Act, which gives adequate power for regulation, monitoring, supervision and control of all banking activities. Accordingly the RBI is empowered to

- issue licences to banks to operate all or some banking functions
- issue orders to wind up the operation of a branch or a bank
- authorise banks, bank branches or other organisations and their offices for holding, buying and releasing foreign exchange under powers vested with the RBI under FEMA

- give directions to banks for mergers, take-overs, etc.
- conduct inspections at bank premises, or clients of banks
- obtain data from banks regarding banking operations
- inspect the books of banks, levy penalties, issue directions and cancel licences for operation of banks
- provide guidelines for finalising interest rates for loans and advances of banks
- exercise the responsibility of an arbitrator in case of disputes between banks, while conducting clearing houses, and with regard to unethical conduct of banks.

On the basis of various powers vested with the RBI, the central bank has become the most authentic data source of current economic activities. It is also one of the most powerful central bankers in the world. As banker to government, a few major responsibilities of RBI include the following:

- Fiscal management: revenue collection and release of government funds
- Public debt management: the issue of government securities, and managing the books relating to buying and selling of such securities
- Custodian of foreign exchange: approvals for capital account transactions under FEMA; the act authorises the RBI directly for current account transactions
- Food advances: managing advances to the Food Corporation of India for funding the procurement of grains and rationing food items to the people of the country.

Perhaps, in days to come, one can expect the disaggregation of roles and responsibilities of the RBI, resulting in changes to separate functions such as regulatory, supervisory, advisory, agency and control functions, in order to inject more independence and professionalism.

THE FOREIGN EXCHANGE MANAGEMENT ACT, 1999 (42 OF 1999)

This was as part of the liberalisation and globalisation of the economy to consolidate and amend the law relating to foreign exchange, with the objective of facilitating external trade and payments and for promoting the orderly development and maintenance of the foreign exchange market in India. This act replaced the Foreign Exchange Regulation Act, 1973. FERA had the support of another law called the Conservation of Foreign Exchange and Prevention of Security Act, 1973 (COFEPOSA), to enable the detention of people suspected to be involved in smuggling and the hawala[31] trade. Doubts about the continuing stringency of the act after FEMA, under which a violation is not criminal as in the case of FERA, were clarified by the Supreme Court. In the judgement in the case of Dropti Devi v. Government, it is mentioned that if the activity of any person is prejudicial to the conservation or augmentation of foreign exchange, the authority is empowered to make a detention order against such a person and provision of the COFEPOSA continues. Thus COFEPOSA enables law-enforcing agencies in the state to detain banks' personnel or members of the public involved in the hawala trade, as far as banking transactions in foreign exchange are concerned. Thus it calls for the proper training of employees of banks to prevent negligence and enforce due diligence while handling forex transactions.

The FEMA approach to forex transactions is to classify them as either capital or current account transactions. The former are regulated by the government and the latter are delegated to the RBI. However all notification issued by the government is circulated by the RBI, along with its own circulars for current account transactions. Another key definition is for the term Non-Resident Indian. There are Indians holding Indian passports but living abroad in order to make a living, or travelling abroad, and there are also those persons of Indian origin holding foreign passports. A person of Indian origin is defined as someone whose parents or grandparents were born in India or held an Indian Passport. Such people can hold a foreign passport and a PIO card issued by Indian consulates. This enables people of Indian origin to purchase property or later on settle in this country. However, there are a number of third generation citizens in other countries who are not aware of this privilege.

---

[31] Method of transferring money through an agent to people in other countries without involving the banking system

The act includes regulations on foreign direct investment in India and overseas investment from India. While most current account transactions are handled by banks and other authorised persons as delegated to them by the RBI, control of large value capital account transactions is decided at the RBI.

In day-to-day banking activities some of the most common forex transactions subjected to FEMA are

- Currency exchange
- Remittance
- Release of foreign exchange for travel, etc.
- Bank accounts and retail loans for non-resident Indians
- Trade-related remittances for export and import, bill discounting, letters of credit, etc.
- Remittances received as donations falling under contributions from overseas entities regulated by the Foreign Contribution Regulation Act, 2010
- Loans from abroad - external commercial borrowing
- Investment into India by institutional investors or companies
- Investment abroad, loans or operating subsidiaries

THE TRANSFER OF PROPERTY ACT, 1882 (4 of 1882)

This is one of the most important British Indian pieces of legislation that affects the entire loan system of banks even today. The act is taken out of The Indian Contract Act, 1872 (9 of 1872). Most of the loans to farmers and small business are sanctioned on the strength of the land and property offered as security. The legislation defines terms like immovable property, mortgage and mortgage by deposit of title deeds, sale, lease, gift, actionable claim, etc. The definition of the term 'property' is given in another legislation called The Securitisation & Reconstruction of Financial Assets and Enforcement of Security Interest Act, 2002 (54 of 2002) (commonly referred to as the Sarfaesi Act). The legislation is also closely linked to The Indian Registration Act, 1908 (16 of 1908), where one can look for details relating to compulsory registration, etc., and the Land Acquisition Act, 1894

(1 of 1894), replaced by The Right of Fair Compensation and Transparency in Land Acquisition, Rehabilitation and Resettlement Act, 2013 (30 of 2013). The legislation is relevant for creation of valid mortgages, seizing them and selling them, the need to search earlier mortgages before entering into a new one, and properties that are not acquirable. The TP Act warrants revision as suggested by the IBA working group, to make the legislation relevant and useful for banking operations.

SARFAESI (54 OF 2002) -(THE SECURITISATION & RECONSTRUCTION OF FINANCIAL ASSETS AND ENFORCEMENT OF SECURITY INTEREST ACT, 2002)

Banks faced the problem of delay in realising the securities mortgaged from loan defaulters by way of sale. A need was felt for legislation like the Sarfaesi Act. The Sarfaesi Act provided bank officials with the enthusiasm to proceed hopefully against defaulters. The legislation was intended to enable sale of the security without the intervention of court. However, defaulters approached the court with flimsy excuses such as the highhandedness of bank employees, law and order problems, failure to inform and non-completion of the due process of auction, etc., sufficient to delay the sale. Both bank guarantees, often interfered with by courts of law at the time of invocation, and the Sarfaesi Act, due to court interference in stalling sales, lost their appeal as a means to boost bank functioning.

The Sarfaesi Act has solved many shortcomings in the Transfer of Property Act and it enabled the maintenance of the Central Repository of Secured Assets (CERSAI), setting up of recovery agencies, resolution agencies and securitisation of assets. The identity of a loan defaulter after the due notice period, ceases to be private information. The myth of the banker's contract of secrecy regarding the accounts of customers has been exploded. In this context the Right to Information Act, a subsequent legislation, confers adequate freedom and power to the RBI to divulge the names of defaulters.

The Central Registry of Securitisation, Asset Reconstruction and Security Interest of India (CERSAI) (a Government Company licensed under Section 25 of the Companies Act, 1956) has been incorporated for the purpose of operating and maintaining the Central Registry under the provisions of the Securitisation and Reconstruction of Financial Assets and Enforcement of Security Interest Act, 2002 (SARFAESI Act). The objective of setting up the Central Registry is to prevent frauds in loan cases involving multiple lending from different banks on the same immovable property.[32]

The amendment to the Sarfaesi Act (1 of 2013) empowered banks, as secured creditors, to bid for themselves on any property, provided no bid was received even at the reserve price, in earlier auctions. The Provisions of the Banking Regulation Act are applicable. While banks consider the Sarfaesi Act and its amendments as favourable steps to realise due amounts lying in mortgages and other securities, borrowers feel the legislation helped the growth of a lot of ruthless recovery agents, as against supportive bank officials who are more likely to treat them with understanding during their difficult times.

THE COMPANIES ACT, 2013 (18 of 2013)

The Companies Act, 2013 recognises one person companies under the act and limited liability partnerships under the Limited Liability Partnership Act, 2008. With these two changes, the business environment for small and medium enterprises (SME) has become more attractive. Earlier, the formalities for the formation of companies used to discourage companies, while partnerships had the problem of losing personal assets upon liquidation. Thus most entrepreneurs used to form any number of private limited companies and partnerships and carried on business conveniently depending on which form was ideal for circumventing government regulations and tax obligations. The new Companies Act makes the organisation structure less cumbersome for prospective start up entrepreneurs. The Act allows only public limited companies to raise capital by public issue.

---

[32]   RBI guidelines on SARFAESI dated 1st July 2014

THE LIMITED LIABILITY PARTNERSHIP ACT, 2008 (6 of 2009)

The LLP reduces the burden of formation of a private limited company. It will be easier to regulate more homogenous corporates under the Companies Act. The limited liability partnership is a legal person with perpetual succession separate from the partners. The partners are no more responsible than the firm. They are not the agent of other partners but only the firm. Over 100,000 firms have registered since the act came into force. Large numbers are in business services and a quarter of its number comes from industries such as real estate, construction, trading and social services. As far as capital contribution is concerned, real estates and construction LLPs are at the top as per the statistics available at the Ministry of Corporate Affairs. Partners are originally given a Designated Partnership Identification Number (DPIN) but after 2011 this number has been integrated with the Director's Identification Number (DIN). Unlisted public companies and private limited companies can now convert to LLPs if convenient.

THE INDIAN SUCCESSION ACT, 1925 (39 OF 1925)

The Indian Succession Act, 1925 (39 of 1925) applies to all citizens except those that have been specified in the Hindu Succession Act, 1956 which covers Hindus, Sikhs, Jains and Buddhists. For Moslems, The Muslim Personal Law (Shariat) Application Act, 1937 is applicable. In the case of interfaith marriages, provisions under the Special Marriage Act, 1954 are applicable.

The Taluk office issues heirship certificates on the basis of the genuineness of the person claiming to be the successor. This legislation is important for banks as settlement of outstanding dues in the bank accounts of deceased persons is guided by the provision of this act. However, the RBI has made a ceiling up to which banks can dispose of claims without insisting on production of this succession certificate. Further, the nomination facility available with banks in India and provided by the Banking Regulation (amendment) Act, 1983, allows the public to name a single individual to receive the amount lying in their name. By this process, banks get rid of the usual procedure for settlement. But the nominee carries the responsibility to share dues with all eligible legal heirs. The habit of writing a will is not very common in India. There is abundant scope for developing this culture among the people so that assets are smoothly transmitted to legal heirs upon the death of an individual.

THE INSOLVENCY AND BANKRUPTCY CODE, 2016

Banks have been waiting hopefully for enactment of the above bill which is expected to put into operation a simplified process for recovery of bank dues. The code features creation of a formal entity to regulate insolvency proceedings. Creditors including banks or employees can apply for the insolvency of a debtor. The time allotted for a revival plan is 180 days, maybe extended by another 90 days in special cases. If the revival plan is acceptable to 75 per cent of the creditors it will be put into action. If not, the company will be put into liquidation. The legislation covers individuals, partnerships and entities set up under the Companies Act, 2013. The positive outcome expected is to assist a failed unit to take a decision for a quick exit and return to action afresh with a new venture. Perhaps, if not impeded by any other constitutional provisions, it will become one of the fastest insolvency regimes worldwide. The bill has been passed by parliament and enacted as The Insolvency and Bankruptcy Code, 2016.

An Insolvency and Banking Board of India is established as regulator and there will be Insolvency Professional Agencies to facilitate the operation of the legislation. Accordingly, the relevant portions of the Companies Act, Sick Industrial Companies (special provisions) repeal Act, Limited Liability Partnership Act, SARFAESI, DRT Act and Indian Partnership Act will become amended.

The code will bring solace to optimists on a whole host of issues plaguing the creditors trying to realise from delinquent borrowers, but pessimists may perhaps keep their fingers crossed and wait to see how courts handle cases relating to the code. On passing of the bill by both houses of parliament the Financial Times stated[33], "The reform will give banks a clear path to

---

[33]   https://next.ft.com/content/4faaa62c-17f7-11e6-b197-a4af20d5575e

wresting control of insolvent companies unable to repay their debts. Its adoption is seen as a major breakthrough that will allow banks to recover their dues in a timely manner, in contrast to the current system in which they often wage protracted legal battles in an attempt to recover what they are owed."

OTHER IMPORTANT LEGISLATION:

There is much legislation perhaps more important but not discussed above, since it falls more under operations and is outside the scope of this book. The following table provides a quick look at some of them.

Sl.No.	Legislation	Relevance
1.	Negotiable Instruments Act 1881 (Act 26 of 1881)	It is essential to know about the role and responsibility of a banker while handling cheques.
2.	Limitation Act 1963 (Act 36 of 1963)	The act prescribes the period within which legal course has to be sought from the date of documents. However, court can condone in genuine cases.
3.	Income Tax Act 1961 (Act 43 of 1961)	The legislation that empowers government rights over other secured creditors. In fact they are also empowered to gather specific information from banks who are supposed to keep customer details confidential.
4.	Constitution of India	i) The provisions regarding proper hearings before an employee is removed from service. ii) States government's power to raise loans from banks or stand surety of government undertakings. iii) A person is not disqualified just because he has a criminal conviction but only when he or she has a conviction involving moral turpitude.

5.	Sick Industrial Companies (special provisions) Act 1985 (Act 1 of 1986)	The legislation was intended to identify sick companies and the possibility of nursing them back to health. With bankruptcy legislation simplified, the relevance may be waning.
6.	Civil Procedure Code 1908 – arrest for execution (Act 5 of 1908)	The police have the power to arrest a delinquent borrower for execution of a court decree. This privilege is provided by the legislation.
7.	Contract Labour (regulation & abolition) Act 1970 (Act 37 of 1970)	While appointing contract labourers or outsourcing, certain regulatory requirements need to be complied with.
8.	Information Technology Act 2000 (Act 21 of 2000)	Important changes in communications like acting on electronic instructions, digital signature, etc., are covered in this.
9.	Prevention of Corruption Act 1988 (Act 49 of 1988)	Defines a public servant as any person in the service or pay of a corporation established by or under a central provincial or state act. Hence employees of public sector banks are public servants as defined in the act.
10.	Protection of Human Rights Act 1993 (Act 10 of 1994)	The legislation enables setting up of a human rights commission to look into protection of human life, liberty, equality and dignity. This is important with regards to transactions with customers and employees.

Conclusion

There is a large amount of legislation and much of it overlaps causing inconvenience to compliance. Landed property is one of the most common forms of security available and is accepted by banks especially in the case of small business loans. Since the process of demarcation, the indexing of the entire landscape is not yet over, and land records have to improve. Another issue is managing the tax laws. They are not found to be simple and give scope for exemption, avoidance, etc. The attitude of judges in cases involving repayment of bank loans is significant and critical for the reformation of the Indian banking system.

9. RECENT INITIATIVES FROM THE RBI

Certain important initiatives taken recently by the Reserve Bank of India are expected to improve the functioning of banks in India. These initiatives, discussed in this chapter, are mainly the systemic changes which can help the RBI to exercise better control on banks' activities and also in controlling inflation. If these changes are supported by simplification of the tax management system by government, the result would be a phenomenal yield. Permanent Account Numbers (PANs), allotted by the tax department for taxpayers, and banks insisting on the PAN for carrying out major banking transactions, has helped in preventing unaccounted money entering the banking system. Better late than never, these changes are hopefully ongoing, in order to take banking in India under better control and into better focus.

1. Setting up of a Central Repository of Information on Large Credits (CRILC)

Large credit means exposure above Rs.50 million (5 crore). The credit exposure from the banking system includes both funded and non-funded. Funded exposure can be in the form of running accounts or instalment accounts. Commonly known running accounts are cash credits or overdrafts. Instalment loans are known as demand loans, term loans, etc. Non-funded exposures are taken on by banks by issuing bank guarantees and letters of credit. Banks allow interchange ability between BGs and LCs and rarely between funded and non-funded. For the banking system, in the case of both funded and non-funded facilities, the risk is the same. The difference is in the utility of savings in the case of funded exposure. In order to have a view of a customer, having a total exposure above Rs.50 million from the entire banking system, the RBI set up a repository of information on large credits (CRILC). The common index used for identification is the individual PAN or PAN allotted to a group. The RBI is thus is in a position to have a view of an individual customer's exposure to banking across banks. The database is shared with banks.

At first the concept of total exposure assisted bankers in communicating exactly what an individual borrower owed to the banking system. Auditors treat BGs and LCs as off-balance sheet items and exclude them from credit facilities. The CRILC database helps in locating non-performing loans of customers in other banks and starts handling each customer differently thereafter. It helps banks to initiate early action before an account becomes non-performing. As discussed earlier, a non-performing asset is one which fails to service the interest or repayment of principal for 90 days. It is prudent to take corrective action before an account is declared an NPA. For this purpose, every account is monitored for showing symptoms of non-performance for more than 30 days. Banks and the customer have two months' time to take corrective action. After 61 days of default, bankers are expected to form a joint lenders forum and take a decision on the future course of action on the basis of scope for restructuring, if not a wilful defaulter. Those borrowers who do not cooperate by getting actively involved in taking a future course of action, are designated as 'non-cooperative' borrowers. A separate database is available for such non-cooperative borrowers to prevent them from re-entering the banking system.

The signs of incipient sickness identified are the bouncing of cheques, devolvement of LCs, invocation of BGs, non-renewal of credit facilities even after 90 days, inability to achieve even 40% of sales projected and promoters selling their stake in the business. On the basis of discussion with the customer and in the joint lenders forum the future course of action can be finalised. If resuscitation is not possible, the quick sale of a running unit may be better for the economy, lenders and the borrower. The asset reconstruction company are expected to play a major role in buying such units and converting them into efficient units. This is the process flow emanating from the CRILC.

Change in the lenders' attitude The database is ready from June 2014 and is being improved upon. This initiative calls for a change in the way an unfortunate borrower has so far been handled. Proactive action, rather than reaction after an account becomes non-performing, is expected from bank officials.

Useful database The database will be providing a uniform industry code, sector code, asset classification and single PAN. Analysis of bank loans will be more meaningful than in the past when customers had multiple PANs, imperfect industry classification by different banks, etc. The sharing of credit information becomes easier.

Role of reconstruction companies Experience from these companies suggests that they were accelerating the downfall of already sick entrepreneurs. They use the provisions of law and rudely handle the arrangements for sale, in ways not expected from civilised bankers. A different quality to the officials of these companies is required. Since the role of this company is similar to that of mercantile agents, they are prone to get into unholy alliances with other banks or with prospective buyers or borrowers. Their role needs to be enhanced so that an unfortunate borrower gets back their unit resuscitated.

Joint lenders forum Hitherto, bankers, in their keenness to acquire business, used to overlook the credit history or troubles of the prospective borrower while taking over a unit. Existing regulations on takeover of units from other banks restricts the shifting of NPA accounts to another bank. The situation motivates bank officials not to classify an account as NPA if the borrower has been successful with offers from other banks to spruce up the working capital. Both traditional SME and start up units suffer from improper working capital management. Therefore, the meeting of the joint lenders forum after a trigger from the RBI, helps bankers define an NPA account as such or proceed with a pragmatic solution for restructuring of the unit.

Non-cooperating borrower Bank officials at the operating level lacked this backing so far. When the situation worsens, borrowers become non-traceable or show no interest in the bank. This provision to list a borrower as a non-cooperative borrower puts the responsibility on the borrower. They are different from wilful defaulters.

Wilful defaulter While borrowers are expected to adhere to the covenants of a loan, normally they do not oblige but get away. People misuse the banking system. If a non-cooperative borrower siphons away funds for elsewhere, they are listed as wilful defaulters. Banks have access to the list and thus can discourage them from taking up a fresh banking relationship.

Identity issues The new database provides for a group master and it will help in identifying entities mushrooming under inter-company activity bubbles. The Companies Act also requires that every director has a Director Identification Number (DIN) so that similar-sounding names are not causing problems over identity, while listing non-cooperating borrowers or wilful defaulters.

Details and depth of the database The amount of exposure is collected in hundreds of thousands of rupees to two decimals which means the data can be accurate up to thousands. It is updated quarterly and a single bank consolidated soft transmission ensures timely data taken from the core banking systems without any adjustment or overwriting.

Corporate borrowers and links to politicians One issue faced by bank officials was from the large corporate borrowers who had fairly strong relationships with politicians, who try occasionally to influence decisions. With politicians having the potential to become part of government, the situation is tricky. However, this open database, by setting a wall, prevents such influence. Bank officials hardly take the risk of approving loans to defaulters.

2. UnHedged Foreign Currency Exposure (UHFCE)

Though the problem of borrowers from the banking system not hedging their foreign currency exposure has been recognised by the RBI from 1999 or earlier, a workable order to measure and own the risk was only issued during the monetary policy announcement in 2013-14. Earlier, there were instructions to banks to have a policy that put in place systems to discourage units that do not hedge their foreign currency exposure. It was also recognised that this was one of the known reasons for units, unable to manage any unexpected variation in exchange rates, becoming non-performing assets of banks. Such unmanaged loss damages not only the unit, but the bank and banking system as well. Therefore if the banks are not able to impress upon the customer to fully hedge their forex exposure, the banker is expected to make additional provision from their profit. Hitherto loss or gain on account of forex risk was borne by the company. The RBI encourages customers, by introduction of this direction, to reduce such unhedged risk and directs banks to obtain the data on UHFCE. The data on such unhedged exposure enables the RBI to take better decisions as to what forex position it should take, to avoid fluctuation in the Indian rupee.

Ascertain the UHFCE The first effort is to ascertain the loss on account of the unhedged forex exposure. Banks have been advised to obtain from borrowers a certificate from chartered accountants on the exposure, the portion unhedged and the probable loss worked out on the basis of volatility of currency provided by the FEDAI, as a share of their profit.

Provide for the loss Once the likely loss is ascertained, banks are advised to make additional provision for that portion of outstanding loans between 20 to 80 basis points (0.01%) over and above the rate of provision prescribed for standard accounts[34].

Impact on capital adequacy While the provision on standard assets and on the unhedged exposure will affect the profitability of banks, an additional measure prescribed is to increase the risk weight on that portion of loans, which will also affect the capital adequacy ratio of banks.

Entities involved Operating units like bank branches have a responsibility to educate borrowers about the loss on account of currency fluctuation which is different from their business loss, for which they have their own strategies. The second most important role is played by the chartered accountants who audit the accounts of the customers and certify the forex exposure. The third entity is the FEDAI who have been authorised to work out the volatility of foreign currency so that banks work out uniform rates for their customers. But the most important role is played by the management of banks, on whom

---

[34]   https://rbi.org.in/scripts/BS_ViewMasCirculardetails.aspx?id=9908#5e

the implementation of the instruction in letter and spirit depends. They are also important in the process of collecting correct data from their borrowers regarding forex exposure.

3. Interest Rate Policy

Interest rates on both deposits and loans are regulated by the RBI. In the past all banks offered the same rate of interest. Presently one can find different rates of interest offered by different banks for deposits. Similarly, interest rates on loans used to be regulated by category and a minimum and a maximum was fixed for those loans which were not prescribed. This gave a very limited leeway for banks to offer a differential rate of interest for good borrowers. Later the RBI wanted individual banks to have their own policy of fixing interest rates based on a 'benchmark' rate. Thereafter, the base rate system was introduced from 2010. These rates appeared to be more arbitrary and not based on their cost of deposit, margin, risk premium and factoring tenor. Moreover, the practice failed with regard to automatic transmission of falls in the bank rate and other rates by the RBI as part of its credit policy.

The RBI introduced the interest rate from April 2016[35], based on the Marginal Cost of Funds Lending Rate (MCLR). The instruction explains how to arrive at the cost of funds, spread and factoring of risk and tenor premium in the interest rate. The cost of funds depends on the ability of banks to mobilise low cost funds often mentioned as a portion of CASA (Current Account Saving Account) in their total deposits portfolio. Too much spread too thinly will cause a fall in profits. Since the provision for mounting NPA and efficiency of employees impact the spread, in order to offer the most competitive rate of interest for loans, bank managements have their work cut out for their operating functionaries in the new interest mechanism.

---

[35]   https://rbi.org.in/SCRIPTs/BS_PressReleaseDisplay.aspx?prid=35749

<u>Zero per cent interest</u> In 2013 the RBI banned banks and dealers[36] from alluring customers with zero per cent interest, by offering a longer moratorium period, or interest-free EMI, etc. They have instructed banks to provide a better bargain, to make the customers fully aware of these benefits and also pass on the benefits to them fully and indiscriminately while sanctioning a loan for the purchase. This has been prescribed so that customers can take informed decisions. They have also banned any charge for reasonable usage of ATM cards or debit cards issued by banks for making payment.

<u>Fact sheet on loans</u> Another important direction issued by the RBI recently related to the introduction of communication with the borrower at every stage of loan processing and changes in terms and conditions on a fact sheet[37], containing simple details of loans and the applicable interest rate. This has been introduced from 1st April 2015.

4. Expansion of banking

Recently, two types of banks were introduced to the Indian banking system, namely Payment banks and Small Finance banks. These banks are designed to provide simple banking functions by being more reachable. They may prove to be a game changer in the expansion of banking services to anyone and everyone in the country. The setting up of the Imperial Bank of India, the nationalisation of commercial banks, the introduction of Regional Rural Banks, and support of cooperative banking, etc., were attempted by various governments to extend banking to all Indians. All these structures tend to behave in a similar fashion when it comes to the expansion of banking. With the IT revolution in every aspect of the life of common man, these two have a potential to provide a better result than earlier experiments: mobile phone service providers and India Post with their very large reach in the country may be able to take banking forward easily. Already, branch authorisation has been made very liberal and reporting has been simplified. Meanwhile, the RBI has made its notification for offering licences 'on tap' for universal

---

[36]   DBS.CO.PPD No. 3578 /11.01.005/2013-14 September 17, 2013
[37]   https://www.rbi.org.in/Scripts/NotificationUser.aspx?Id=9508&Mode=0

banks in the private sector, by which an eligible applicant who wants to start a bank can apply any time. Briefly, Payment banks can provide savings up to Rs.100,000 per individual and remittance services but do no lending. On the other hand, Small Finance banks can accept savings and also provide small loans to small business units and farmers through high technology, low cost operations, sell mutual funds, authorise forex dealers, etc.

Conclusion

While recent efforts are clean and clear in objective, there is a need for change in the attitude of bankers and government to yield results. While expansion of IT has taken away many of the issues in the past, pragmatism, employee integrity and the privacy of customers' data continue to challenge development. The RBI can simplify audit reports in consultation with the Institute of Chartered Accountants, and adopt simple Know Your Customer practices in other countries. They can also advise gold dealers and jewellers to lend or accept deposits against a banking licence.

10. UNCERTAINTIES

'A scenario for indecision and mismanagement of time'

Both public and bank officials function in a scenario of uncertainties. These uncertainties can be seen from the excitement of a customer when a bank account is successfully opened, a loan request is approved or when a confirmation of the receipt of remittances by the beneficiary reaches the remitter. Interest rates are stated differently. Bank holidays vary in different states within the country. Interest rates also vary for different purposes though the security is common. There are other causes of confusion as well. Some banks are similarly named and some banks are owned by another bank but apparently competing with each other.

Similarly, employees are functioning in a scenario of uncertainties and one can witness the excitement when accounts are settled after each day's job without counterfeit notes, loan proposals recommended are approved by superiors, employees are transferred to another centre or when employees receive their due promotion, etc.

Investors are excited when results declared by banks are as per their expectations and the management has not fudged the figures to bring up surprises. Bank managements too are uncertain about the probable change of instructions on accounting income, provisions for loss, and subsidies offered by the government on certain types of loans. Further, sometimes the instructions from regulators and management provide the scope for statutory auditors to interpret information differently from bank officials, adding to uncertainties that exist until the audit is over.

While many of these uncertainties are common in other industries too, the discussion here is limited to those which can be removed by improving the clarity of decisions, transparency in processes and exchange of essential communications. As long as the regulators do not rein matters in to remove the scope of any misinterpretation or misconceptions emanating from instructions, the customers, employees and bank managements suffer by being at the receiving end.

Interest rates

In the olden days, bankers' interest used to be quarterly compounding, interest was applied half-yearly on saving accounts and no interest was offered on current accounts. However, ledger folio charges on the basis of actual folios used were levied on current accounts. In those days, the interest rate was denoted in 'per cent per annum'. All costs of banks used to be embedded in the interest rate and no other levies were made from the loan accounts or deposits. Recoveries were made for remitting insurance and guarantee premiums. But today it is not so.

Customers are not sure about the interest amount. There is tax on interest income applied on some deposits but not across all deposits. This vitiates the comparison of earnings on deposits by two different individuals at the same bank or by the same individual with two different banks.

The Equated Monthly Instalment (EMI) at the same rate of interest is different for loans taken from various lenders such as banks, non-banking companies or credit card companies. The customer can get a personal loan from a bank, NBFC or from his bank's credit card. He will be puzzled at the instalment amount and interest worked out on the loans. Banks are working out interest on the basis of the daily outstanding figure in loan accounts while NBFC and other private loan or credit card companies do not factor in repayments other than the instalment repaid on due dates, for working out interest.

Keeping in mind that an average customer in India is not as well educated as a customer in a developed country, uniform practice is necessary so that ignorant customers are not exploited. Interest rates on personal loans can vary from 10-12 per cent in banks and up to 45-55[38] per cent when the loan is taken using the credit card of a bank. The loan approval process is simple in the case of credit card loans.

Compounding periods are different and the published interest rate does not give the whole picture. Credit cards marketed by banks offer loans at monthly rates. Banks apply interest monthly, effectively bringing compounding interest monthly. Interest on deposits made in the Public Provident Fund available at bank branches under government schemes is compounded yearly. There is also some usage of the term 'flat rate' which means the rate of interest is applied for the full amount for the full tenor without recognising the repayments made in between. In such a situation the interest rate may appear to be low. In a typical case of a twelve month EMI repayment loan, on a flat rate of 7.5% p.a., the customer will be paying effectively more than 12.1% annually. A similar loan taken from a bank would have cost the customer only 5.6% simple interest rate. The processing charge realised usually at 1% on the principal loan amount, would further increase the cost of the loan.

Loan processing charges thus become a factor to be streamlined. Banks are yet to develop a system of costing the loan sanctioning process. Banks definitely save time if customers approach them along with all the required papers and the bank is able to complete the approval after a single round of discussion. However, loan processing charges are levied equally for those who come with the required papers and for those who make frequent calls for many days before the decision is taken. There is no system of qualified professionals vetting loan proposals before they are received by banks. If such a system was in place, the duration of time spent for a customer in processing loans could be uniform and it would be sensible to levy one-time loan processing charges that make loans of longer duration and larger value loans sound economical.

---

[38]   Worked out on the basis of the monthly rate of 2.5-2.95 percent and the cash handling charge

The uncertainties about interest rates arise from the difference in the rate applied on similar loans and on account of various situations as follows:

- Even though primarily the risk lies on the individual who seeks the loan, the purpose of a loan taken in the retail segment makes a difference in the interest rate of loans, e.g. consumables, housing, vehicle, medical purposes or personal emergencies. The repayment fully depends upon the personal integrity and creditability of the borrower.
- Subsidy offered by the government on loans granted to a select group of individuals - based on religion, gender, income, location, etc. It depends upon the bank official to input the personal details of a customer for a loan correctly, e.g. the rate of interest for an educational loan can vary from 7.5% to 13.5% in a public sector bank. The interest rate for a gold loan can vary on the basis of purpose - for kitchen, garden and personal expenses, for loans that are regular in repayment and not, etc.
- The person taking the loan, even though the security can be the same, e.g. a loan against a fixed deposit for the depositor, and for others against the same security.
- Floating rates of interest on loans - most loans are approved by this method so that change in a bank's base or benchmark rate or MCLR automatically affects the interest rate applicable. This makes the cost of the project uncertain and the instalments too.

These are just the most common situations but the scenario provides for many such. There is scope for the regulator and bankers to improve the situation, keeping in mind the characteristics of customers in general.

Reporting of loans

There are many aspects of a loan such as limit, facility, outstanding amount, exposure, funded, non-funded, ad hoc or additional, contingent exposure, etc. The limit is the ceiling up to which the loan can be availed. The term facility means loan form, which can be separately monitored. There can be a ceiling or limit for each facility. For a single customer, there can be a cash credit facility, overdraft facility and demand loan facility. All facilities put together make up the total limit. The outstanding amount refers to the actual loan amount repayable with reference to the particular date.

While assessment can vary from bank to bank, it cannot vary beyond a point. Therefore a single limit of credit flexible within working capital and within capital may remove the ambiguity. This overall limit can include the funded and non-funded as well. Between audit practices and the risk exposure of a bank in respect of non-funded exposures, the process of issuing BG, LCs, etc., and the accounting practices relating to those, need to be presenting a true and fair view of affairs to stakeholders of both customers and banks.

The accounting system followed by banks considers non-funded exposure as an off-balance sheet item even though customer-wise, risk has been accepted by banks against common security attachable by banks. These off-balance sheet items can become loan amounts in the balance sheet on any day they are invoked. Therefore, the method of processing this liability needs to change so that the promised obligation is carved out of the credit limit and kept, like deposits held by the customer, in favour of the beneficiary of the LC or BG for the amount of the obligation along with the margin money.

Thus there are uncertainties about the real obligation of the customer to the banking system used for MIS. On some occasions it is the limit that is used for reckoning, for some other purpose it is the outstanding amount. Non-funded exposure like that outstanding on account of bank guarantees and letters of credit are not reflected in the balance sheet. The interchangeability permitted by banks between fund based and non-fund based, within the overall limit, further makes the MIS reports unclear. Using exposure as the only method of reporting may be advantageous and auditors could also change practice, to include their non-funded lines on the liabilities side of their balance sheet.

Banking arrangements

Common banking arrangements are sole banking, multiple banking and consortium lending. Both from the point of view of customers and bankers, the option of sole banking, multiple banking or consortium finance is important. Keeping a single bank for all their banking needs, allows customers to save time, ensures privacy and encourages a longstanding relationship. Banks on the other hand grow together with the customer and remain aware of activities. It is a customer's choice.

In the case of multiple banking, the customer simultaneously operates from more than one bank without any formal arrangement for the sharing of information. This arrangement has the advantage of getting the best service and rates out of the banks. Bankers often may not even be informed by customers of their banking arrangements with other banks. By introduction of CRILC, this issue would have been more or less resolved. However uncertainty continues as regards exchange of information with regard to consortium lending.

In consortium financing, the regular meetings of financing banks and sharing of information helps to reduce duplication of work. Thus uncertainty of banking arrangements continues till sharing information is easy and practical. Moreover, consortium procedure is made simple and meetings can be held using video or audio facilities. Uncertainty as to who should decide on the need to go for multiple banking, consortium or sole banking needs to be settled.

Banking data and reliance on classification

Banks have to place or tag their customers in various groups to provide data for different analyses. The successes of the information system rely mostly on the knowledge level of the bank officials in creating a proper customer profile. Ambiguity arises and the job is not easy when it relates to a customer who has to be tagged differently on the basis of ownership, priority lending and identified sensitive sectors.

a) Public sector and government companies - In India the government is involved in everything from space research and power generation to running hotels and universities. Therefore, there are possibilities for all types of organisational structure managed by government. There are government companies, public sector companies, autonomous bodies and government departments engaged in enterprises and engaged with banks. A company is said to be a public sector enterprise[39] if 51 per cent or more of its share capital is held by the government. Autonomous bodies are outfits directly under any government department but operating like a commercial institution. Uncertainty primarily arises from the classification of a company under any of the above. There also arises uncertainty on the applicability of the power to borrow in respect of government officials. The drawing arrangements vary from company to company. There is a need to clarify this and bank officials right at the account-opening stage need to be aware of this in order to make bank data more accurate and hence reliable for analysis.

b) Priority sector advances - The government and the RBI have decided to ensure that a portion of bank finance goes to certain categories of borrowers among the industrial, agricultural and service sectors. Currently there are six categories of borrowers under priority sector lending. Eligible borrowers will have to provide banks with a number of testimonials to establish their eligibility. Conditions for classifying loans under priority sectors are available at the RBI site[40]. An eligible borrower may not be certain whether he or she satisfies the eligibility conditions to be considered to belong to a priority sector and about the outcome when they approach a bank.

Category	Number of conditions by which one can be eligible for a loan under priority sector
Agriculture	8
Micro and small enterprises	4
Education	2
Housing	3
Export (foreign banks)	1
Others (weaker sections)	11

Thus the uncertainties hovering over this sector-based analysis are the eligibility, identification and correct classification in the system, causing inaccurate data to be provided for analysis.

---

[39]   http://www.archive.india.gov.in/spotlight/spotlight_archive.php?id=78#mf1
[40]   http://www.rbi.org.in/scripts/FAQView.aspx?Id=87

c) Sensitive Sector - This includes loans given to real estate, commodities and capital market. Housing loans do not come under real estate, which is primarily the development of land and construction of buildings as apartments. There is no system of indexing as a real estate at the time of registration of a home. Thus classifying a home loan account as real estate or not relies upon the intention shared by the customer with the bank official.

d) Branches and population group - Expansion of banking forms an important part of economic development. In this respect, the development plans of the government are worked out on the basis of habitats, classified into population groups called rural, semi-urban, urban and metro. India is politically divided into states and union territories and they are further divided into districts. The following local administration bodies are responsible for the development of the region:

- Village level Panchayat
- Block level Panchayat
- District level Panchayat

The branch expansion plans of the RBI are linked to the opening of new bank branches on the basis of centres grouped as follows:

Category	Population (as per 2001 census)	Centre
Tier 1	Above 100,000	Metro : above 1 million Urban : below 1 million
Tier 2	50,000 - 99,999	Semi-urban
Tier 3	20,000 - 49,999	
Tier 4	10,000 - 19,999	
Tier 5	5,000 - 9,999	Rural
Tier 6	Less than 5,000	

The total number of branches varies from RBI data on functioning offices, perhaps including administrative offices and processing centres, e.g. the RBI as at 31st March 2016 for the SBI indicates 16,784 functioning offices, compared to the bank's annual report showing 17,400 branches. Similarly,

ICICI bank data from the RBI is 4,450, compared to the bank's annual report indicating 4,442, and in the case of HDFC Bank Ltd, the RBI data indicates 4,579 compared to 4,520 as per its annual report.

The branch where the customer has opened his first account provides a customer identification number (CIF) and the branch for the customer is designated as the home or parent branch. The home branch can be changed and customers can open any number of accounts for fresh deposits and loans with the same CIF at any office of the same bank.

Branches can be referred to centre-wise, population group-wise and panchayat-wise. Branches may include processing centres or not. The customer can maintain a bare minimum balance account at the CIF centre branch and his operationally active accounts in some other centres. The reports perhaps impede the planning process for regional economic development because of data inconsistency.

Uncertainty in the nature of loans

The structuring of a loan depends upon the intention of the borrower. There can be some uncertainties because of the way it is handled by bank officials, or because of the extant guidelines. Some of them are:

a) Loans against fixed deposit This may be one of the simplest uncertainties. Security is taken while granting loans as an alternate recourse to realise dues. Therefore when someone wants to take a loan against a fixed deposit of the same bank, the rate of interest on loans against fixed deposits varies if the same deposit is in the name of the loan seeker, or someone else who has willingly offered the security. Another examination of the process could help to remove this uncertainty. Ultimately the deposit holder has willingly conveyed his agreement to set the proceeds against dues in case the borrower fails and for the bank, the loan is fully covered.

b) Financing customers by discounting trade bills against inland letters of credit issued by other banks There is an interesting way of obtaining bank finance for small enterprises by obtaining inland letters of credit.

The bills are drawn on a bank in India. The seller, after carrying over the goods on road transport companies, takes the transport receipt and other related documents and discounts the bill drawn against the letter of credit for payment. These LCs usually have a long period of use. The seller's bank obtains payment from the buyer's bank within the country. Sometimes both the buyer's and seller's bank are the same. If the seller and buyer are operating in the same city, even the transport receipt for actual movement of the goods may not be available. Instead of the buyer taking finance for goods in transit, this inland LC process, vulnerable to fraud, is availed. The buyer can issue a cheque and provide the same comfort to the seller to release goods which could be discounted or collected as agreed between the buyer and seller, instead of going for a letter of credit arrangement.

c) Intra-group firms offering guarantees to banks An individual, a firm or a company guaranteeing a bank loan is common in India. Though the liability on account of this guarantee is usually not accounted as a liability of the guarantor, on the strength of this guarantee, a loan liability is created in the banking system for the borrowing company. In effect, the guarantor's banker has depleted the value of his security unknowingly for finance provided by the borrower's bank. If the borrower's bank invokes the guarantee, the ultimate loser will be the guarantor's bank. Confusion can be avoided if the guarantee of the guarantor's bank is preferred instead of the guarantees provided by individuals or companies. Thus a reduction in the value of assets of the guarantor's bank is compensated for by the increase in the value of assets of the borrower's bank in the banking system.

d) Appraisal, Internal Risk assessment and Rating by External agencies These three processes apparently look alike. But their perspective is different. Banks in India approve large value loans especially, usually based on appraisal of the loan proposal, internal credit risk assessment by bank officials and external rating of the applicant company by RBI-approved credit rating agencies. Even though the information provided by the company is the same, the result provides different perspectives of the applicant company. Uncertainty arises when they are compared or mapped to reflect the same or a similar view.

The RBI has approved certain rating companies and their rating, known as an External Rating, reflects the future potential. Since they are not in the process of sanction or affected by loan approvals, the independence offered by the rating agencies has its own merit. They also factor in the efficiency of the management, their discipline and ability to honour their commitments.

The Credit Risk Assessment of a borrower is carried out internally by ascertaining the strength of the borrower on the basis of the audited financials, conduct of accounts, corporate governance and practices. It also factors in the outlook for the industry based on the probability of default in a particular industry, along with geography and other macroeconomic factors that may affect the performance of the unit. The major part of it comes from the financials.

When it comes to appraisal, the attempt is to obtain all other information that is relevant for considering the proposal from the unit and from other financiers. Many a time, the impression of the external rating company officials, and the internal risk rating officials can be misleading, when inferences can be different because of certain critical facts not available from any published information (e.g. a death or chronic disease for anyone in the family of the proprietor affecting production or sales, etc.). Depending upon discussions with the prospective borrower on ways to reduce the weak points, the appraiser takes a view on the proposal.

Uncertainty exists when all three reports lead to different conclusions.

e) Uncertainty from bank guarantees When the beneficiary and applicant of a bank guarantee belong to the same bank, there is probably uncertainty of obtaining payment promptly. The payment of a guarantee is countermanded or delayed indefinitely when proper procedure is not followed or a court issues a stay order. Banks have to take care of the interests of their customers. For the issuing bank, countermanding may be a favourable twist and for the beneficiary bank, prompt collection of payment may be a favourable twist. When both are the same bank, any outcome may complicate the impression on the official handling it. The threat of losing an important customer looms large.

Uncertainties because of communications not sent

Another important cause of uncertainty in the banking business is the failure of banks to communicate appropriately with customers. It is necessary to ensure that customers are kept up to date about their obligations and rights under the contract, both in the case of deposits or loans. Some of the regular communications to be sent are the periodical statement of accounts, notice of instalments due in respect of loans, due date when deposits mature, maturity of deposits, failed standing instructions, and any revision of interest retested. Such communications help banks to confirm and update the change of address of customers indirectly. Similarly, notices of dues sent to customers help banks to rule out any opportunity for defaulters about ignorance of the dues. Insufficient attention to the exchange of information puts banks in the way of uncertainties and disputes. Often communications are not sent and if sent at all, they fail to answer customers' questions, such as 'How much exactly is due?', 'When am I expected to pay?' or 'Is there any single contact person with whom I can discuss my issues?', etc. By not sending information promptly to customers banks only escalate their operational cost.

Uncertainty caused by third party entities

The uncertainty of responsibility exists when banks engage professionals such as engineers, lawyers and chartered accountants in order to make the job of bank officials easier. Bank officials rely on the opinions of these professionals heavily and use their reports to defend their credit decisions. Even though the services of these professionals are available for a fee, they carry limited responsibility. However, they are in a position to influence credit decisions. The responsibility for verifying and monitoring the integrity of these professionals lies with the bank officials who take credit decisions. Like auditors, the professionals owe their dealings to the bank officials. This situation often leads to the provision of reports favourable to the needs of the bank official currently requesting their service. These valuers[41] show a tendency to be favourably disposed towards the bank official who favours

---

41   Professional engineers who certify the value of property

them with more valuation jobs. In the process, the certified value of a property fluctuates according to the situation that is preferable to the bank official. An inflated value at the time of considering a loan proposal helps to prove that the security for the loan is adequate. Similarly, a deflated value when a property is considered for auction attracts more bidders. Such low value at the time of auction often is contested by the defaulted borrower and the true owner of the property in courts as a deceit or to prove that the bank official acted in connivance with a prospective buyer. The uncertainty lies in the process, however banks can fix responsibility on those professionals and make them accountable.

Others

Audited Balance sheet This is one of the most important documents presented to a banker along with the request for a loan. An auditor's report is expected to state that the figures represent a true and fair picture of the state of affairs of the company. But Indian audit reports include disclaimers, and also do not always present helpful observations. Audit firms are small and they are appointed by the company. Therefore, they are not encouraged to make frank statements detrimental to the company. However, bankers have to make their judgement based upon the balance sheet, its notes and other discreet enquiries before making the decision on credit. Since there is space for using discretion by bankers while interpreting the balance sheet and other documents, there is the possibility of difference of opinion between banks on loan eligibility. This uncertainty can be removed only when the Institute of Chartered Accountants guides their members to make audit reports easily comprehensible and statements made are of plain opinion in simple language comprehensive to the less educated person. To illustrate:

- The company will continue its operational existence
- The company's banking facilities are adequately secured
- Fixed assets are reviewed for impairment and carrying values are recoverable
- Stocks are stated at the lowest of cost or net realisable value

Post-dated or undated cheque There is a practice of handing over post-dated cheques (cheques drawn with a future date), undated cheques or blank cheques (with signature only) by the consumer to shops offering goods on instalments, financiers, hire purchase companies or to banks while offering personal loans to individuals having a bank account with other banks. Due to a change in legislation relating to the negotiable instruments act, a holder of cheques can get orders to arrest the issuer in an easy way. Thus cheques became attractive as security for retail loans. There was a demand for cheque books from customers in banks, undermining the fact that cheques are like bombs[42]. They can detonate at any time causing uncontrollable damage. In the feature film 'Catch me if you can'[43], issuing cheques without providing funds is referred to as 'paper changing', perhaps from a fraudster's angle.

Many entrepreneurs lost business due to this severe and rapid advance against them and applied for bankruptcy to avoid arrest. Consequently banks too suffered. The legislation intended to boot out the retail loan defaulters, in effect injected many uncertainties into the banking system in the country, such as the issue of safe custody of cheques and presenting them in a timely manner, the payment of cheques at remote centres when presented by people who are not known to the bank, and the increased risk of forgery of customer signatures.

Moving away from cheques to online systems of clearing and standing instructions reduced usage of cheques and the uncertainties surrounding them.

Bank holidays Even though there is a demand to treat banking as an essential service, it is not. But it is a public utility service. Declaring banks as an essential service will impact the employee's right to strike from work. Employees can go on strike and they used to strike from work on average for one or two days in a year. But the point here is the uncertainty coming from such non-working days due to strikes and holidays in India.

---

[42]   http://www.gobankingrates.com/checking-accounts/
your-checkbook-identity-theft-time-bomb-waiting-off/

[43]   http://en.wikipedia.org/wiki/Frank_Abagnale

However, taking into consideration religious sentiment, bank holidays are not on the same dates all over India. They differ on the basis of every state government's decisions. Even though almost all major banks are connected by the core banking system, these holidays cause problems to travellers as well as businessmen. Adding further uncertainty is the practice of changing dates after the dates are published midway during the year. Bank employees at the front office may not be able to provide information about holidays in other states.

There used to be a half working day on Saturdays which has been removed. Now banks in India work on all days except Sundays and on the second and fourth Saturdays of the month. There is scope in this area to retain the expected actual number of working days and work around additional leave and uniform holidays. Even though ATMs are doing a wonderful service on holidays in cities and towns, customer needs may not be limited to ATMs.

Conclusion

These are some of the uncertainties that take away the time of employees and customers. They are the cause of indecision and customer complaints. Most of them can be rectified if the regulator takes them up with government and banks and brings out the required changes at the policy level and at supervisory level. The consultants Ernst and Young, in their book "Global Banking 2020", indicated twelve uncertainties for global banking. They are: changes in the regulatory environment, the economic shift towards emerging economies, globalisation, type and degree of competition, financial crises, future availability of the lender of last resort, government debt, availability of the securitisation market, retirement scenario, the unpredictable role of technology, customer empowerment through the internet, and government bail-outs to protect creditors' rights. Banks in India additionally may face a different set of uncertainties that emerge from the changes that are happening due to political events, economic development and global issues affecting emigration and forex flows.

11. COMPETITION

Indian banking evolved into its present stage as a net result of government initiatives such as legislation, organisational changes, regular directions given to them, and the way the employees who managed these banks responded to those initiatives. There is no doubt that banks are very well controlled by regulators and government. However, conditions have not generated the need for efficiency, whilst the banks' existence was made easier by their patronage of both regulator and government.

India thrives on unity in diversity. The government is democratically elected. There is no space for superiority of meritocracy or bureaucracy over government in decision taking. Therefore, decisions affecting banking also depended upon the views of the governments that have come into power since 1947.

It is evident from history that the Indian banking system was left untouched without any major changes except during the times of Prime Ministers Mrs Indira Gandhi and Dr Narasimha Rao. During Mrs Gandhi's time, the major portion of the entire banking system was brought under the control of government by way of nationalisation, while during Dr Rao's time, his finance minister Dr Manmohan Singh liberalised licensing and provided opportunities for the private sector in developing banking. That resulted in the operation of the four top banks, namely the ICICI Bank, HDFC Bank, Axis Bank and IDBI Bank.

Since globalisation and liberalisation was adopted to accelerate the growth of the economy from 1990, India has been able to achieve consistent growth of its wealth and presence across the world. However, when it comes to banking in India, there are not so many good words to be said. After Dr

Manmohan Singh's initiative of boosting the role of private banks in Indian banking, Dr Raghuram Rajan as governor of the Reserve Bank of India also is acclaimed for his initiatives to clean up the banking system which was ridden with bad loans. In general it is believed that the government will have to leave banking to the private sector in order to make Indian banks efficient. However, the efficiency need not come just by a change of ownership. It can be by way of stimulating competition, which exists only on a level playing field. Moreover, the sector where Indian banks currently have a lot to do is that of household savers and the SME segment. Globalisation has taken care of liberalised FDI and overseas investments for globally operated business.

Beneficiary of competition

The customer is the face of business and definitely it is they who expect to benefit. The benefits can be enhanced if customers are made aware of the services banks can offer that could improve their living conditions. This responsibility lies with the banks and the process has to be part of their marketing strategy. Once the public are aware of the benefits of banking and banks are accessible to them, they will be seeking bank support. There follows competition, when consumers choose the most ideal and suitable to them. On the other hand, by serving a larger number of customers, banks will have the opportunity to economise their transaction costs. Product innovation will follow. Customer education on banking services therefore is most important.

Competition in providing essential service

If there are sufficient banks offering almost all services expected from a bank at the same cost, then competition may not exist. In such a scenario, banks function like ration shops and proximity becomes the key deciding factor for customers to choose a bank. Therefore branch expansion to remote areas will be an important factor. Banking statistics do not state that there are enough banks for the people. The setting up of the SBI, then nationalisation of all major banks, liberalisation of bank licensing, setting up a hybrid version in the form of regional rural banks, globalisation of banking, injection of IT into the banking industry, offering small banks and pay banks, etc., are steps taken since independence. The present government has initiated certain steps of which circulation of the Aadhar card as an identity for members of the public is going to be a significant game-changer in managing subsidy, circulation of unaccounted money, etc.

Banker of the first choice If I have saved some money shall I prefer to go to a jewellery shop to buy gold, or to my banker, for keeping in any savings schemes? If I have to go to a bank, what is the name of the bank that comes to my mind as my bank of first choice? This is the challenge to all banks in India when competition surfaces. Some banks by default lure customers because of their size and many years of existence. The State Bank of India, with its subsidiary banks, is better positioned to become the banker of first choice, as they have a larger network of branches, ATMs and safes too. Proximity, safety, easy handling, convenient products and mutual growth are some of the factors a customer looks for in banks. The situation in cities may be better than in villages where bank branches are very few. In urban centres where the public have choice, new private banks contest the position with a somewhat homogenous clientele, and contrary to government banks, customer segmentation is difficult to implement. Therefore, the younger generation looks at the ease of doing business, mutual growth and flexibility of timing. In that situation, new generation banks and foreign banks are preferred.

As government banks tune up with more IT products, new generation banks will have to look to better placement outside the urban centres. At that stage, when there is more than one bank for selection and IT is the backbone for operations, any bank can be the bank of first choice. That is when competition exists, which draws upon the efficiency of management strategies. It may be interesting to take a glance at the top ten banks and how they have taken up the government campaign for new accounts under the scheme of Prime Minister Jan Dhan Yojana. The top ten banks have declared in their annual reports that they have opened 109.4 million accounts, of which the SBI has opened 53.2 million accounts, new generation banks including the IDBI Bank opened 6 million and the remaining five nationalised banks opened

50.2 million. Broad basing of the clientele is important as once an account is opened with a particular bank, the customer rarely tries to move except in the case of a bitter relationship. The present system of account opening will not encourage people to shift either. The public need to be weaned away from moral attachment, instead they have to be lured by financial incentives.

The role of regulator and government has to ensure that the banks offer the quality of service they promise customers. This is necessary to avoid bad competition or exploitation of weak customers. Practically, an individual customer may not take on a giant corporate organisation to redress the grievance. The need for a functioning authority that can take up issues faced by customers and discipline the deficient service provider is essential and urgent.

Current scenario for customers in India - supply side

Not all Indians who are old enough to operate a bank account do so. And even among those who have bank accounts, very few use them for various banking purposes. Just having a bank account to receive salaries or government subsidies, etc., may not do justice to the role banking is intended to play, to encourage the people and the economy to prosper. A fully-fledged banker customer partnership or hand-holding support needs to be in place, in order to mobilise surplus income from citizens and provide them with instant financial support whenever they need it the most. There is one more aspect one cannot overlook about the population of India. Of the 1.23 billion people, only 26.3 million file tax returns and only 12.5 million really pay tax. This is just to establish that generally people are hesitant to be in the tax net. Often they view tax as a nuisance. Banks are also seen as friends of these taxmen and people may be hesitant to open accounts if they can live without one. Therefore there are many accounts opened just to receive government support in the form of a grant or subsidy, etc. This is not banking for someone who is concerned with economic development. This belief about banks causes a large volume of business transactions to still be handled on cash terms. ATMs in urban centres are attractive for their convenience.

There is churning in the offing with present government initiatives. Banking may be moving to a vaster, fertile field. That would cause an era of competition and efficiency. Potential growth is entwined with economic development in different segments of the society. If banks take the initial steps for development, the economy will boom. The initial steps include branch expansion, creating awareness of banking, process simplification, developing the right attitude among employees and creating confidence in commercial banking.

Setting up bank offices near to people (branch expansion)

A bank existing near people's vicinity creates interest and people will become interested in the bank and the employees there. Gradually, they will start saving with the bank and later become takers of other products including loans. The familiarity of local people with the bank and bank personnel generate the demand for bank services. But if banks consider profitability branch by branch as a deciding factor for opening a new branch, expansion will be difficult. This approach resulted in branches getting opened in prosperous states like Gujarat and Maharashtra in the western region. Out of 60,347 branches opened by commercial banks, 17 per cent of branches were opened in these two states. During 2015-16, 21 per cent of new private banks and 13 per cent of public sector banks were opened in these two states. There is a need to plan and spread commercial bank branches near to every household and not on the basis of population. Depending upon the number of branches and taking into consideration the minimum essential requirement of a branch manager and housekeeping staff, ample employment has to be created. In fact among the new generation banks the HDFC Bank has opened quite a good number of branches and augmented its employee strength.

Educating people to demand service (customer service) Banks do not send communications to customers on information that a customer needs to know, or other useful information to create a demand for banking product or services. Awareness among people about products and services available in the market is important for creating a competitive market. Bank websites provide information on their products and services but most of their websites are not attractively designed and navigation is not easy. This is a significant part of bank management. In fact, Global Finance magazine has awarded best website design to the site of the ICICI Bank Ltd and the Asia Pacific Regional Bank was sub-category winner - best consumer digital banks.

Simplicity of processes In order to step up the pace of growth of banking, banking processes need to be simplified using cost effective sustainable IT solutions. When all is said and done, ultimately it is the courteous employee who beckons customers again and again to a branch. Their roles need to be strengthened to enable them to manage more customers than in the past.

Attitude of employees to sales The frontline officials of banks are often criticised for not attending to customers promptly, or engaging in gossip, etc. They should be aware of their image and responsibility to the public. The relationship is long term in nature. Customers may become poor and the poor may become awfully rich during a cycle of thirty years. But if bank officials' attitude is that of being helpful, each interaction turns into a bond that helps to sell products and services in a growing market. A lot of scope exists for banks in India to improve upon this area by giving proper training to their employees to develop a helpful attitude towards customers, irrespective of the business they are conducting with the bank.

The business of security Deposit insurance is an important aspect of developing banking. The sum assured to a depositor in case of bank failure is one lakh rupees (equivalent to 1300 USD). This has become irrelevant as a bank rarely if ever has been allowed to go into liquidation by the regulator in India in the recent past. Thus security comes from the regulators and government rather than from the bank. In respect of public sector banks however, even this concern may not exist as they are owned and managed by government. A distinguishing feature of competition among banks therefore does not exist. Steps need to be taken so that security of banks' deposits is assigned to banks alone.

Another aspect of security is that of keeping personal articles of individuals in safe custody. Every household will have some personal items to keep safe. These can be land documents, jewellery, keys to important storage or even documents such as a will, etc. Offering such a service will encourage people to enrol for more banking services.

The other side of work pressure: Chaotic processes and intervention in employees' routines leaves them less time to market and get new connections. They often find solace in pursuing other banks' customers at higher rates. Banks have to work on the basis of comprehensive market surveys on the lines of decennial population, and rely on product innovation.

Ideally looking forward - demand side

Until all banks are brought under similar control and regulation with the required freedom to manage their affairs, competition cannot be said to exist. It is also necessary to plan for the probable short term and for long term changes unfolding on the horizon. Ideally, looking forward, some of the following have to happen soon for which the government and the RBI may have to take the initiative.

Account portability The facility to avail services from any office of a bank is a convenience to the public. This is possible if the personal information provided by customers is available at every centre. Core banking has made this possible. Moving further, if a customer has the option to shift his banking to another bank without going through all the formalities of account opening, that would be a welcome change. Then the customer could switch over at their convenience to another bank where they get better service without difficulty. This scenario will demand efficiency from banks and competition will begin to settle.

Grievance redressal mechanism Pursuing grievances is a frustrating experience and in all probability, people avoid approaching banks for their banking service requirements. A monitoring or regulatory authority which speaks for the public is necessary and such an entity will firstly confirm the existence of comprehensive rules and thereafter can point out banks' lapses on omissions and commissions. They shall be in a position to establish employee lapses and organisations' lapses. Quick redressal of grievances will provide the impetus for competition, with adequate systems and courteous conduct in place. In the long run, banks save time because of the shift to a better customer service standard.

Emergency loans It is not material whether a bank adopts the franchise model or traditional business practice, the public will be interested in all banking services at a single place or interface. Emergency credit in the form of personal loans, instalment purchases, cash on EMI, etc., are offered by banks, credit card companies and retailers on different terms and conditions. The same purpose is served. The difference lies in the means of administration of such loans. All such emergency short term loans have to be brought under similar terms of lending so that the customer chooses, on the basis of cost and eligibility rather than other factors, to obtain credit. By bringing changes to the way such loans are administered, the retail trade will flourish as purchases can be completed on the fly.

Single point interface for customers Multiple options, different layers and centralisation may be economical or productive. But they are often baffling. In a scenario where customers can be illiterate to globally active corporate entities, the relief provided by a single point interface to customers is invaluable. Like evangelists, they can stay between the customers and bank systems.

Conclusion

Competition has to be at the heart of the business of banking. Competition begets efficiency. Competition can be said to exist when the players are homogenous and the market is equidistant from all of them. The RBI and the government have to draw up proper plans to be rolled out at the earliest time. Most banks have over a century of existence but out of 48 commercial banks only ten have assets of more than 50 billion USD. As hope of India's bouncing back still exists, banks will have to take the route of competition.

SECTION 3

12. TOP TEN INDIAN BANKS

− *Champions of Indian banking*

The scenario in which banks operate in India has been discussed from the perspective of a practical banker, and readers would have read about the dim view of Indian banks held by the investors and economists of the world. Predominant public sector banks are blamed for their inability to control the growth of non-performing loans, and their low profit generation despite the high rate of interest margin prevailing in the market. Most views centre on the thought of privatisation which will bring in competition and infuse the required leadership to make banks globally competitive.

Various thoughts have been considered by governments in the past. As a result, changes in the bank licensing system to facilitate the opening of banks in the private sector became part of the liberalisation process in 1991. Eight new private banks commenced operation by 1996. They have completed two decades of operation. They tested their strategies along with those banks in the private sector, government-owned large banks and foreign banks. Some of them became aggressive and some floundered and merged with bigger banks after a promising start. Of those eight banks, only five are now in existence.

Even though there are 48 commercial banks[44] operating in India as on 31st March 2016, only ten of them have assets of more than three trillion rupees or 50 billion USD approximately. Analysis of these banks is insightful for

---

[44]   Table 1 showing the list of 48 banks

those who look for a successful direction for future banking in India. The analysis is based on data in the annual report presented to their shareholders. Figures, unless specifically indicated, are converted to USD on the basis of the RBI's reference rate for the Indian rupee. This is basically to remove the inflation factor in their growth. In India both the financial year and fiscal year run from 1st April to 31st March. Accordingly the latest data is taken from balance sheets dated 31st March 2016.

There are five groups of commercial banks in India. Three of them are owned by the government, such as the State Bank of India and its group popularly known as the **SBI Group**, then there are nineteen banks nationalised by the government and known as nationalised banks, and there are two more banks grouped as **other public sector banks**. One of them was started by the government and another, by virtue of its shareholding, became a public sector bank. The other two groups are in the private sector. Some of them came into existence after liberalised licensing in the nineties and are known as **new private banks** and all other commercial banks are known as **old private banks.**

The largest bank in terms of assets[45] is the State Bank of India (SBI), that came into existence in the present form in 1955. True to its name it has been working closely with the government right from the time of British rule, first as a princely state bank and then as the Imperial Bank of India. Two of the nine new generation private banks occupy the second and third position among the top ten banks on the basis of their assets. They are the ICICI Bank Ltd and HDFC Bank Ltd. The Bank of Baroda and Punjab National Bank are the next two banks with assets of more than 100 billion USD. Three more nationalised banks find their place among the top ten. They are the Bank of India, Canara Bank and Union Bank of India. The Axis Bank Ltd, a new generation bank, occupies the eighth position and the IDBI Bank Ltd, a new generation bank in the public sector, is the tenth largest bank in India, having assets of more than 50 billion USD as per their solo balance sheet on 31st March 2016.

---

[45]   Table 2 showing the top ten banks

The objective of the analysis of these ten banks in this chapter is to look at their strength to take Indian banking forward. The size of their assets is of paramount importance from that perspective. The other parameters that are used for analysis are the following:

1. **Total assets** indicate the dominance of a particular bank in the Indian banking system and the Indian economy
2. **Group assets** shows diversification and divided risk management
3. **Loan Assets to Total Assets** indicates the inclination of banks' policy and plans towards the core business of lending
4. **Operating profit in relation to employee costs** indicates the ability of the management to harness the best of logistics and support for better employee productivity
5. **Market view** indicates the evaluation of the bank by investors
6. **Age** represents proven adaptability and resilience

Non-performing loans, net profit and capital adequacy are not included in this study for the following reasons:

i) <u>Non-Performing Loans/Assets</u> Perceptions about non-performing loans by investors, the regulator, customers and banks are practically different. From the point of view of a regulator, it is an accounting system, but banks who have been able to watch a borrower at close quarters view this as an indictment to a valuable customer in society. A genuine entrepreneur or individual also views this as a disproportionate share of indignity given to them for happenings beyond their control. The global picture is different from the economic wellbeing of the people of this country and hence not comparable. While transparency and accounting aspects are important, a lot has to happen before a view is taken on the basis of numbers.

ii) <u>Capital Adequacy</u> is something imposed on Indian banks for aligning with the global standard after bank failures in the west. Even though Indian banks are not functioning in the environment in which banks in the west function, Indian banks are looked down on for their poor capital and reserves. But most of the banks are owned by the government, for whom it is a budget allocation. That rules out the question of liquidation. If profit generation is something that is to be considered, the practice of classification of loans and investment as non-performing has a wider impact. This is discretionary and comparison showing inconsistency with previous years or other banks may not provide any revelations. Until a good regulatory system ensures that there is equal opportunity for banks, and banks are given equal opportunities to generate their own capital, comparing their capital adequacy ratio may not be so telling when it comes to their ability to compete or survive.

iii) <u>Net Result or Profit</u> has not been reckoned as a parameter, as a lot of management discretion is used to arrive at the net result. Such decisions may not be evenly applied between banks and not even for the same bank every year. Therefore comparing these figures may not reflect any shortcomings in the bank's efficiency or its potential for the future.

1. Total Assets

As on 31st March 2015, 89.78 per cent of the total assets of banks are with government banks including the SBI and new generation banks. While these banks have improved their share during 2014-15, the share of foreign banks and old generation private banks reduced from 11.33 per cent to 10.22 per cent. There are nine new generation banks and twenty-five government banks that are active and their consolidation or alignment represents the direction banking may take from now onwards.

The top ten banks held 58.23 per cent of the total banks' assets as of March 2015. As part of cleansing the books there has been a reduction in the balance sheet size of many banks in 2015-16. Therefore growth during the financial year 2015-16 has been only 1.45 per cent compared to 7.62 per cent in the previous year. By March 2016 these ten banks had grown their assets to 1.13 trillion USD. During the last two years alone, the six public sector banks (PSB among them), increased their assets by 43.20 billion USD and the three new generation private banks grew by 50.15 billion. The tenth largest, the IDBI Bank Ltd[46], presently grouped as one of the 'other

---

[46]   The IDBI Bank Ltd is under the process of privatisation; presently it is categorized among 'other public sector banks'

public sector banks', grew by 1.64 billion USD. Altogether, these ten banks increased their assets by 95 billion USD during the last two years.

Among these ten banks, the HDFC Bank recorded the highest growth of 13.04 per cent over the previous year. Other banks such as the Axis Bank and the ICICI Bank increased their assets by 7 and 5 per cent respectively. Among public sector banks, the PNB and the SBI recorded more than 4 per cent growth.

In real value terms, the SBI and the HDFC added assets worth 13.35 billion USD and 12.31 billion USD to their last year figure. Other banks such as the ICICI Bank, Axis Bank and PNB added 5.48 billion, 5.33 billion and 4.21 billion USD assets in one year's time. The RBI direction for cleansing balance sheets had its effect on banks' financials particularly in the financial year 2015-16. These five banks increased their assets by just 40 billion USD in 2015-16 compared to 101.57 billion USD during 2014-15. Not only that, but the assets of the Bank of Baroda, Bank of India and Canara Bank together contracted by 24.35 billion USD.

The SBI continues to be the largest in size with 341 billion in assets and the next in asset size is the ICICI Bank, less than a third of its size. Going by the growth trend during the last two years, the HDFC may emerge as the largest in the private sector and the second largest among all banks in India. Between the largest and tenth largest, the IDBI Bank, the latter is only a sixth of the size of the SBI.

Among developments in banking that are taking place is the absorption of five associate commercial banks by the SBI, and the IDBI Bank will be moved to the private sector. After the merger the total assets of the SBI will increase to 432 billion USD and that will put the SBI management in control of 25 per cent of the assets of Indian banks.

2. Group Assets

Banks have been allowed to take up non-banking activities by forming subsidiaries for improving their profitability since 1991. Accordingly most banks have tie-up arrangements or formed subsidiaries and joint ventures for various activities. This will help them to increase their income by cross-selling the products of non-banking subsidiaries to their customers. Therefore, when group assets are reckoned for a ranking, the intention is mainly to understand how well a typical bank has been able to increase their profit earning capability utilising their customer database.

Most of the banks have Indian subsidiaries and all these ten banks, except the HDFC Bank and IDBI Bank, have overseas subsidiaries. Group companies add 107 billion USD to the assets of the SBI. But most of it comes from the five associate banks[47]. The next highest contribution from group companies, of 30 billion USD, goes to the ICICI Bank. In this respect the HDFC Bank itself being a subsidiary of the Housing Development Finance Corporation (HDFC), most of the para-banking and non-banking activities are managed by subsidiaries of the parent company. Therefore, there are just 3.32 billion USD additions from the group companies to the assets of 106.73 billion USD of the HDFC Bank.

Generally group companies operate activities such as mutual funds, factoring, credit cards, life insurance, general insurance, pension funds, asset management, housing finance, merchant banking, securities broking, securities investment, trading, arranging private equity, venture funds, etc. During the last two years the total group assets of these top ten banks increased by 16.90 billion USD, which is comparable to the total assets of the six smallest commercial banks in India. Most of the business carried out by subsidiaries is attractive to people living in urban centres. The Indian urban population, as per the 2011 census, is 377 million, which means there is a huge potential in place for these top ten banks in the coming days.

3. Loans to Assets

Lending is the primary function of banks, for which they mobilise deposits. So loans are the core business activity. Earning comes from that stream. Therefore the ratio is very important. Even the variation between two years requires examination. While a gradual increase in the ratio is welcome,

---

[47]   Merger of associate banks with SBI is in progress

a sharp and sudden rise in the ratio indicates an increase of riskier large value borrowers. This can be due to forced lending and the probability of undercutting of interest rates cannot be ruled out. This increase in the growth of bank loans during an election year has been noticed by analysts in the past.

The ratio for all Indian commercial banks, on the basis of audited financials as on 31st March 2015, was 62.60 per cent, whereas the top ten banks had a ratio of 66.09 per cent. However, due to the cleansing exercise, the ratio of these ten banks reduced sizeably to 62.28 per cent by March 2016[48]. Overall the loan portfolio of these ten banks shrunk by 32.47 billion USD. The 'Loan to Assets' ratio of public sector banks reduced by 6.28 per cent and that of the private banks increased by 2.55 per cent over last year. The loan portfolio of the HDFC Bank increased by 11.79 billion USD while that of the SBI reduced by 31.25 billion USD.

The HDFC Bank and the Union Bank of India have a Loans to Assets ratio above 65 per cent, while the SBI and Axis Bank have a ratio marginally below 65 per cent. For the SBI, the ratio reduced from 77 per cent in 2015 to 64.81 per cent in 2016 but their total assets increased by 13.35 billion USD. On the other hand, the loan portfolio of the Bank of Baroda and Bank of India contracted, as did their balance sheet size. Both banks were pushed two notches down in the overall ranking. The PNB is the only bank among public sector banks in the top ten to increase its loan portfolio and assets during 2015-16. Since the loans portfolio was not in proportion to the increase in assets, the Loan to Assets ratio of the PNB reduced from 63.02 per cent to 61.77 per cent. The Union Bank and the PNB have shown consistency in the ratio during the last three years.

Having almost two thirds of all loans of Indian commercial banks as of March 2015, these ten banks' potential is bright for selling more loan products in the near future.

---

[48]   Table 3 showing loans to assets

4. Operating profit and employee costs

In a service industry, the productivity of employees is the most important factor. It indicates the performance of the management, as to how they get the best out of their large human resources. Not only by control of pay and allowances, but the positive ambience of their work environment and motivating factors for promising employees, are the results of good management functioning. From recruitment until retirement, this entire part of the life of an employee is in the hands of management. While payment of wages is the main attraction for getting better quality and performance, provision of all other conveniences affects the performance of employees. Therefore, the ratio of 'per employee operating expenditure' to 'per employee operating profit' provides better information on the management's performance. The data, including the strength of employees, is taken from the annual reports of banks. If the average of the number of employees at the beginning and end of the year is taken for working the ratios, the ratio for ICICI Bank will be 188 per cent instead of 224 percent as mentioned in Table 4.

The data for 2015-16 for all of these ten banks put together indicate that only 117 per cent of the operating expenditure forms operating profit[49]. Five of them have higher rates. The ICICI Bank has the highest rate of productivity at 188 per cent followed by the Axis Bank with 159 per cent. The IDBI Bank, HDFC Bank and PNB have more than 120 per cent. The SBI with employee strength equalling the total of all three private banks in the top ten league, secures 104 per cent of operating expenses as operating profit. The Bank of India, the sixth largest employer, is behind all other nine banks, with a rate of 65 per cent.

Some sort of benchmarking with the best performers has to be undertaken by the management of those banks which are behind. Basically, the comparison shows how superior banks are able to balance their direct expenditure on employees against all other indirect expenditure.

The second aspect of the analysis reveals the strategy of bank management to ensure that banks produce consistently reasonable profit by exercising

---

[49]   Table 4 showing operating profit and average number of employees

control on overheads and ensuring other income adequately makes up for the lower interest income. Other income comes in the form of fees and commission for banking-related services rendered. But nowadays, recovery from written-off accounts adds to the other streams of income.

On the basis of analysis of the data for the last three years relating to operating profit and operating income, during 2014-16, it is found that the HDFC Bank has improved its efficiency by 32 per cent compared to the growth of 4 per cent of all ten banks together. Necessary adjustment has been made for the increase or decrease of the employees over their 2013-14 strength. The Axis Bank comes in with the next highest rate, of 23 per cent. Both the PNB and ICICI increased their employee strength but increased their efficiency at the rate of 8 per cent and 9 per cent respectively. The Union Bank of India almost maintained its efficiency at the same level after factoring in the increase in their employee strength. The Bank of India, IDBI Bank and Bank of Baroda increased their employee strength but reduced their efficiency level by 19 per cent, 4 per cent and 2 per cent respectively. For the IDBI Bank Ltd, the growth of interest income and other income was good enough. The fall in other income for the Bank of India resulted in it becoming the worst performer among the ten, unlike the PNB which could gain by other income even though it was affected by the reduction in the interest income. In the case of the SBI, the ratio improved but after making adjustment for reduced employee strength, it could improve by just one per cent.

Now we move to the third aspect of efficiency of management, namely results due to consistency of policies of management. Better results are achievable by banks having stable management and policies. During 2015-16 banks in India had to make abnormal provisioning for writing off bad accounts as part of cleansing their balance sheet and five banks among the top ten declared net loss. The Union Bank, Axis Bank, ICICI Bank, HDFC Bank and SBI have been making profit consistently. The three private banks in the top ten declared around 55 per cent of their operating result as net profit while two profit-making public banks declared around 30 per cent of their operating as net profit.

Some of these insights are useful for the future. The ninth-ranked Union Bank appears to be consistent and has not been impacted by the cleansing exercise. Perhaps it can be the role model for benchmarking for other nationalised banks. The consistency of performance comes from the chairman, consistency of leadership, and continuing with the same vision and organisation structure. The Union Bank of India and State Bank of India continue to have chairmen from 2013. On the other hand, the Bank of India, Bank of Baroda and IDBI Bank had some continuity of leadership and management issues.

5. View from the market

One factor that is going to affect these banks in the pursuit of their goals in future is the view their investors hold. The indicator is their share price in the stock market as against their book value per share. The statements in the annual reports for the financial year 2015-16 are taken[50] for our analysis. The share price in the market is influenced by the availability of shares for sale in the market, the strength of their balance sheet, return on equity and return on average annual assets. In addition, better value is also available for those shares where the employees are incentivised to perform well by offering employee stock options. This feature of payment based on performance will be a motivation to the employees and boosts profit for the bank but it also encourages some financial camouflage. The shares of banks owned by government, even though not available for acquisition, or management control, are sought for short term investment of the liquid funds.

The market price of individual bank shares is sensitive to purchasing sprees by RBI-approved Financial Institutional Investors and management's control over non-performing loans. Banks that have the potential for expansion and better structure for business growth also boost their share price.

In this analysis the book value of shares is taken from the annual reports of these ten banks and is compared with the price of their stock in the Bombay Stock Exchange market. The BSE is one of the largest exchanges in the

---

[50]   Table 5 showing equity related ratios

world and has more than 5,200 listed companies. Bank stocks influence the entire stock market. A look at the ratio of market value of share to book value indicates investor friendship.

During 2015-16, the BSE Sensex moved downwards by 9 per cent and Bankex fell by 12 per cent. The Bank of Baroda, HDFC Bank, IDBI Bank and Union Bank fared better than the Bankex as of March 2016. The real market expectation on these banks can be gauged from their ratio of market value to book value. The HDFC bank is at the top with 373 per cent followed by Axis Bank's 199 per cent, ICICI Bank's 153 per cent, Bank of Baroda's 111 percent and SBI's 110 per cent.

Among the factors that would have contributed to this score would be their earnings per share, net interest margin, and return on assets over and above the impression of the new management team. The HDFC Bank's figures regarding Return on Average Assets, Return on Equity, Earnings per Share and Net Interest Margin was higher than other banks. The Axis Bank was the second highest in ROA, ROE, EPS and NIM. The third best performer as regards the ratio of market value of shares to book value was the ICICI Bank, which followed with better ratios after the Axis Bank on ROA, ROE and NIM. Earnings per share of the Union Bank were higher than that of the ICICI Bank. Among the public sector, the performance of the Union Bank has been consistent and in some areas, such as NIM, EPS and ROE, was better than the largest bank, the SBI.

The three private sector banks are viewed by the market positively. And among government-owned banks, shares of the SBI and Union Bank are at a higher value than others. The shares of the Bank of Baroda, a bank that has unfortunately been affected adversely by the cleansing exercise, have been viewed positively by the market.

6. Age

In 2016 the publication[51] of the World Bank regarding doing business worldwide, ranked India at 130th among the 189 nations taken up for the study. However, India has been ranked at the 42nd position for obtaining credit. This is a reflection of the development of banking in India, where overall its ranking is behind 129 other countries. In this chaotic scenario, banks have done a good job[52].

Against this background, when we look at these ten banks, there is no doubt that they have done a mammoth job for banking in India. The SBI has been in its present form of existence for the last six decades. The other five nationalised banks have been there for more than four and half decades. Private banks such as the ICICI Bank, HDFC Bank and Axis Bank have been there for two decades. And the IDBI Bank has been in its present form for a decade. Many of the banks have existed for a longer time in a different form. Their successful existence only proves their ability to adapt to changing government and government policies. The longer they have survived, the longer they can withstand future variations in shares too.

The SBI is ranked as 55th among Banker's 1,000 banks. Among twenty banks that were nationalised, only five could manage to come within the top ten. Similarly, out of eight new generation banks found in the private sector, only four could make it into the top ten. Even the many-decades-old private banks that escaped from nationalisation could not mature to make it into the top ten, indicating that their model is not so promising for the future. That means that nationalisation helped banks to grow better. These private banks now face competition from much stronger nationalised and new generation banks.

The age of a bank indicates its ability to face the competition but the size of the bank is very significant when it comes to growth. Nationalised banks got the support of the government and new generation banks among the

---

51   http://www.doingbusiness.org/data/exploreeconomies/india/~/media/giawb/
     doing%20business/documents/profiles/country/IND.pdf?ver=3

52   Table 7 showing last three years CEOs

top ten had the backing of large financial institutions like the ICICI, IDBI, UTI and HDFC. Associate banks of the SBI also enjoyed its strength. Other private banks belonging to both the old and new generation are not able to gain the momentum for appreciable growth. The new generation bank which recently joined the Indian banking scene may be able to be guided by this factor of growth, and for old private banks it may be useful to go for a merger or tie-up so that they do not remain too small to last long.

Individual Banks - some interesting information

These ten banks have made their own imprint in the banking industry and the economy of India. They are there at the top with sizeable assets. Their history is different. Some of their ownership has undergone changes in the past. Their founding objectives are also different. Each one of them had their own unique strategies and developed resilience to work according to the government and regulatory controls. From the perspective of future banking in India, it may be interesting to know about these banks individually from their history, customers' point of view, investors' point of view, their brand value and the effectiveness of their leadership with regard to their large number of employees.

1. STATE BANK OF INDIA - 'a banker to every Indian'

The State Bank of India is popularly known as the SBI or 'STATE Bank' and is undoubtedly the largest bank in terms of assets, group assets, branch network and the number of employees. It is the 232nd largest company listed among the Fortune 500 companies[53], an improvement from 260th last year. It is the only bank from India to make it into the Fortune 500. The SBI is placed as the 55th largest bank with 26 billion USD Tier 1 capitals among the Banker 1000 global banks.

According to RBI data, the bank has 17,400 functioning offices as of March 2016 which is nine times more than the number of branches of

---

[53]   released in July 2016

the tenth-ranked IDBI Bank. The state bank group has both banking and non-banking subsidiaries. The SBI group has 448 billion USD assets and generated revenue of 41 billion USD last financial year. In terms of assets, the SBI is three times bigger than the next biggest, the ICICI Bank. It is the largest employer in India after Indian Railways and the defence forces. Global Finance magazine[54] recognised SBI as the best bank in India providing trade finance and the best among emerging markets of banks in Asia Pacific 2016.

The SBI came into existence in 1955 by taking over the functions of the Imperial Bank of India. The latter was formed by the British government in 1921 by merging the three presidency banks of Bengal, Madras and Bombay. The history of the bank thus goes back to the days when presidency banks were the mainstay of Indian banking during British rule.

According to the book entitled "The Rise, Progress and Present Condition of Banking in India" published in 1863 and written by the Bank of Bengal's Deputy Secretary and Treasurer Mr Chas. Northcote Cooke, the Bank of Calcutta was opened for business on 1st May 1806 and in January 1809 the bank was granted the charter and renamed as the Bank of Bengal. The secretary was from the Bengal civil service.

The Bank of Bengal, and later the Imperial Bank of India, played a pivotal role in India's banking until 1955, even after Indian Independence. During this period, the central banking function was separated and the RBI was set up in 1934. After Indian Independence in 1947, the most important step taken in banking by the government was the setting up of the State Bank of India in 1955 by an act of parliament, taking over the functions of commercial banking from the Imperial Bank of India. The bank continues to play the lead role in areas such as currency distribution, conducting of clearing houses and other agency functions on behalf of the RBI, in addition to branch expansion and business growth.

Being the largest in assets, volume of business and branch network and having a long history of existence, employment in the SBI continues to

---

[54]   https://www.gfmag.com/about-us/

appear glamorous and attracts superior talent available in the country. The career path for employees provides opportunities to go up the ladder and ultimately reach the position of the Bank's Managing Director or Chairman. Some of the employees even get opportunities to work in their offices in other countries.

Between 1955 and 1959, the SBI initiated steps and brought into its fold eight princely state banks. However, they were allowed to continue as banking subsidiaries of the SBI. These banks are referred to as 'Associate Banks of SBI' and form the major part of the SBI Group. Later, among these eight banks, two of them merged with each other and two were absorbed by the SBI. Presently there are only five of them working independently. Some of these associate banks are larger than some nationalised banks. The process of merger of these five associate banks with the SBI is in progress while this book is in the manuscript stage.

Customers' point of view

Customers look at a bank from the point of view of their safety, security of their savings, accessibility, transparency in their dealings and ease of doing business.

The large network of offices of the SBI and its subsidiaries and the more than fifty thousand teller machines make the SBI more accessible to the public. No other bank has this large a network. For a layman, the name **'State bank'** reminds one of its government ownership and patronage. The bank is active in services to government, such as distribution of government subsidies, government loans, government tax saving schemes, or for payment of taxes to government. It is also perceived as a bank with deep pockets. Since the bank is run by employees and not considered to patronise any particular community or group, that makes it more transparent in its dealings. Together with its numerous subsidiaries, the SBI is there in every aspect of banking and is directly or indirectly connected to the majority of people in the country.

Investors' point of view

It is a banking company formed by an act of parliament and the government share in the capital is more than 60 per cent. Around 7 per cent is with the resident individuals and the rest are with NRIs, FIIs and other corporate investors. Government control of the bank may not be a strong point for investors in the stock market but its 25 per cent hold on the Indian banking industry is definitely seen as its great strength.

The brand

Its invisible value exists in the form of its large client base, historically-known role as a government bank, very large pool of human resources and adequate capital funds to bring about change by investing in banking or non-banking, both in India and abroad. The emblem of the SBI is one of the most popular brands in India. Its latest technology push has seen the SBI emerging in the digital marketing world. Of late it has been one of the stable banking partners with the younger generation.

Leadership

The bank is managed by a board of directors headed, during the majority of its history, by employees who are appointed by the government to be chairman. Other members are also nominated by the government. The bank has adapted to changes happening in the banking sector, be it at the time of the first nationalisation of fourteen major banks in 1969 or liberalised bank licensing in the nineties. It has also adapted to the IT revolution in banking and has kept its leadership position intact all through its history. Its conventions, practices, and the quality of employees of the bank, keep it middlingly aggressive. The objective of expansion of banking was originally mandated to the SBI when it was set up in 1955. The government had to come up with two rounds of nationalisation of banks and a retreat to liberalisation for more private banks. Whether professional managers from outside the bank would have developed SBI into a better bank is something which one has to wait and see.

The future

With a lot of scope to perform better by benchmarking its performance sector-wise with the best in the industry, the bank must be in a position to become greater than it is now. Whether ownership will change the situation or the leadership will change are tricky questions to find answers to. Whether a bank utilises the full potential of its human resources is another big question. The productivity of employees measured on the basis of return against amount spent is 104 per cent, compared to the ICICI bank's 188 per cent and Axis Bank's 159 per cent, and discloses a lot of underemployment. The SBI's return on average assets is just 0.46 per cent compared to 1.92 and 1.72 per cent of the HDFC Bank and Axis Bank. The bank is successfully discharging a pivotal role in Indian banking.

In conclusion one has to appreciate the role and responsibility discharged by the bank for over two centuries. The bank is well placed with its large amount of assets, the strong relationship with government and the wide network of branches and ATMs. It is truly a national bank with a large number of branches in almost of all parts of the country. The bank needs to find answers for the management and leadership issues in order to go forward to the league of bankers with higher productivity.

2. ICICI BANK - *a private sector bank with a development bank underneath*

In terms of both assets and revenue, the ICICI Bank is the second largest bank in India. On the basis of the number of functioning offices, it is the seventh largest among all banks, and just behind the HDFC Bank among banks in the private sector. The bank is ranked 97th for its 13 billion USD Tier 1 capital among the 'Banker 1000' global banks.

According to RBI data the bank has 4,442 functioning offices as at 31st March 2016. The total assets and revenue of the group at 138 billion USD and 15.29 billion USD respectively is the highest after the SBI Group. The bank has both banking and non-banking activities and also Indian and foreign subsidiaries. The subsidiaries contributed more than 27 per cent to the group assets and generated 49 per cent additional revenue for the year 2015-16. Only the SBI has a comparable 32 per cent share of group assets and 42 per cent of revenue from subsidiaries.

The finance minister, Dr Manmohan Singh, during his budget speech on 24th July 1991, mentioned certain rigidities, some weaknesses in India's finance system and the need for reform to transform the finance system into a more efficient, competitive banking system with proper capital adequacy, provision for bad debts, etc., including a larger role by the private sector. These thoughts developed into a new licensing norm for banks in the private sector. The ICICI Bank Ltd was one of those new banks in the private sector that came into existence in 1994. It was promoted by one of India's popular development finance institutions called the Industrial Credit and Investment Corporation of India (ICICI).

History repeats itself. The ICICI was set up in 1955, the same year as the SBI was set up as a commercial bank, with the support of the Government of India, the World Bank and others, when development finance in India was in a crisis after the IFCI and the State Finance Corporation were found wanting in providing long term financing. In this situation of crises, the ICICI Bank Ltd came into existence in 1994. However, by 1998, the parent company reduced its share in the ICICI Bank to less than 50%. By 2002, the ICICI Bank Ltd absorbed the ICICI.

The ICICI Bank Ltd acquired a private bank called the Bank of Madura Ltd, operating in southern India for almost 57 years with a network of 263 branches. Later, the Sangli Bank Ltd and Bank of Rajasthan Ltd, operating in the western region, merged with the ICICI Bank. In the process, between 2002 and 2016, the ICICI Bank multiplied its assets 57 times and by March 2016 emerged as the largest among banks in India after the SBI group.

Thirty-two per cent of branches of the ICICI Bank operate from three states in the western region: Maharashtra, Rajasthan and Gujarat, and ten per cent from the southern state of Tamilnadu, where the Bank of Madurai had concentrated its operations. The Loans to Assets ratio is inferior to two other new generation banks in the private sector, namely the Axis Bank and the HDFC Bank. During the last two years, government banks such as the SBI and PNB averaged better growth on their assets than the ICICI Bank.

Customers' point of view

The ICICI Bank has 4,442 offices and 13,766 ATMs spread across the country, compared to 17,400 offices and 59,011 ATMs of the SBI group. The background for setting up banks like the ICICI Bank was to provide a banking facility similar to services provided by foreign banks operating in India. With IT as the backbone of its operations, the bank is popular among the financially better-off younger generation. Though the bank may lack trust on account of not being a government bank, its extraordinary growth, thanks to existing customers of merged banks and its current positioning in Indian banking, provide for the required faith of the people of this country. Unlike the situation in other countries, where features of deposit guarantee play a key aspect in a customer's choice for saving, bank failures being very rare in India, this aspect can be overlooked. It is a bank that provides almost all financial services to its customers through its branch network, subsidiaries and joint ventures.

Investors' point of view

The HDFC Bank and Axis Bank have outperformed the ICICI Bank in Return on Equity, Return on Assets and Earnings per Share, on the basis of performance during the financial year 2015-16. The Net Interest Margin at 3.49 has been one of the best among the top ten banks. The market value of shares was 153 per cent of their book value compared to 373 per cent and 199 per cent of the HDFC and Axis Bank Ltd. Almost 65 per cent of shares are held by ADS depository and FIIs and others. Residents hold 6 per cent and the remaining 29 per cent are with domestic institutional investors and corporates.

The brand

The ICICI Bank carries an appreciable brand value and is placed among the top tier in the finance industry in India. The leadership provided by the bank, in taking banking in the private sector in India during the past two decades to the present level, has gained the trust and faith of the people of the country. Having a number of subsidiaries for financial services also adds to the brand value.

Leadership

Their leadership has been clearly visible since banking in the private sector was opened up. The leaders were able to keep the bank in the limelight. Their pursuit of an ATM network in the beginning made other Indian banks foray into ATM banking vigorously. The founder chairman Shri N Vaghul had the experience of working for the State Bank of India and for the ICICI. He was supported right from the beginning by Mr K V Kamath[55], and the present CEO Mrs Chanda Kochhar. This ensured continuity of the same vision since inception. This consistency is lacking among traditional banks both in the private and public sector. The bank has the best ratio of operating profit to operational expenditure per employee, indicating the ability of the management to exercise an adequate degree of control on the activities of employees, who are the most precious asset of a bank.

The future

The ICICI Bank is comfortably placed to take on emerging challenges in Indian banking. However, the State Bank of India, HDFC Bank and Axis Bank continue to challenge the bank's ability to maintain its position. The SBI is three times bigger while the HDFC Bank and Axis Bank are growing at a faster rate. Having managed the mergers of large size banks into it and having a strong IT base, the bank is better positioned for the future. Perhaps the bank's model adopted for growth by building on their franchise will be tested against the traditional model, adopted by the HDFC Bank and Axis Bank.

3. HDFC BANK – *a private bank with global accolades and the longest-serving CEO*

The HDFC Bank began with a mission to be a "world class Indian Bank". In just over two decades, the bank has become the third largest bank in

---

[55]   presently the president of the New Development Bank floated by BRICS nations

India. It is ranked 115th among the Banker 1000 banks on the basis of its Tier 1 capital. The HDFC Bank has more than 106 billion USD assets and along with its subsidiaries, its assets are approximately 110 billion USD. According to its annual report for 2015-16, the bank has 87,555 employees and thus becomes the second largest employer among banks in India.

The bank is promoted by a popular housing finance company in India called the Housing Finance Development Corporation which has a housing loan portfolio of approximately 2 trillion rupees (30 billion USD). The bank continues to be a subsidiary of the HDFC. During the course of its existence, the HDFC Bank took over three new generation banks: Time Bank, Centurion Bank and Bank of Punjab, and one old generation bank called Lord Krishna Bank. Mr Aditya Puri continues to be the CEO of the bank right from the time it was set up in 1994.

During the last ten years, the HDFC Bank has opened 3,147 branches and only the SBI and Canara Bank have opened more among the top ten banks. The bank appears to be planning for a very strong presence in Indian banking. It has increased the number of branches and employees and maintained a high loan to assets ratio. The bank has displayed the highest level of control on its loans as is evident from its highest Net Interest Margin of 4.30 and the lowest gross non-performing loans among the top ten banks as on 31st March 2016. On the basis of its highest rate of growth of assets of the HDFC Ltd during the past, the bank can soon be expected to become the second largest.[56]

Customers' point of view

The HDFC Bank has 4,579 functioning offices and 12,000 ATMs as at 31st March 2016. The numbers are similar to those of the ICICI Bank Ltd. The bank has been very aggressive in extending its branch network. During the last two years, the bank opened more than 1,100 branches compared to 600-700 branches opened by its nearest competitors such as the ICICI Bank or Axis Bank. The additional branches opened every year will definitely

---

[56] June 2016 quarterly results show HDFC Bank Ltd has become the second largest in terms of assets

help the bank in extending its reach to people. This is supplemented by the consistent addition of ATMs to its network and also the increase in its number of employees. Like the ICICI Bank, IT is its backbone, and this new generation bank has been attractive to the younger generation. The bank's inventory financing platform was reckoned to be a significant innovation in banking by the Global Finance magazine. The HDFC Bank, like the ICICI Bank, may not be disadvantaged by its existence in the private sector because of its consistent performance, policies on expansion and strategies that are explicit.

Investors' point of view

Foreign Institutional Investors (FIIs) hold more than seventy per cent of the shareholding in the bank's promoter, the Housing Development Finance Corporation Ltd. FIIs also hold a considerable portion of the shareholding of the HDFC Bank. The ratios of Return on Average Assets, Return on Equity, Net Interest Margin and Earnings per Share of the HDFC Bank are the highest. All these aspects are reflected in the higher market value of shares. As at 31st March 2016, shares were quoted at 3.73 times their book value. Both directly and indirectly, foreign institutional investors are the major shareholders.

The brand

The HDFC Bank and its promoter, the HDFC, are very popular. Factors that enhance the visibility of the bank are the regularly increasing number of branches, ATMs, and its penetration in two high potential sectors in retail banking: mortgages, which are the core business of its promoter, and auto loans through inventory financing of automobile manufacturers in the corporate sector. In addition, its exposure to employees of corporates extends its reach to a large population and results in more profitable business streams.

Leadership

The HDFC Bank has the longest serving CEO and professionals control its operations. It has managed a few mergers and its growth strategy has worked successfully in making it one of the largest banks in India. The focus of the management can be appreciated from its high Net Interest Margin, low Non-Performing Loans and a high Loans to Assets ratio. Perhaps its leadership may undergo a test of its strategy, structure and systems when there is a change of the CEO.

The future

Between 2015 and 2016, the bank has moved its position from the sixth to the third largest bank in India, and moved yet further to become the second largest bank on the basis of June 2016 quarterly results. Still, as a group, the ICICI Bank is bigger. On the basis of consistent growth in almost all dimensions of employee strength, branch network, profitability and control on non-performing loans, Tier 1 capital and market capitalisation, the HDFC Bank is expected to play a predominant role in Indian banking. However, its consistency may be tested when there is a change in leadership in the future. As of now its nearest rival, with equally good growth during the last two years, is the eighth-ranked Axis Bank with just about two thirds of its assets and revenue generation.

4. BANK OF BARODA – *India's international bank*

The Bank of Baroda (BOB) is the largest among the nationalised banks, the term referring to all banks that have been taken over by the government in 1969 and 1980. It has 5,487 functioning offices according to RBI data, of which 2,613 have been opened during the last ten years, even though the bank has been in existence for more than a century and in the custody of the government for almost half of that time. The bank was the second biggest on the basis of 2015 figures, but slipped to fourth position as the result of a fall in the total assets due to reduction in the loans, assets, deposits and provisions by approximately 12-15 per cent in dollar value. This downsizing was a result of the RBI's drive to cleanse the account books of Indian banks by March 2017.

The operation of the BOB is predominant in the western region, particularly in Gujarat, Maharashtra and Rajasthan. The bank is known for its international presence, spread over sixteen countries such as Tanzania, Uganda, Kenya, Mauritius, the Seychelles, Botswana, New Zealand, the UAE, Fiji, the UK, Oman, Ghana, Australia, Trinidad & Tobago, Guyana, and the USA.

The Bank of Baroda was nationalised in 1969 along with another thirteen banks and government shareholding is around 56 per cent. It was originally a princely state bank established in 1908 that figured among the ten banks recommended to join the State Bank of India by the Committee for Rural Credit Survey for the development of banking in India. However the BOB continued as an independent entity and did not form part of the State Bank group. Currently the BOB, with 101 billion USD assets, is more than four times bigger than the biggest associate of the SBI, namely the State Bank of Hyderabad with 24.81 billion USD assets as at 31st March 2016. This may be a point in favour of independent operation rather than allowing the bank to work under a group.

Customers' point of view

Public sector banks carry an image of trust and security and the BOB is entitled to that trust from the public. Its branch network is concentrated in the business-intensive western and northern region. Its overseas branch network adds to its advantage.

Investors' point of view

BOB stocks are traded in BSE and NSE in India. The book value of a BOB share with a face value of Rs.2 was Rs.166.83 and BSE traded at Rs.163.00. The Tier 1 capital of the bank as on 31st March 2016 was 6,736 million USD and its value in rupees increased over the previous year. It is admirable that the book value and market value are almost at the same level when for most of the public sector banks, the market price is far below the book value. The equity market is sensitive to the levels of NPAs declared by bank managements and their strategies to reduce them in future. The management of the BOB will be under close observation by investors, with regard to their ability to manage the non-performing loans of the bank.

The brand

The BOB carries the brand value of a public sector bank. The bank carried out a branding exercise in the past, erecting uniform signage across its branches. They have a brand ambassador to boost the bank's image. The management feels the exercise is helpful in pushing its retail business.

Leadership

The bank is led by government-appointed employees who carry with them decade-long experience in banking. Among the twenty banks that were nationalised by the government since 1969, the BOB could emerge as the largest, which indicates the leaders had done a better job than their peers in other nationalised banks. The cleansing exercise initiated by the RBI showed the bank management in a poor light as its figures on deposit and loans shrank by 5 billion and 7 billion USD respectively during the two year period between 2014 and 2016. In rupee terms, the fall in deposits for the year 2015-16 was 5 per cent and in advances was 8.5 per cent. In the process the bank was also pushed to its fourth position, having been in second position. Perhaps the lack of professionalism among the middle and top management could have allowed the puffing up of the numbers in the past.

The future

The Bank of Baroda may not be the only bank that has exposed its management by the cleansing exercise. It may become irrelevant later in the bank's history, if the bank is able to carry out the required correction to its course. Another area of concern would be the regional concentration of the bank. The future of the BOB may also depend upon entering into a tie-up with other banks in areas where it does not have branches, gaining more mileage from its overseas outfits and pushing more technology products. It is also important to ensure that the bank does not retreat to its previous system of managing accounts once the cleansing exercise phase is over.

5. PUNJAB NATIONAL BANK – *a public sector bank that begin in Lahore*

The Punjab National Bank is a nationalised bank popularly known as the PNB. It is the largest after the SBI on the basis of its branch network and ATMs. It has 6,875 functioning offices as on 31st March 2016. More than one third of them were added during the last ten years. While eight out of the top ten banks operate from Mumbai, the PNB operates from New Delhi. Twenty-five per cent of its branches operate from the erstwhile Indian state of Punjab, presently divided into separate states known as Punjab, Haryana, Himachal Pradesh and Chandigarh. The bank has overseas subsidiaries in nine countries. It also has subsidiaries as primary dealers, housing finance, investment services and insurance broking.

The PNB had seven mergers and the latest of them was in 2003 when the Kerala-based Nedungadi Bank, originally established in 1899, was merged with it. The Nedungadi Bank had 174 branches. Another significant acquisition before this was the merger of a nationalised bank called the New Bank of India in 1993. The New Bank of India was nationalised in 1980 and originally had commenced its operations from Lahore like the PNB.

According to the bank's annual report for the year 2015-16, the PNB had approximate total assets of 100 billion USD and group assets of over 107 billion USD. On the basis of group assets, the PNB is bigger than the fourth ranking Bank of Baroda. During the last two years the PNB's group assets increased by 12 billion USD with an average annual growth rate of 6.17 per cent. Only the HDFC Bank and Axis Bank, among the top ten, have a better rate than this.

Customers' point of view

For an estimated 35 million Indian Punjabi people across the world, the PNB is a common name. The bank's nearly seven thousand branches and nine thousand ATMs, along with its overseas offices, provide access to its customers. It has also reasonable presence in the southern part of India thanks to its merger with Nedungadi Bank.

Investors' point of view

PNB shares, like most of the public sector bank shares, have a market value of less than the book value. A two rupee share was quoted at Rs.84.70 on 31st March 2016 when the book value was Rs.181. FIIs holding is around ten per cent. The Net Interest Margin was 2.60 as on 31st March 2016. Non-performing loans are high. The Tier 1 capital has slipped from 6,767 million USD to 4,962 million during the last two years.

The brand

The PNB's logo is very distinct, with its font typical of Indian language. It has good visibility in the states surrounding Delhi. The bank's mission is - "To be a Leading Global Bank with Pan India footprints and become a household brand in the Indo-Gangetic Plains providing the entire range of financial products and services under one roof." In spite of the challenges posed by the existence of the Punjab and Sind Bank, a nationalised bank, and the State Bank of Patiala, a regional associate of the SBI, the PNB enjoys a greater identification with the Punjabi diasporas. Another bank which could have perhaps challenged its Punjabi identity was the new generation Bank of Punjab. But the latter bank lost its Punjabi identity upon its merger with the HDFC Bank. Therefore, the PNB's position as a bank for the Punjabi diasporas across the world is intact. This is promising and reflected in their figures.

Leadership

The PNB, like other public sector banks, is led by senior employees from the PNB or from other banks. As a result of the cleansing exercise carried out by all banks under direction from the RBI, the assets of the PNB did not shrink. In 1986, the bank handled a 100 million dollar scam in one of its branches in the UK. It handled many mergers in the past. On the basis of these, the bank is able to be in the top ten, indicating a better middle and top management. Given freedom, the PNB holds a large captive market on tap.

The future

The focus of the bank was on the Indo-Gangetic plain of Northern and Central India, evident from the fact that around 66% of their branches operate from that area. After Punjabis, the other Indian communities engaged in business domestically and globally are the Sindhi, Saurashtrian, Kutch and Gujarati. They centre their operations in Mumbai and in the states of Maharashtra and Gujarat. The PNB has just two per cent presence currently in that region. Eight out of the top ten banks operate from the western region. Therefore, there is a potential for phenomenal growth in the western region, once the bank expands its activities into that area.

6. BANK OF INDIA - *a public sector bank that was started in India*

The Bank of India, denoted as BOI, is the sixth largest bank in India and third among nationalised banks in terms of Total Assets. It has 5,195 functioning offices as on 31st March 2016 and almost half the branches have been opened during the last ten years, even though the bank has been in existence for more than a century. The employee strength of the bank is around fifty thousand. The group assets of the bank are 93 billion USD. The gross revenue at 6.89 billion USD for 2015-16 is less than the next two big banks: the Canara Bank and Axis Bank. Last year the bank could increase its number of branches by just 68 even though during the last ten years it had opened 2,345 offices. It has eleven subsidiaries/joint ventures including five overseas subsidiaries.

The BOI was promoted by a group of people including the business house of TATAs, in 1906. It was nationalised in 1969. Later, in 1986, the BOI acquired one bank from the southern state of Kerala. Other than that, the bank has grown organically. The BOI also has branches operating from all states except in the Lakshadweep islands. The home state of Maharashtra accounts for almost 18% of its branch network.

This is one bank that has been hit hard by the cleansing exercise of the RBI. It reduced its Deposits, Advances and even the Tier 1 capital as well.

It could not even open any significant number of new branches. There was an increase in the strength of employees during 2015-16. Among the top ten, it slipped from fourth to sixth rank in terms of total assets. In terms of gross revenue, it is placed at eighth. Of the top ten banks, it has the lowest ratio of market value to book value of shares as on 31st March 2016. The net interest margin is 2.11 compared to 3.24 of the ninth-ranked Mumbai-based Union Bank of India.

Customers' point of view

The bank has the advantage of being a public sector bank and has more than 5,000 branches and 6,777 ATMs as of March 2016.

Investors' point of view

The book value of a BOI Rs.10 share was Rs.262.77 as on 31st March 2016 but the shares were traded at Rs.97.05. The bank has shown resilience in the past to bounce back from crises.

The brand

The BOI is a regionally popular brand and is often confused with another very low ranking nationalised bank, the Indian Bank.

Leadership

The impact of the cleansing drive tells upon poor professionalism in the middle and top management, even though it is a century-old bank. The bank's systemic failures in internal controls came to light in 2000 in a bank scam engineered by Ketan Parekh when the BOI lost over a billion rupees. In the next two years, the Bank proved its resilience and is among the top ten.

The future

The bank continues to be a regional bank. Despite being in the top ten, it is vulnerable to regulatory changes. Therefore, the future will be fully dependant on how early standardisation, systemisation and transparencies can be employed in operational processes. It also needs to tie up with banks in those areas where it has no branches to become a national bank.

7. CANARA BANK - *the biggest bank from the south*

The Canara bank is the seventh largest bank in India in terms of assets. As on 31st March 2016, its group assets are above 85 billion USD and generate revenue of more than seven billion USD. It has almost six thousand branches and more than nine thousand ATMs. The Tier 1 capital of the bank is approximately 4,490 million USD. Unlike most banks in the top ten which operate from Mumbai, the Canara bank is headquartered in the South Indian state of Karnataka, the state that houses popular IT companies.

The bank commenced its operation in Mangalore in 1908 and was nationalised in 1969. The bank took its name Canara (Kannada) from the coastal region which includes the port city of Mangalore. Almost 50 per cent of its branches are in the southern region. The bank does not have much group activity or any overseas subsidiaries. In states like Gujarat, Maharashtra and Rajasthan, where business potential is very high, Canara Bank, just like the PNB, has just 2 per cent presence.

RBI's cleansing exercise has not adversely affected the bank as much as the Bank of Baroda and Bank of India. The deposits and advances in rupees have only changed marginally. But in dollar terms, there has been no major growth during the last two years. In branch expansion, the bank has opened 3,167 branches during the last ten years, second only to the 6,856 branches opened by the SBI. The HDFC Bank is another bank which has been vigorously opening branches like the Canara Bank. During the last two years, the employee strength of the bank has gone up by approximately five thousand.

Customers' point of view

Like Punjab National Bank which is popular from its network of branches in Northern India, Canara Bank is one of the most popular banks in the southern states of Kerala, Karnataka and Tamilnadu. Its century-old existence is indicative of its strength and resilience.

Investors' point of view

Government ownership is more than 66 per cent and FIIs have invested around 7 per cent. Diversification or overseas operation is negligible as the flagship company holds 98 per cent of its group assets. It has two regional rural banks also to manage. Performance of its share in the stock market is reflected in the ratio of market value to book value of shares which is around forty per cent as on 31st March 2016.

The brand

Canara Bank is a popular bank among southern Indian states because of its branch network. However, the better penetrating power of new private banks and merger of a nationalised bank with the PNB have stymied its positioning as the largest bank among nationalised banks and as the nearest competitor to the SBI which is five times bigger. A few years back, the bank, having been in existence for a century, worked on enhancing its brand image. The Canara Bank had a redesign of its logo and signboards, etc., highlighting the shift from 'branch customer' to 'bank customer'.

Leadership

As in the case of other nationalised banks, the Canara Bank is led by senior employees from the same bank or from other banks. During the course of its history, the bank achieved phenomenal growth from 1982 to 1988 under a young Canara Bank officer named Mr Ratnakar as chairman. During his tenure, the bank employees bubbled[57] with enthusiasm and its growth took it to a position next only to the SBI. It was a demonstration of leadership and showed that public sector banks can be responsive to good leadership. But there is a need to put in place failsafe systems so that employees can take in large deposits.

---

[57] http://indiatoday.intoday.in/story/canara-bank-net-profits-soar-under-b.-ratnakar-chairmanship/1/337371.html

The future

The bank has proven its ability to face challenges in the past. The cleansing exercise did not damage the bank as much as it did the Bank of India and the Bank of Baroda, confirming that the middle management and top management are more professional than their counterparts in those banks. In the area of operations, the bank has Bengaluru, the IT hub of India, as its main hinterland. If the bank can push technology and systems to become international class, it can harvest the advantage of its location. It can also expand its operations to those countries where most of the employees in the IT companies immigrate from or emigrate on work visas.

8. AXIS BANK - *a cautious but aggressive private sector bank*

The Axis Bank was promoted in 1994 by a few government-owned entities such as the Unit Trust of India, General Insurance Corporation, Life Insurance Corporation of India and other government undertakings in general insurance. It is the eighth largest bank in India as on 31st March 2016. It has 2,991 functioning offices of which 2,335 were opened during the last ten years. From 2015-16, the bank added 315 branches. The bank also has 12,743 ATMs. The group assets are about 80.20 billion USD and the bank generated revenue of about 7.74 billion USD from 2015-17. It is the seventh largest employer among banks, with employee strength of 50,135. Both in dollar terms and rupee value, the bank has increased its deposits, advances and Tier 1 capital. The Tier 1 capital of the bank as on 31st March 2016 stands at 7,847 billion USD and it is ranked at 156th among the Banker 1000 banks.

It is a new generation bank that came into existence as the UTI Bank Ltd. The bank later changed its name to the Axis Bank to distinguish it from the sponsor the Unite Trust of India commonly known as the UTI. While the ICICI Bank and HDFC Bank have been able to grow by merger and acquisition, the Axis Bank has not been able to take over any other bank or banks and the bank continues to grow on its own. The group companies of the Axis Bank add just one billion USD, whereas the ICICI Bank Group companies add 30 billion and the HDFC Bank Group companies add 4 billion. Thus one can call the Axis Bank a pure new generation private sector bank.

On most of the growth parameters such as Return on Average Assets, Return on Equity, Net Interest Margin, etc., the performance of the Axis Bank is very close to that of the HDFC Bank Ltd. But when it comes to size of assets and Tier 1 capital, the Axis Bank is way behind the HDFC Bank by 30 billion and 3 billion USD respectively. The Axis Bank has a long way to go to be on a par with the other two that started together.

Customers' point of view

The Axis Bank is a new generation bank functioning with IT as its backbone. Customers see other fast-growing banks, such as the Yes Bank and Kotak Mahindra Bank (though not in the top ten), as an alternative to the Axis Bank, as the latter has fewer branches.

Investors' point of view

Axis Bank shares are an attraction to investors as the market value is double the book value. Only the HDFC Bank is better than the Axis Bank on the basis of Return on Average Assets, Return on Equity, Earnings per Share and Net Interest Margin as on 31st March 2016. 41 per cent of shares are held by FIIs.

The brand

The Axis Bank is considered as a private sector bank and the public would have forgotten its lineage from the government investment company called the Unit Trust of India or UTI. The Axis Bank is promoted by the UTI, LIC and a few other insurance companies. Initially, the bank was named the UTI Bank. In 2007 it changed its name to the Axis Bank and thus lost the 'public sector connotation' from its name. There was a branding campaign for the change, with new signboards and logo to distinguish the new entity. Its place in the banking sector is based on its performance. That on its own strength is the real brand value of the Axis Bank.

Leadership

The bank is managed by professionals and it provides good shareholder value. The bank has the highest profitability per employee after the ICICI Bank Ltd, measured on the basis of ratio of operating profit per employee to operating expenditure per employee. The management is yet to be tested for its ability to manage cross-culture arising from mergers and acquisitions.

The future

The future of the bank depends mainly upon its expansion and its ability to develop a good team of professionals with high ethics and standards. The bank that was established in 1994 almost at the same time as the HDFC Bank Ltd and the ICICI Bank Ltd were set up, could only become the eighth largest bank in India. The other two are almost vying for a dominant position in the Indian banking scenario. The bank may have to put up with its fewer branches for growth and with the inexperience of managing mergers. The present growth of the bank has to be seen from the perspective of the aspect of change of leadership. Compared to the HDFC Bank Ltd and ICICI Bank, led by professionals who were there from the beginning, the Axis Bank has passed the test of a change of guard. If its lagging behind the other two is an offshoot of this change of leadership, circumspection may be required among all the banks as this is also the problem faced by nationalised banks.

9. UNION BANK OF INDIA – *a public sector bank started only by Indians*

The message Mahatmaji gave on the occasion of the inauguration of the Union Bank of India's head office building in 1921 was:

"We should have the ability to carry on a big bank, to manage efficiently crore of rupees in the course of our national activities. Though we have not many banks amongst us, it does not follow that we are not capable of efficiently managing crore and tens of crore of rupees."

The Union Bank of India is the ninth largest bank in India in terms of assets as of March 2016 and it is the sixth bank out of 27 public sector banks currently in India. The bank provides employment to more than thirty-five thousand employees and has 4,336 functioning offices as on 31st March 2016. The bank has a deposit base of 51 billion and a loan portfolio of 40 billion USD as on that date. The Tier 1 capital was more than 3,361 million USD. And the total assets of the group exceed 61.36 billion USD. It generates revenue of 5.46 billion USD. The next biggest bank is smaller by more than 15 billion USD.

Customers' point of view

The bank holds the advantage of being a government-owned bank operating from Mumbai. Its long years of existence among the business and industry oriented states such as Maharashtra and Gujarat is another attraction for traditional banking. Not known for any gimmicks or aggressive marketing, the bank has been espoused by customers who like safe banking. It has one overseas subsidiary in the UK and branches and representative offices in the UK, Belgium, China, Australia and the UAE. The bank reduced its number of ATMs during 2015-16.

Investors' point of view

More than sixty per cent of the bank's shares are held by government and the share owned by FIIs is around 8 per cent. The ratio of market value to book value of shares works out to 46 per cent, which is the case with most public sector banks. As per financials as on 31st March 2016, the Union Bank is the only bank among nationalised banks in the top ten, that has positive ratios of Return on Equity, Return on Assets and Earnings per Share.

The brand

The bank has existed since 1919 and in 2008 changed its logo[58] for the second time, to be trendy, along similar lines to the branding exercise carried out by the Axis Bank and the Canara Bank. The tagline of the

---

[58]   http://www.afaqs.com/news/story/22039_Ninety-years-on-Union-Bank-refreshes-itself

bank - "good people to bank with" - continues. The bank may perhaps be disadvantaged by its acronym, the UBI, which is shared by another 28th ranked nationalised bank based in Kolkata called the United Bank of India, the latter beset by high NPA and erosion of capital. The Union Bank has fewer branches and employees compared to other banks in the top ten. Perhaps this has reduced the visibility of the bank, which has been active in the Indian banking scenario for almost a century.

Leadership

It is led by senior employees from other banks and is yet to set up a niche market for itself in the Indian banking industry. A safe player among public sector banks, the Union Bank is not known to have plunged into anything in the past in order to accelerate growth. The cleansing exercise also has not impacted the results of the Union Bank adversely, indicating some professionalism in the middle and top management of the bank. During the last three years, there was no change of leadership and that could be reason for the consistency.

The future

The bank's future depends upon its ability to push all-round performance by merger and acquisitions and by continuing to maintain the quality of control of operations. The bank may have to work to increase its visibility, which has been reduced by its poor employee strength, slow branch expansion and capital support.

10. IDBI BANK - *another public sector bank*

The IDBI Bank Ltd came into existence when the ICICI Bank and HDFC Bank began operations as a new version private bank promoted by the Industrial Development Bank of India (IDBI), a development finance bank set up as a subsidiary of the RBI. In 2004, the IDBI got merged with its subsidiary bank and thanks to government ownership of the IDBI, the IDBI Bank ceased to be a private sector bank. It is now referred to as an 'other public sector bank', isolating it from banks in the SBI Group and nationalised banks. There are two other public sector banks, namely the IDBI Bank Ltd., and the Bharatiya Mahila Bank. The former is going to be privatised and the latter is slated for merger with the SBI.

The IDBI Bank, in its present manifestation, completed its twelfth year of operation and it is expected that the bank may go back to the private sector as this is being considered by the government. In 2006 it took over a private sector bank called the United Western Bank Ltd, which had 230 branches, mainly in the western region. Currently, the IDBI Bank has 2,040 functioning offices and six subsidiaries and joint ventures that are loss-making. The group assets of the IDBI Bank stood at 56.38 billion USD as at 31st March 2016 and generated revenue of 4.76 billion during 2015-16. The Tier 1 capital of the company stood at 4,005 million USD. The bank employs around 17,570 employees.

Customers' point of view

Since the bank has not made any major retail permeation, it will be a major player in wholesale banking and a major player in infrastructure, financing, debt syndication and securitisation, etc. The educational website of the bank is very informative for customers.

Investors' point of view

The government holds 76.50% of the bank's shares. As on 31st March 2016, the bank's ratios are not impressive and the market value to book value of shares is around 50 per cent. Since the original object of setting up the IDBI Bank was to have a strong bank in the private sector, the bank may soon have to redesign its business plan.

The brand

Among corporate customers the IDBI Bank enjoys an impressive position but not with the retail segment.

Leadership

The bank is headed by senior employees from the public sector although it had professional managers running the show when it was a new generation private bank. Its leadership in the near future is going to be most influential to its very continuance.

The future

The bank is a big player in development banking, with a penchant for retail banking. Presently, as one among the top ten banks, its assets are good enough to make it a leader in the potpourri model. It has very few branches but the capital to take more over. It has an organisational design good enough to take on its private sector peers, such as the ICICI Bank, HDFC Bank and Axis Bank. The bank lost considerable time in the past two decades in the constitution of stable management, fixing its focus on development banking and commercial banking, and managing government control, then for some time that of private shareholders.

Conclusion

Individually all of the top ten banks have spruced themselves up and adapted to changes to make them distinct among 48 banks. The recent changes brought out by the RBI encouraged banks to be more transparent, financially sound and manage risks with better management information systems based on more accurate data. From the discussions so far, two important things can be observed. One is the importance of stable systems and professionalism in middle management in banks, and another is the unchanged vision of the management over long periods of time by continuing with the same team. Added to these two are the advantages of experience gained over time and endurance to handle forces emanating from the government and government machinery.

Stable systems and procedures, along with professional middle management, repel too much intervention in their work. This is the case in the State Bank of India and the Union Bank of India, whose balance sheets did not shrink as a result of the cleansing exercise.

The growth of the HDFC Bank Ltd and ICICI Bank Ltd illustrated the merits of the same team continuing and continuance of their vision compared to other new generation banks such as the Axis Bank Ltd and IDBI Bank Ltd.

Between public sector banks and new generation banks that could grow to be in the top ten, the difference lies in the professional managers heading the operations. It is for the government to look at changing the public sector banks. This will take care of improving employee productivity.

The strategy adopted by the SBI in the past and currently by the HDFC Bank Ltd, to grow by expansion of the branch network, typically looks a better bet in Indian circumstances. FIIs have a major role in market capitalisation and the government needs to facilitate public sector banks to make them attractive to FIIs. The government appears on the liability side of banks in the form of capital and on the asset side for their SLR investments. There is scope for bringing about changes and unleashing banks from this hold.

Finally, it may be concluded that all of these ten banks are way ahead of other banks and are capable of staying put and leading Indian banking to new heights. Each of these ten banks has unique superlatives. They are ideally placed to go global. Encouraging them to expand by merger or tie up with other banks may make each one of them cast aside their regional status and become nationally important institutions, making Indian banking truly efficient.

13. CASE STUDIES

For students in banking, there is a popular phrase - 'the theory and practice of banking'. Flexibility is necessary in day-to-day banking operations. So far whatever a practical banker, the author, could recollect on banking has been discussed on the subject of one of the oldest banking systems in the world - Indian banking. The previous pages will have given an impression of what Indian banking is. Now it is time to share a few stories in order to understand how bank employees and customers have lived with Indian banking.

CASE STUDY No. 1

The tortoise rather than the hare

Summary of events

Mr Ram Singh joined the National Bank as a Probationary Officer in 1966 at the age of 26. He completed his two year probation and was confirmed as an officer. In the next twelve years, he was elevated three times and become a Chief Manager of the Bank, which is usual for officers displaying exemplary performance in most of the government banks. Soon he was rewarded with a posting to the bank's London branch. In the very next year he was promoted to Assistant General Manager, which is the second highest grade.

In the next two years, he was given two more promotions. He became Deputy General Manager and then General Manager in this short span of time. Even though he was promoted three times, his posting continued at the London branch. In those days, government banks had less than a dozen General Managers and it was such a senior position that they were considered for appointment as chairmen of other banks the same size or even bigger. Having put in seventeen years of service, he had reached an enviable position among his peers, both within his bank and similar government banks. He was just 43 years old and continued heading UK operations. In the next two years, developments such as the change of government in India, and fall of governments in other countries where his bank taken exposure, led to his removal from service. He was 45 years old. This chairman was prematurely terminated one month before his exit in February 1985. At the same time, his name was associated with one of the biggest bankruptcy cases of its day and with a global fraud committed by one of the bank's customers.

His appeal to court for a stay of his termination was heard favourably but they failed to reinstate him. The court exposed the termination simplicities in vogue in the case of public sector banks and questioned the applicability of the traditional 'law of master and servant' even after the country gained independence.

The case also throws light on one or two major aspects that reflect negatively on Indian banks. The first one is the lack of a professional approach in handling personnel matters. The abnormal promotion proves the failure of systems and the possibilities for interference with traditions or systems. The accelerated promotion cut short a requirement of approximately twelve years of experience, which saw him at three different managerial levels.

The second one is the unfortunate way in which brilliant employees are subjected to a "fight or flight" situation created by their superiors, perhaps to answer the needs of the hour or to respond to the government who appoints them. Such a scenario causes the loss of meritorious managers who could have been guided to work within their long standing framework or design.

Job security of employees When Mr Singh's case was discussed by the court, they came to an important point of law - The 'law of master and servant'. Times had changed. Every citizen has the right to be told why he or she was dismissed, and to have their views and circumstances heard appropriately in order to understand what may have placed them in a hazardous situation where they may have been wronged. This right is guaranteed to every citizen of the country. There cannot be any service condition that provides the unfettered right to dismiss employees without assigning reasons valid in the context of article 14 of the Constitution. They also discussed the simplicities of the termination procedure and acts of misconduct often spelt out as 'loss of confidence' without stating an apt reason or justification, whether it applies to public sector or private sector employees. The aspect of overriding "public interest" vs. industrial jurisprudence, administrative law, the principle of natural justice, etc., was discussed. They also discussed the difference between a public servant and a government servant. Management of banks should stop thinking that they can continue as "masters" and dismiss a "servant". With financial power not on their side, victimised employees take their management to court.

Collateral damage During his tenure as general manager, a crisis took place in the bank following the bankruptcy of a customer on whom his bank had taken sizeable exposure. As a result of a political upheaval in December 1983, the army deposed a democratically elected government with which the customer had large dealings. The customer reportedly lost a large sum and became bankrupt. The customer happened to be a good client of the deposed government and enjoyed their patronage. On losing such favours, the customer lost his ability to get fresh business and the financing bank failed to realise the dues. The customer was arrested in India. A case of fraud was filed against him. His company in the UK went into compulsory liquidation and he was declared bankrupt in January 1985. The volume of funds involved being high, the bank's loss was discussed at government level and the chairman was prematurely removed from service.

The new chairman recommended termination of service of the general manager to the board of the bank, stating that loans sanctioned by the board on his recommendation had become unrealisable. The official was alleged to have been indiscreet in extending credit to the bankrupt client. The official proved himself unworthy of the confidence reposed in him, and the credit and reputation of the bank suffered as a result. Having found no scope in the interests of the bank to delay taking action against the official, he was considered as rendered unworthy of confidence and could not be retained in their service. His services were terminated by the issuing of a letter along with a cheque for a sum which represented the salary for the usual notice period of three months for a simple termination.

The bankruptcy of the customer, who was an Indian supplying goods and services for various concerns including governments globally, raised uproar in parliament and the media carried reports. The minister of finance had to assure parliament that the severest punishment would be inflicted on the guilty when it came to the loan sanctioned to the now-bankrupt customer. They suspected collusion between the bankrupt customer and the employees of banks. Other banks too had taken exposure on this client. One judge, in a case relating to this, had even inserted statements indicating the alleged involvement of the politicians in power at that time with the client who became bankrupt. The case was taken up by the investigating agencies of the country in March 1985, a fortnight before the official was dismissed. The High Court in a case in 1986 did not approve of the way he was dismissed and the bank was advised to compensate him. Of course the court made it optional for the bank to reinstate him or compensate him.

Issues that come to one's mind are the way the official was elevated out of the ordinary norms usually followed by banks, exposing a sorry state of affairs in the personnel management of a large bank. Secondly, instead of bowing to public sentiment, the case could have been handled in a way whereby the business loss could have been dealt with – whether or not it involved fraud.

Analysis

Personnel Management in Banks

The employees in banks comprise two types - clerks, also referred to as assistants, associates, etc., and officers, at junior, middle and senior levels.

Public sector banks recruit on the basis of successful completion of a process made up of an IQ test and interviews. In the case of officers, sometimes a round of group discussion is also part of the process of selection. They are supposed to display superior mental ability in order to solve problems with speed and accuracy and are more organised in planning their work in the best possible way for timely completion of tasks. Other traits carried by people who score well in such exams are a serious attitude to the work at hand, emotional stability and above all whether they take on difficult work or impose it on their subordinates. Longer service reducing their ability to work is a factor significant in banks in India, where an alternate employment market does not exist, and the bank has to carry the high cost of low productivity officers in their organisation. The officer dismissed here was recruited on the basis of such tests and would have displayed such values.

The officer, on recruitment, is usually given training for two years of probation and thereafter works as a deputy to senior officers. It usually took twelve years after probation to reach the grade of a chief manager in the past. These twelve years are adequate for exposure work in branches, administrative offices, training centres, etc. Until the time he was promoted to Chief Manager at the London branch, things appeared to be normal. During the eighties, the grades above this post were the Assistant General Manager who usually supervises the operation of 30 to 40 branches, and then the Deputy General Manager who controls and supervises three to four such regions – approximately 120 to 200 branches. At DGM level the official gets involved in many meetings and discussions with top management who guide the bank with policy making and strategies. A couple of years' service minimum would ensure that the official is mature enough to occupy the seat of a general manager. General managers in public sector banks were usually posted at head office where they supervise various segments of business such as personal banking (consumer banking in modern day terminology), commercial banking (corporate business), international banking (foreign office operations and forex transactions in India and abroad), personnel management and other operations such as audit inspection, etc. In this case, the officer continued in the same assignment and did not undergo any of the exposure usually experienced to shape him as a general manager. As the general manager of international operations, he was located outside the head office. The bank was running the risk of him now, without adequate experience, being eligible for taking up other general manager posts or to be considered for positions such as executive director or CEO of the same bank or other banks. He had no opportunity to learn the characteristics of the people of the country at any level other than that of Chief Manager. Sadly, the failed system of personnel management and the absence of proper systems of checks and controls to expose such excesses, exposed the unprofessional way in which this government bank had been run.

Instead of enhancing the grade of the official, the bank management could have managed to support him by providing senior officials who had undergone the usual level of career progression. This could have saved the bank, allowed the detection of early warning signals, and saved the employee from committing the excesses that lead to losing his job.

Corporate fraud sensationalised

The difference between banking and money lending is yet to sink in, in the mind of the public and of bank executives at senior level. Many of the executives at a senior level came into service when loans were granted against adequate security, depriving a large part of the population of banking support. The important role of banks in economic development is not comprehended. Banking is built on understanding the risk and probability of loss in taking exposure. Merits accrued to the nation other than through the enterprise financed need to be weighed up while considering a loan proposal. The government wants employment opportunities to grow. They want to increase the skill level of their people. They want to provide people with opportunities to save for capital. As regulator, the central bank has to ensure that in the pursuit of attaining the government's mission, the banking system does not collapse. Between these two principles, banks need to be accountable for their functioning. They cannot be just fair-weather friends to people. Having perfectly drawn up a policy on lending, ensuring compliance to such policies and controlling the operations of employees is the responsibility of management. If a loan has failed, it should have lost either on the basis of the failure of an uncertain scenario visualised at the time of sanction, or on the failure of an action by an unskilled employee or control mechanism. Having provided for the degree of uncertainty in a loan proposal and comprehended the loss in case of any unfavourable development, the bank should handle a failure on its merits. It should look for any intentional deceit committed by the employees or the client, or by specialists from inside or outside the organisation, but carry the loss as a vocational hazard and move forward. Both the client and the employee are human beings and prone to temptations. But periodic scrutiny of records as to the compliance to the bank's policies and procedures, and the greater the exposure the more frequent the scrutiny, would work against such temptations and reduce loss, given early detection picked up by scrutiny.

In this case, both customer and employee were treated as fair-weather friends. One can imagine the warmth offered to the customer during the 'good times', that led to a great growth of business for the bank and accelerated elevation in the grade of the official. Leaving a single individual to run the show was a significant shortcoming on the part of the management. Another glaring shortcoming that came to light from the management side was the elevation of the official to general manager, overlooking the prerequisites for the position. The customer took control of the branch and the bank official took control of the bank, thus leaving aside the normal practice of banking.

A corporate fraud had been committed and the government as owner of the bank sacked the CEO and the employee. The need for banks in India to be run professionally without the intervention of the government as owners, via both written or unwritten advices, becomes important. The generic relationship starts right from the time someone is appointed as the chairman and CEO of a bank and his/her continued role is limited to the period in which government approval is maintained rather it is phrased 'during the pleasure'.

Had the CEO not been responsible for the appointment or promotion or posting of the officials, he would have discharged his or her responsibility to the government better. In order to maintain such a distinct relationship, it is necessary to separate the board from the CEO in every sense. The board must restrict their role to that of listening to the CEO and his team. If government ownership is imperative under Indian economic conditions, a unique proposition one can imagine is to have a single board for all government banks, or a variable structure of a single board comprising professionals and specialists, to ensure implementation of uniform systems and practices.

In brief, the lesson one has to learn from the case study is as follows:

i) Human resources management needs to be made secure from tampering

ii) Assignment of employees must be based on experience and mental framework to work confidently at higher levels of risk and responsibility

iii) The chief executive officer and the chairman of the board need to be distinct

iv) Criminal cases and banking losses need to be viewed distinctly

v) Employees are not to be sent out at the whims and fancies of management; the employees as public servants hold a fiduciary responsibility to report any excess by seniors.

CASE STUDY NO. 2 - DOING BUSINESS WITH INDIAN BANKING, THE UNCERTAIN SYSTEM

Believe in God; there is a course designed for you too

Summary of events

Mr Raj Kumar wanted to invest his savings in India and he considered property investment to be the best option. So, when he heard about a property under sale at a bank, he contacted the bank for details. The property was for sale as the bank was in the process of realising the bank dues from the owner of the property, who had mortgaged to obtain a business loan. Since there was no successful bid even at the minimum approved price for auction, the property sale did not take place. At this point, Mr Raj Kumar approached the officials and conveyed his willingness to make the payment and purchase the property.

The bank proceeded with the deal and issued a sale notice using the statutory power vested with them under a legislation known as SARFAESI. The legislation was passed by government with the intention of helping Indian banks to shortcircuit court proceedings.

The owner of the property approached court for quashing the sale, at first arguing for acceptance of the case on the grounds that he was deprived of the privileges of being informed of the sale by way of private treaty. Once the case was accepted he wanted to quash the sale. In eight years' time, ultimately the sale was quashed. The bank did not get anything more than the amount originally received by way of sale, the buyer of the property was compensated for the amount paid to the bank along with interest lost over the eight year period, and the defaulter gained more than nine years' time to arrange for alternate sale of the property and refund the buyer.

If banks have to wait for such a long time for the settlement of dues for which, despite having legislation to speed up the process, the probability of a defaulter to opt for legal recourse is higher than the possibility that he or she would try to settle the dues. Banks also do not have a professional team of solicitors or attorneys to take care of the need to follow the nitty-gritty of extant legislation in the country. Instead it is the bank employees, alongside their usual work, who are obliged to handle such cases. Often the advocates hired by them are paid less than the counterparty advocates who stand to gain by winning the case. The former gets a fee while for the latter the fee will in all probability be proportionate to the windfall or gains. The larger the amount, the greater counsels are hired.

How the judiciary bends a simple straight case of repayment of loan is the interesting part of the case.

The story

Mr Soja had a textile unit and was operating successfully with the help of finance from a government-owned bank. The loan was obtained by mortgaging his property and assets purchased out of bank finance. As long as the inventory he was holding matched the terms of the loan, the unit was running unhindered. However a fall in the level of inventory was not followed by a consequent fall in the loan outstanding. The bank sensed the collapse of the unit to be imminent. Instead of opting for discussion and carving a path for restructuring, hope and optimism delayed the resuscitation and the inevitable happened. Mr Soja got into a vicious circle of spending more time arranging for funds to save his unit while spending less time with the company. This accelerated the date when the final shutters in the factory had to come down. In those days, proceedings against non-performing loan customers were not as swift as they are now. Bankers avoided taking a legal course in order to realise their investment as much as possible.

The prudence of selling at the earliest opportunity and winding up did not occur to him. He hoped to arrange for funds from his fairweather friends or elsewhere and wanted to settle the bank dues. He wanted to avoid a sale in disastrous circumstances and sought time from the bank. The bank also waited and did not impede his movements knowing his past performance.

Years passed and the bank was obliged to proceed after declaring his account as non-performing in its books. The enactment of the SARFAESI Act added fresh ammunition for banks to take on defaulters. The practice of restructuring or leasing the unit to professionals for turning it around is not common in India even now. The Bank declared the unit as non-performing in 2002.

Banks cannot seize property and sell it quickly. It requires the intervention of a court or tribunal set up by the government. Consequently, by the time the sale takes place, the borrower may not be available, the equipment or machines may not fetch their true value and bidders rarely attempt to buy property which is under a dispute or sold in the aftermath of a disastrous situation. Bank officials issue a notice to the borrower and file a suit for attachment of the property, selling it to realise bank dues. After three years of waiting from the time the account was declared as a non-performing asset, the bank took recourse using provision under the new legislation called SARFAESI, took possession of the property and realised its dues. It may be interesting to go through the statement of objects and reasons of the new legislation.

'Our existing legal framework relating to commercial transactions has not kept pace with the changing commercial practices and financial sector reforms. This has resulted in slow pace of recovery of defaulting loans and mounting levels of nonperforming assets of banks and financial institutions. Narasimham Committee I and II and Andhyarujina Committee constituted by the Central Government for the purpose of examining banking sector reforms have considered the need for changes in the legal system in respect of these areas. These Committees, inter alia, have suggested enactment of a new legislation for securitisation and empowering banks and financial institutions to take possession of the securities and to sell them without the intervention of the court. Acting on these suggestions, the Securitisation and Reconstruction of Financial Assets and Enforcement of Security Interest Ordinance, 2002 was promulgated on the 21st June, 2002 to regulate securitisation and reconstruction of financial assets and enforcement of security interest and for matters connected therewith or incidental thereto. The provisions of the ordinance would enable banks and financial institutions to realise long-term assets, manage problem of liquidity, asset liability mismatches and improve recovery by exercising powers to take possession of securities, sell them and reduce nonperforming assets by adopting measures for recovery or reconstruction.'

The mandatory notices were issued in 2005 and the bank took possession of the property in January 2006 with the help of 'resolution agents'. These agents were professionals taken into the panel of banks by their head offices, to provide support to bank officials in taking possession and realisation of assets. The bank conducted an auction for sale of the property but no bidder came forward. Alternative recourse offered in the legislation is to go for a sale on a private treaty. The bank finalised the sale with a willing party who was willing to accept it at the lowest price fixed for auction. The sale took place in December 2006, after completing all the processes of notices, waiting period for response, in-house approvals, etc., which stretched to one years' time. (Later this auction process got a boost as 'e auction' became acceptable, and bidders may be from anywhere in India.)

The borrower, having found no fault in the auction process as envisaged under the legislation, now took recourse through the provisions in the

Constitution of India. He petitioned to the High Court to exercise power conferred under Article 226 of the Constitution of India and issue an order to cancel the sale. This right, vested with the High Court, is held as something that cannot be taken away by any legislation. Thus the SARFAESI Act provision too cannot override this right. The case moved from single bench to high court and then to supreme court in a span of eight years from 2006 to 2014 and eventually it was decided to cancel the sale and restore the property to the loan borrower.

The case was viewed on two major counts 1. The borrower and original owner of the property was not informed about the private treaty entered between the bank and the buyer, even though the course of action available to the bank as per the legislation was well known to him. 2. The bank had not tried for the best price, even though it was apparent the bank took up the auction process only after having offered the borrower four years' time and opportunity.

The decision of the Supreme Court made the buyer and borrower happy while the banking system suffered from an agonising wait for twelve years before finally settling the case. The borrower was made happy by having his property restored to his ownership and the buyer was not significantly inconvenienced as he was compensated by interest at an annual rate of 18% (or a compounded interest rate of 11.29%).

Analysis

All three losers Firstly, there is the businessman who took the risk of taking a bank loan. He did not have the experience of remedy to mitigate his risk. The bank had its risk mitigated by taking the borrowers' property. On 'D Day', the property was lost. Most small business models work on traditional management skills. It was left to him to pursue the business and seasoned traders may well find loopholes and exploit them. When in disarray, beliefs, hopes and superstition take charge over reality and the appropriate systems. The bank, secondly, also loses. Finally, loser number three is the buyer. He was new to the realities of India and was compromised for failing to understand the style of doing business successfully in India. He simply looked at the opportunity of acquiring a property of adequate size for the expansion of his recently-started business. All three failed. None could claim success. But of course these failed entities provide 'bread and butter' over a long period to those people involved in the judicial network and services providers like the resolution agents.

Failure of the judiciary represented by the twelve years taken to 'end time' including his initial four years of indecision, taken to finish the obligation to the bank. All three judgements did not recognise the four years' time enjoyed by him to decide on the future course of action - sell the property, lease the business or restructure his business, before the bank took his property to auction. His first obligation should be to the bank that has helped to develop the business and the first partner to settle on a future course of action should be the financing bank who could have helped in restructuring his business on the basis of credible propositions. This was not recognised by the judiciary. During these twelve years, the borrowers' investment was inactive and did not provide any returns to him. Accordingly, many advocates and judges received their fee from the entrepreneur in dire straits. The bank too wasted taxpayers' money in the form of time and labour spent by its employees and lawyers. The judiciary did not recognise the importance of commerce and commercial institutions set up to improve the living conditions of people. They upheld the attitude of borrowers to delay, defer or not honour their obligations. For a moment if we assume that a country that does not support such cases exists, one can envision that in that country, commerce and commercial institutions would not thrive. People would value time. In the case under consideration, Mr Soja would have sold at the earliest instance, fetched a better price for his assets and cleared the loans to the bank with a deadline acceptable to them. He would have learned from his error and experienced better growth during these twelve years of inaction.

Failure of resolution agents The bank had empowered some agencies who have the capability to possess assets for realisation of bank dues, which are in effect depositors' money. The speed at which they execute can definitely encourage a positive, quick decision by the entrepreneurs on the future course of action. The entrepreneurs would fear failure and only take manageable risks. They would not be encouraged to take exposure to unknown risk. A good set of commercial institutions would flourish. They need the support of an agency who can help in handling the recovery of defaulters who are not interested in restructuring or compromise – a non-cooperative set of customers.

The absence of a market for a company on sale In this case, Mr Soja would have been looking for someone who could have taken his company on a lease or merge with them at a fair price. The availability of such a market for taking over not-so-successful units would encourage more entrepreneurs to start and try their luck by investing their capital. He did not have the benefit of such a market. The chamber of commerce and industry or SME associations need to develop such a system whereby everyone can take care of their bad times and need not play to the bank officials' whims.

Inadequate room for banks to focus on credit quality Risk assessment in banks is important and risk sharing is clearly understood. Banks, when they take exposure on enterprises, need to know the risk they are exposed to. This requires adequate knowledge. Enterprises expect banks to guide them, especially in their fledgling years. Whatever risks they feel are not ascertainable and not manageable, should be adequately covered by insurance, so that borrowers' assets are hardly affected by the failure of an enterprise. The role of banks is different from that of money lenders. Every official in banks must imbibe this truth. The money lender may look at the security while granting loans, but the banker should look at the risk. Had Mr Soja been told about the possible risk he would be encountering, the course of events would have been different.

Unlimited scope to fail the banking system In the end one has to accept there is unlimited scope for failing the banking system. There is the uncertainty of litigation. In this case, it took twelve years to know its fate. This would discourage officials from going ahead promptly with bad loans. Another cause of failing banking is the delay in impressing upon the borrower information about the condition of the loans. The delay worsens matters and loss to the bank increases as time elapses. Many banks consider NPA to be the result of an unpardonable offence committed by employees and endeavour to delay in declaring an asset to be an NPA. The cleansing exercise of the RBI made some corrections. One more aspect that pulls up the banking system is the handling of NPA and performing accounts in the same manner. It is like bringing up children with a different mental calibre together. While focus on a performing account will be on up-selling, the focus of the NPA account will be on how early the individual can be returned to his or her family. Also, how quickly the bank can regain its funds and free the employees' time. Most important is the uncertainty of proposed action by banks on a failed account. It is necessary that customers get notices on the dues and circumstances and timelines of step-by-step action. This will remove the uncertainty and hope of escape from or delay in honouring commitments.

Conclusion

The importance of commerce and commercial institutions in uplifting the standard of living of the people can be summarised by these few words of a banker[59]. "The effects of commerce upon the general civilisation of the world are too manifest to escape observation. Wherever it has flourished, nations have enjoyed prosperity and plenty; and refinement and liberty have naturally followed. Commerce changes the character of a people; it dissipates crooked and mistaken notions; it produces a more expansive liberality of mind; it increases social intercourse and teaches man his true rights". It is therefore inevitable in India that all institutions and systems need to be directed towards improving commerce and commercial institutions, particularly banking.

---

[59]   From the book "The rise progress and present condition of Banking in India" written by Chas Northcote Cooke, Deputy Secretary and Treasurer of the Bank of Bengal published in 1863

14. MODELS

After going through the book one may embark upon the idea of searching for a model that will be ideal for the Indian banking system to go forward, taking into consideration the fact that India is not just a nation but a nation of complex polity, equally vibrant in many areas unrelated to economic development. Therefore, experience must be given its due share of importance, if one is interested in going forward and shaping a structure for banking. The way the top ten banks emerged offers a lot of insight in this regard. The two case studies discussed also provide a closer view of the reality in which customers and employees operate, and sufficient insulation to banks from the disturbances of external agencies needs to be built into the envisaged model.

The reader would perhaps agree that in order to develop an appropriate structure for banking, certain important factors that played a critical role in restricting the growth of banking at the desired speed need to be considered. Some of those that appear most important to me are given below:

i) Political system of the country India is a democratic country and democratic thoughts stay above welfare thoughts. Bureaucracy is influenced by the poverty of employees who are vulnerable to petty favours and they need not be those who find happiness from work or who hold ethics above everything. Corruption is common. Constitutional rights reign supreme even over legislation. The judiciary plays an important role. They are not known for quick resolution and thus they render the value of time and the value of commercial institutions of import insignificant while upholding the value of fundamental rights.

ii) The theory of majority The majority decides everything in a democratic set-up. Most of the decisions are based on committees that also work by majority. The principles of common sense, wisdom, minimum welfare standards or expert opinion do not find their appropriate place in decision-making, particularly in government and government undertakings which form the majority of commercial institutions. The large population votes people to power. They form government. The government appoints the finance minister who controls the entire financial system and institutions, including appointment of the governor of the central bank and government-owned banks. There are committees for selection but members of the committee are decided by the ministry headed by the minister. Ultimately it is those who are responsible for selecting the finance minister and the government who are responsible for the functioning of banks.

iii) Attitude of the people Faith in traditions and conventions often made people superstitious rather than rational in their judgements. Discretion reigns supreme over logic. Unequal distribution of wealth paves the way for people to subordinate their thoughts beneath the thoughts of the wealthy. The craving for wealth and influence of the wealthy play a significant role in keeping the poor attached to ideas such as 'duty before self' and they stay superstitious.

iv) Systems inferior to individuals The importance of putting in place time-tested systems as permanent solutions for issues that hamper progress towards the welfare of the people is not recognised by the people. Ad hoc solutions or philosophical and ambiguous remarks instead of rejection often are considered as wisdom and indicative of a helpful attitude. This allows an air of uncertainty to pervade everywhere that decisions matter.

v) Economics of divide The economic divide does not end with wealth alone. It is predominant in other areas such as language, geography, religious group, literacy level, social level, etc. Thus there is no keenness to compete in the absence of an equal opportunity platform.

What all these points sum up is the need for involving people in revamping or putting in new systems. This is applicable even to banking. Indian banking continues with the banking system introduced during British rule, spanning three centuries. Even after independence, none of the governments tried to change the banking system except Mrs Indira Gandhi when she was Prime Minister and Dr Manmohan Singh when he was Finance Minister. The former nationalised all major banks to bring them into the custody of the government, to align the banking system with economic development plans. Dr Singh, having found this government ownership of banks led to some rigidity and complacence in the Indian banking system, inducted private banks. The government has to decide whether control of the banking system is preferable by ownership or without ownership.

From the performance of the top ten banks, one cannot conclude whether ownership mattered to the performance of banks. Typically the SBI, the bank that was closely aligned to rulers all along, still continues to be dominant, pervasive and the provider of affordable banking to the common man. It is managed most of the time by government nominees from the bank itself.

Experiments of introducing cooperative banking, rural banks, local area banks or other versions did not grow as much as was expected due to the impact of some of the factors mentioned above. It is therefore necessary that a design for the future banking system has to be based on the footsteps of the top ten banks and only the full version of commercial bank branches at proximities can make banking grow successfully and push economic activities.

Principles for developing Indian banking

The following principles may have to be kept in mind while redesigning Indian banking.

i) **Involve the people at grass roots level** Not only to utilise banking services but also in setting up the banks. Therefore, the involvement of the panchayat at village level, block level and district level is inevitable to make banking services available to the entire population. Provision for loss during the initial years may have to be borne by the government, in the way that the integration and development fund was set up in the SBI for recouping losses from new branches for a period of five years. A similar arrangement with all banks may be considered necessary.

ii) **Recognise the importance of people's attitude** People prefer gold ornaments to bank savings. They trust currency notes for the settlement of debts. And land documents are considered as the only stable security. These basic attitudes of people have telling bearings on banking operations in India. As a result gold and jewellery shops carry parallel banking activities. The forgery of currency notes is encouraged by the insistence on currency notes rather than settlement of debts through bank accounts. In the absence of a market for other fixed assets, land continues to be the prime security and investment for people; however, it is difficult to root out the possible involvement of evildoers in transfers of land.

iii) **Recognise the potential for transfer of technical know-how via banking** It is important to recognise the transfer of technical know-how and the inflow of foreign capital which will help industries to reduce production costs. For this, global banking and merchant banking need to be adequately encouraged.

iv) **Recognise the importance of the populist agenda of governments** It is the government of the people who voted for them that rules banks. Direct injection of money to weak sections or selective groups of people may be necessary as it would boost economic activities. It is important to administer these subsidies and government loans like education loans directly rather than for them to be seen as dole money. The function of such schemes is the same as that of pump priming or helicopter money, etc. Bankers need to be involved actively while such schemes are conceived, in order for fully accountable administration of the schemes to take place.

v) **Recognise the importance of the size of banks** Efficiency comes from better supervision and competition. While supervision can be made functional through administration of accountability of management, competition will exist only between similar banks. In order to have similar banks, it is necessary that similar types of banks and similar liberties exist.

vi) **Recognise the importance of educating people about the utility of banking services** The functioning of banks depends on how much demand is made on them. And depending upon the demand on them, banks reorganise themselves to serve their customers. There is a need to educate people on the potential of banks to make a living for them. Bank accounts need not be just for receiving dole money but for saving with attractive interest, the safe keeping of valuables, and to obtain short term funds in order to benefit from offers coming from local shops and establishments. For the enterprising, banks are capable for partnering with them for viable ventures. Education is important. Projects need to be approved by bank officials and vetted by experienced large professional firms.

Three features of banks that matter to the banking system are: the appropriate size of a bank branch; consumer groups according to needs; and management aspects such as ownership, leadership, and employee integrity.

Size of a bank branch Today the size of a bank branch has become insignificant. Technology has dramatically reduced the necessary size of the structure. There was a time when a single branch of the State Bank of India had more than 3,000 employees. The Core Banking System, centralised processing centres, centralised document management systems, email communications and such developments helped banks to reduce the minimum size to one or two employees. However, basic organisational rules of maker-checker, supervision and control cannot be derided. A minimum economic size is to be decided from the personal security and safety point of view also.

Consumer groups There are three groups of customers who look for banks' assistance. They are households, entrepreneurs and corporates. The households include individuals and their families and they are potentially savers and consumers. The second group comprises entrepreneurs in farms, business, service providers and other professionals. They help in the growth of banking in their area of operation. They also provide employment and create savers. This is the most significant group for developing banking. The third group are the corporates who invest large amounts of capital and provide the infrastructure and opportunity for the second group, also increasing the number of active households, i.e. the first group.

Management features Government is the ultimate controller of the banking system. Irrespective of whether banks are owned by private individuals or government, the regulatory system is superior to ownership. Control systems to ensure that people get what they have been promised are still more significant. Efficiency is the cornerstone for taking a decision on the ownership, management and leadership.

Ownership has great impact on the bank's operations. When banks owned by industry houses were taking care of their side of business while mobilising public deposits, they failed to associate with the all-round development of the economy, subsequently the banks were nationalised. However, the issue was not over. The nationalised banks later become a tool for the government to push implementation of government schemes while depriving commercial enterprises of working capital at cheaper rates. While government schemes were not so viable, commercial loans were expensive. Both resulted in continuous inflation due to escalation of the cost of production and an increase in liquidity. Banks lost their competitiveness. They lost their commercial acumen. Then banks in the private sector were again allowed to flourish. This time the owners or promoters were not industrial houses but investors and government undertakings. Many of them could not survive due to low margins and the restrictive nature of the banking industry. Those among the new private banks which survived had experienced professional leaders at the helm of affairs. Therefore government ownership of banks may not be an issue, but recognising the need for unchanged vision and professional leadership is essential for growth.

Leadership is an individual trait and if the mission is right, success is more or less guaranteed. There is a scarcity of successful leaders. While new generation banks in the private sector were led by eminent professionals, those in the government did not have that advantage. Their remuneration usually is justified by their aggressive performance. The old generation private banks resorted to taking leaders from public sector banks and public sector banks were led by senior employees from other banks including public sector banks. Their growth was more people-specific and most of them served a short term of two years or so, while in contrast new private banks typically had their CEOs continuously providing leadership for more than a decade. Both of these did not experience aggressive growth as promising as that of the new generation of banks in the private sector. Legislation proscribes experienced bankers from heading the State Bank of India and nationalised banks. One cannot agree that the leadership quality of an individual has to be proved by being successful in the same industry. In fact banking is a common business of all people.

Quality of employees is important, and employment in banks requires extra integrity checks as public money is dealt with. Employees with poor ethics may be motivated to do business aggressively but be vulnerable to flouting rules and regulations. Since public sector banks attract employees for a long career, social respectability and convenience, complacency sets in at the earliest. The new generation of banks are not under protection from labour unions but are prone to hire-and-fire systems of management. This causes more inclination to earn from opportunities at the cost of ethics and values. A balance of the two is necessary.

A MODEL FOR INDIAN BANKING

It may not be worthwhile to copy a model that has been successful in any developed or developing country, taking into consideration the vast human geography in India. The banking system should be manageable, available for people and affordable to people. Invariably, all branches should have at least one strong basic banking service and support for other services so that a typical bank branch provides all sorts of banking services to the people living in the surrounding areas. Bank branches need to be aligned to the commerce of the respective village panchayat, block panchayat and district panchayat. Panchayats have the responsibility, government support and people with initiative for economic activity. Coalescing with active people will provide banks with opportunity and boost economic activity in the area. There are 239,000 village panchayats, 6,405 block level panchayats and 589 district level panchayats in India[60]. More than 30 billion USD is going to be invested by the government during 2015-2020.

---

[60] http://www.panchayat.gov.in/ebook/

Types of banks

There are three categories of commercial banks: Retail banks, Loan banks and Global banks. The RBI may be vested with licensing to global banks, whilst licences to loan banks can be given by global banks. Similarly loan banks can provide licences to retail banks.

I Retail banks

This first category comprises the bank branches designed to regularly contact customers and keep a personal touch. They should be barely staffed and supported by one or two tellers or alternatively by machines. Target customers are households in the surrounding area and individual farmers, petty traders, associations, firms, trusts and non-corporate bodies. They can add customers of post offices, cooperative banks, regional rural banks, local area banks, etc.

They mainly provide services for savers, accept short term deposits, approve loans against salary, gold, deposits with or without security, small amounts say up to annual income, repayable within a year. They can also exchange currency notes, issue remittances, and can even handle allocated credit limited accounts (which are operated like a current account). They can issue credit cards and ATM cards, and provide internet banking products.

Core banking being necessary to become a member of a clearing house, they can provide anywhere anytime banking. Ideally, the human resources required must be a minimum of three people altogether. Local staff may be preferred.

Additional services through relationship managers can be provided by insurance, securities, sub-custodial services, and forex transactions handled by money changers.

Even two or three bank branches per village can increase the bank network to a million. On an average, the number of accounts can be around 2,500. That means one hundred customers per day to be served.

II Loan banks

These banks are bigger sized and focussed on the main business of loans. They may not have to keep regular personal contact with the customer. It is indeed good enough if they meet the representatives. Such bank branches need to be reasonably staffed with skilled employees. Target customers are small and medium entrepreneurs, farmers, and small corporates including partnership firms or proprietary concerns. All firms belonging to the above group registered in that district or operating offices in a district can be the target customers. The dichotomy of retail business and loan business if maintained properly may help in preparing target levels of business and preparing strategies thereafter. This may avoid chaotic management.

The businesses that generally come into their fold are: working capital finance, trade finance, cash management products, discounting of instruments, commercial real estate loans, and village adoption. Where target firms are concerned, an ideal annual turnover of up to 100 million rupees or 15 to 20 million USD may be manageable. Potentially, there are 6,400 blocks where such branches can be housed. This would work out roughly to 40 to 50 branches of four or five commercial banks in a district.

Core banking, centralised loan processing systems, document management systems, and trade finance systems may be required to derive the best out of the employees. At least two employees as maker and checker are required for each product.

The branch must be in a position to handle all forex transactions other than the ones carried out by the retail bank, including handling of remittances and import and export. In addition, obtaining approvals from the RBI for capital account transactions must be vested with them.

Such branches can be expected to boost economic activity by providing educational loans, training centres, farm loans, mortgage loans for residential housing, support research centres, etc. They also provide other non-banking products such as insurance, wealth management, share trading, custodial services, and investment banking through respective relationship managers.

In order to make the entire gamut of banking available to the customer, it is necessary that such bank branches have representative outfits for retail banking and agencies for global banks. These banks may be permitted to run and operate retail banks.

III Global Corporate banks

These banks need to be few in number but the size of the business handled has to be large. There are around 589 districts but it may not be necessary to open such branches in all these places. Ideally one or two in a state would perhaps suffice. In this context, the bank will be going to the client rather than the customer visit the branch. Depending upon the number of industries registered with the registrar of companies, and government undertakings set up, the number of branches can be decided. However, the branches require extension windows of the retail and loan bank within the branch to take care of retail and loan business for cross-selling.

Corporate banking services include asset management, custodial service, merchant banking, cash management products, trade finance, forex including maintaining bank accounts of foreign banks and with foreign banks, securitisation, syndication of loans, opening overseas subsidiaries, etc. They need to have separate subsidiaries for Islamic banking, emerging market financing, government business and government companies, currency management, public debts, payment mechanism, product innovation, risk management and rating, treasury products, development banking, etc. All of these subsidiaries may have to work through relationship managers and use the cross-selling route to retail and loan bank customers.

They need to pick up only those units with turnover above 20 million USD. Other than core banking, bank branches should have a customised product-wise system that can be integrated to the core banking software. As regards the staffing of these banks, it depends upon the business potential, and is to be assessed branch to branch. These banks may be permitted to run and operate loan banks as subsidiaries and in turn they may operate and own retail banks.

Conclusion

A very detailed narration of the model may not be accomplished in this book. But the intention of the author is to share several ideas with readers. The role of government and regulator in a redesign best suited to India is overdue. India is no longer under British rule and banks in Great Britain have changed. In the Indian context of unity in diversity and isolated growth, it is important to keep the customer as the central point of a redesign. It is also necessary to provide for the loss potentially involved with the expansion, as profit may not always be yielded. Providing banking facilities at their doorstep is an obligation to the people. Ownership is different from having influence. Even without ownership, the government can influence decisions. The direction for change has to be to put into operation with tougher systems and should be led by professionals with clear business plans and accountability.

* * *

TABLES

Table 1. **List of 48 Commercial Banks**

(Note: Balance Sheet date is 31st March 2016. SBI - State Bank of India Group, PSB - Nationalised Banks, PSBO - other Public Sector Banks, PVT - Banks in Private Sector, PVTN - New Generation Banks in Private Sector; Conversion to USD at RBI reference rate of 66.3329 rupees to one USD)

Rank by Assets 2016	Group	Bank	Assets in Billion USD	Assets in Billion Rs.
1	SBI	State Bank of India (SBI)	340.56	22,590.63
22	SBI	State Bank of Hyderabad	24.81	1,645.97
27	SBI	State Bank of Patiala	19.75	1,310.36
29	SBI	State Bank of Travancore	17.26	1,145.07
30	SBI	State Bank of Bikaner & Jaipur	16.63	1,103.36
33	SBI	State Bank of Mysore	12.51	829.75
4	PSB	Bank of Baroda	101.21	6,713.76
5	PSB	Punjab National Bank	100.61	6,673.90
6	PSB	Bank of India	91.95	6,099.14
7	PSB	Canara Bank	83.36	5,529.61
9	PSB	Union Bank of India	61.01	4,046.96
11	PSB	Syndicate Bank	46.43	3,079.67
12	PSB	Central Bank of India	46.05	3,054.66
13	PSB	Indian Overseas Bank	41.37	2,744.37
14	PSB	UCO Bank	36.92	2,448.83
15	PSB	Oriental Bank of Commerce	35.81	2,375.42

16	PSB	Allahabad Bank	35.55	2,358.28
17	PSB	Corporation Bank	35.41	2,348.63
18	PSB	Indian Bank	30.71	2,037.10
19	PSB	Andhra Bank	30.15	1,999.62
23	PSB	Bank of Maharashtra	24.27	1,609.57
24	PSB	Vijaya Bank	21.92	1,454.09
26	PSB	Dena Bank	20.12	1,334.42
28	PSB	United Bank of India	19.51	1,294.32
31	PSB	Punjab & Sind Bank	15.46	1,025.81
10	PSBO	IDBI Ltd	56.44	3,743.72
48	PSBO	Bharatiya Mahila Bank	0.30	20.20
32	PVT	The Federal Bank Ltd	13.78	914.30
34	PVT	The Jammu & Kashmir Bank Ltd	12.10	802.68
36	PVT	The South Indian Bank Ltd	9.52	631.75
37	PVT	The Karur Vysya Bank Ltd	8.69	576.64
38	PVT	The Karnataka Bank Ltd	8.52	565.00
39	PVT	RBL Bank	5.90	391.61
40	PVT	Tamilnad Mercantile Bank Ltd	5.32	352.66
41	PVT	City Union Bank Ltd	4.71	312.52
42	PVT	The Lakshmi Vilas Bank Ltd	4.33	287.32
45	PVT	The Catholic Syrian Bank Ltd	2.36	156.52
46	PVT	Dhanlaxmi Bank Ltd	1.88	124.63
47	PVT	Nainital Bank Ltd	0.92	60.84
2	PVTN	ICICI Bank Ltd	108.65	7,206.95
3	PVTN	HDFC Bank Ltd	106.86	7,088.46
8	PVTN	Axis Bank Ltd	79.22	5,254.68
20	PVTN	Kotak Mahindra Bank Ltd	28.98	1,922.60
21	PVTN	YES Bank	24.91	1,652.63
25	PVTN	Indusind Bank Ltd	21.11	1,400.57
35	PVTN	IDFC Bank Ltd	11.15	739.70
43	PVTN	Development Credit Bank Ltd	4.33	287.32
44	PVTN	Bandhan Bank Ltd	3.00	199.15

Table 2. **List of Top Ten Banks and their Assets, Group Assets and Tier 1 Capital**

No.	Bank	Total Assets USD Bio[66]	Total Assets Rs.Tio	Group Assets USD	Group Assets Rs.Tio	Group Tier 1 Capital USD Bio
1	STATE BANK OF INDIA	340.56	22.59	447.89	29.71	26.38
2	ICICI BANK LTD	108.69	7.21	138.54	9.19	13.28
3	HDFC BANK LTD	106.73	7.08	110.05	7.30	11.14
4	BANK OF BARODA	101.16	6.71	104.17	6.91	6.74
5	PUNJAB NATIONAL BANK	100.55	6.67	107.49	7.13	4.96
6	BANK OF INDIA	91.96	6.10	93.02	6.17	3.85
7	CANARA BANK	83.22	5.53	85.03	5.64	4.49
8	AXIS BANK LTD	79.15	5.25	80.20	5.32	7.85
9	UNION BANK OF INDIA	61.06	4.05	61.36	4.07	NA
10	IDBI BANK LTD	56.38	3.74	56.38	3.74	NA

Table 3. **Top Ten Banks and their Loans to Assets Ratio**

Rank by Assets 2016	Bank Name	Loans US $ Bio	Loans to Assets 2016 %	Loans to Assets 2015 %
9	UNION BANK OF INDIA	40.25	65.93	67.45
3	HDFC BANK LTD	70.10	65.68	61.76
1	STATE BANK OF INDIA	220.70	64.81	77.00
8	AXIS BANK LTD	51.11	64.57	60.82
5	PUNJAB NATIONAL BANK	62.11	61.77	63.02
2	ICICI BANK LTD	65.58	60.33	60.06
6	BANK OF INDIA	54.12	58.85	64.94
7	CANARA BANK	49.00	58.77	58.39
10	IDBI BANK LTD	32.56	57.75	58.43
4	BANK OF BARODA	57.89	57.23	59.86

[61] At 66.3329 rupees or one USD
[62] NA - Not mentioned in the Annual Report

Table 4. **Operating Profit and Employees of Top Ten Banks**

Rank by Assets 2016	Bank	Employees (March 2016)	Operating Profit 2016	Operating Expenses 2016	O. Profit/Emp.	O. Expenses/ Emp.	(O. Profit/ O. Exp.)/ Emp.
No.	Name	Count	USD Mio	USD Mio	USD	USD	%
2	ICICI BANK	74,096	4,276	1,912	57,709	25,805	224%
8	AXIS	50,135	2,428	1,523	48,421	30,373	159%
10	IDBI	17,570	810	623	46,076	35,436	130%
3	HDFC BANK	87,555	3,221	2,560	36,785	29,235	126%
5	PNB	70,801	1,842	1,503	26,011	21,233	123%
1	SBI	207,739	6,521	6,299	31,392	30,321	104%
4	BOB	51,237	1,329	1,345	25,939	26,254	99%
7	CANARA	54,008	1,077	1,129	19,950	20,913	95%
9	UBI	35,473	863	950	24,318	26,783	91%
6	BOI	49,455	910	1,408	18,400	28,474	65%

Table 5. **Market Value and Book Value of Shares of Top Ten Banks**

Rank by Assets	Bank	No. of Shares	Face Value	End of the Year Share Price at BSE	Book Value of Shares	Market Value / Book Value of Shares
	Name	Ten Mio	Rs.	Rs.	Rs.	%
3	HDFC	253	2	1,071.20	287.47	373%
8	AXIS	238	2	444.55	223.12	199%
2	ICICI	580	2	236.55	154.32	153%
4	BOB	232	2	147.10	132.74	111%
1	SBI	776	1	194.30	176.60	110%
10	IDBI	206	10	69.50	107.41	49%
5	PNB	196	2	84.70	180.61	47%
9	UBI	25	10	130.85	287.51	46%
7	CANARA	18.3	10	189.85	477.19	40%
6	BOI	82	10	97.05	262.77	37%

Table 6. **Equity Ratios and Shareholding**

Rank by Assets	Bank	Earnings per Share Rs.	Return on Equity	Return on Average Assets	Foreign Share-holding	Govt. Share
	Name	Rs.	%	%	%	%
3	HDFC	48.84	17.97	1.92	72.41	2.56
8	AXIS	34.59	17.49	1.72	44.61	29.73
2	ICICI	16.75	11.32	1.49	64.68	10.29
4	BOB	-23.89	-17.64	-0.78	11.45	59.24
1	SBI	12.98	7.74	0.46	11.19	60.18
10	IDBI	-21.77	5.57	-1.07	2.59	73.98
5	PNB	-20.82	-11.20	-0.61	10.38	62.08
9	UBI	20.42	6.84	0.35	8.88	63.44
7	CANARA	-53.61	-10.69	-0.52	7.13	66.30
6	BOI	-83.01	-25.39	-0.94	4.49	68.01

63   Govt. share includes holdings by government companies explicitly stated

Table 7. Change of CEOs and last two years' growth

Rank by Assets	Bank	Growth of Assets 2014-16 in USD Bio	No. of times CEOs changed during last two years	CEO as per 2016 Annual Report
1	SBI	42.38	Same	Mrs Arundhati Bhattacharya
3	HDFC	25.04	Same	Mr Aditya Puri
8	AXIS	15.42	Same	Mrs Shikha Sharma
2	ICICI	9.69	Same	Mrs Chanda Kochhar
9	UBI	2.15	Same	Mr Arun Tiwari
5	PNB	9.04	Once	Mrs Usha Anantha Subraramanian
7	CANARA	1.67	Twice	Mr Rakesh Sharma
10	IDBI	1.64	Once	Mr Kishor Piraji Kharat
6	BOI	-3.55	Once	Mr Melwyin O Rego
4	BOB	-8.49	Twice	Mr P S Jayakumar

Brief Profiles of the CEOs of the Top Ten Banks

1. Mrs Arundhati Bhattacharya has been the Chairman of the State Bank of India from October 2013. She joined **SBI** as a Probationary Officer in 1977 and rose up to the topmost position in the bank. She has a Bachelors and MA in English Literature.

2. Mrs Chanda D Kochhar has been the Managing Director and Chief Executive Officer of ICICI Bank Limited since 1st May 2009. Kochhar began her career with **ICICI** as a Management Trainee in 1984. She holds an MBA and Bachelors degree in Arts from Jai Hind College in Mumbai. She holds a Masters in Management Studies (Finance) from the Jamnalal Bajaj Institute of Management Studies, Mumbai, and is a Cost Accountant from the Institute of Cost and Works Accountants of India.

3. Mr Aditya Puri has been a Managing Director of HDFC Bank Limited, since September 1994. Puri holds a Bachelor of Commerce degree from Punjab University and is an Associate Member of the Institute of Chartered Accountants of India. Mr Puri served as the Chief Executive Officer of **Citibank** Malaysia from 1992 to 1994.

4. Mr P S Jayakumar, also known as Jaya, has been the Chief Executive Officer, Managing Director and Director of the Bank of Baroda since 13th October 2015. He started his career with **Citibank** in 1986. He is an Associate Member of the Institute of Chartered Accountants of India. He is also a Gurukul Chevening Scholar from the London School of Economics and Political Science (1998). Mr Jayakumar holds a Masters degree in Management from XLRI, Jamshedpur and a Masters degree in Commerce from the University of Madras.

5. Mrs Usha Ananthasubramanian has been the Chief Executive Officer and Managing Director at Punjab National Bank since 14th August 2015. She started her banking career in 1982 as a Specialist Officer in the **Bank of Baroda** and also served as a General Manager there. She has a Masters degree in Statistics from the University of Madras and a Masters in Ancient Culture from the University of Mumbai.

6. Mr Melwyn O Rego, BCom, MBA, has been the Chief Executive Officer and Managing Director at the Bank of India Limited since 14th August 2015. Rego served the **IDBI** from 1984 and became Deputy Managing Director and Executive Director from 30th August 2013.

7. Mr Rakesh Kumar Sharma has been the Chief Executive Officer and Managing Director of Canara Bank Limited since 11th September 2015. He was employed in the **SBI** for more than 33 years. Mr Sharma has CAIIB. He has earned a BCom and MA in Economics degrees.

8. Mrs Shikha Sharma has been the Chief Executive Officer and Managing Director at Axis Bank Limited since 1st June 2009. She began her career with **ICICI** Limited in 1980. Mrs Sharma is a Post Graduate Diploma holder in Software Technology from the National Centre for Software Technology in Mumbai. Mrs Sharma earned an MBA from IIM, Ahmedabad and a BA Honours degree from the University of Delhi.

9. Mr Arun Tiwari has been the Chairman and Managing Director of the Union Bank of India since 26th December 2013. Mr Tiwari joined the **Bank of Baroda** as a Scale I Officer in January 1979 and served as the General Manager of the Bank of Baroda. He holds an MSc in Chemistry.

10. Mr Kishor Piraji Kharat has been the Chief Executive Officer and Managing Director at IDBI Bank Limited since 18th August 2015 and serves as its Executive Director. Kharat has 37 years' experience at the **Bank of Baroda**. He is a graduate in Commerce, CAIIB and Law. Mr Kharat also holds an Executive Diploma in Management.

GLOSSARY

Term	Explanation
Aadhaar	The Aadhaar card is issued to all residents in India by Unique Identification Authority of India and widely approved as identity proof for 'know your customer' compliance. Introduced in 2009 as an ambitious project to obtain the biometric data and demographic information on individuals, got a legislative support in 2016, when an act has been passed called The Aadhaar (Targeted delivery of financial and other subsidies, benefits and services) Act 2016. It can be compared to something similar issued in other countries such as the social security number, National Insurance number etc.
Article 226	Indian constitution guarantees certain fundamental right. One of them is under Article 32. When emergency is declared, these fundamental rights can be suspended. Article 226 though not a fundamental right, enables a high court in India to issue writ even during an emergency.
Assets	Assets in banking terms mean something that has the potential to earn income. The annual rate of return on assets indicates the efficiency of the management.
ATM	Automated Teller Machines used to dispense cash and provide basic information on bank accounts. Along with the variants of these machines such as passbook printers and Currency deposit machines Indian banks have become less dependent on employees to provide twenty four hour service to people.
Audit	The terms audit, inspection, verification and scrutiny are used for scrutiny of bank records by various entities. However, term 'audited' refers to financial statements certified by professionals certified by the Institute of Chartered Account of India.

Bankers cheque	Cheque (check in US) is a printed format made available to customer for withdrawing funds after opening an account by bank. The account holder can issue a cheque for drawing money from his or her account. A Bankers cheque (also called pay order, managers check etc) is similar but it is issued by banks. The payee is assured of payment compared to customer's personal cheque. Before the implementation of core banking software, Bankers cheque was payable locally unlike demand drafts (DD) that are payable at specifically named branch office.
Big money	The money in the banking system and forms part of money supply. Most of the money transactions carried out by poor fall outside the system.
Block	The term related to the local administration system followed in India called panchayati raj. It comprises of a gram panchayat, Block panchayat and a district parishad. A gram panchayat at village level is the lowest tier. There are 618 district parishad, 6595 block and 248148 gram panchayats. The people elects democratically members and altogether around 2.7 million representatives forms the set up.
CAR (Capital to Assets Ratio)	This report often referred as Capital adequacy return reflects the proportion of bank's capital funds to assets that are risk weighted at a predetermined rate. There total value of assets in the CAR return varies with the Total Assets in the Balance sheet. Most banks in India have more than 9 per cent capital funds. The capital is grouped into Core Capital, Tier 1 capital and Tier 2 capital. Individual bank's annual report gives details. Paid up capital and reserves shown in the Balance sheet form the Tier 1 Capital. The sum of subordinated debts and various permitted reserves and provisions held for future loss and subordinated debts becomes the Tier 2 capital.
CBI	Central Bureau of Investigation is a crime investigation agency under government of India to enquire into bribery corruption among employees of government and government owned enterprises. Since main banks in India are owned by government, CBI is active entity in Indian banking. Originally this outfit was set up to investigate under war department in 1941.
CBS	Core Banking solution is the software used by banks to perform banking transactions such as loans, opening accounts, deposits, withdrawals etc. Commonly used by Indian banks are products of internationally famous Indian IT companies such as TCS and Infosys.

Centralised database management system	Banks have a data centre centrally that helps the centralised clearing and remittances for any where banking possible. The computer systems banks used in India in the nineties spent almost an hour for Start of the day and End of the day operations and required service of a dedicated officer to take care of the systems at branches. A daily back up of data was also necessary. Banks saves a lot of time with the CBS with centralised database management systems. Centrally managing ATMs became possible.
CEO	Whenever a reference to CEO is made it means the Chairman in the case of public sector banks and the particularly designated Chief Executive Officer in private banks. There are positions in banks such as Managing Director, Executive Director who are in most cases are members of Board but need not be the CEO.
Cheque	In India it refers to the 'check' used for drawing out money from bank accounts.
Class banking	This is a commonly used term when topic under discussion is 'under banking' or 'financial inclusion'. Banks in India are encouraged to adopt mass banking from their traditional class banking. Here 'class' refers to social class based on their birth, place they are born, education, inherited wealth etc. Mass banking refers to bringing in the marginalised and excluded population into banking. In general, the Upper class refers to the dominant community, middle class refers to employees and small entrepreneurs, professionals etc and the lower class refers to people with no regular income.
Computerisation	Computerisation does not refer to full migration to computer systems by banks in India. It refers to the movement away from manual systems. Initially the change was to adapt to ledger posting machines and later to branch banking software and later to networked solutions. There were issues initially from labour unions, availability of satellite communication systems and funds with banks for investment.
Crop insurance	It is a method of mitigating risk in farming. The local state government plays the pivotal role of fixing the premium on the basis of historical data on yield of various crops. Loans to agriculture and allied business are encouraged by government since India is considered as basically an agrarian economy.

Rupee	Indian currency is Indian Rupee and INR is the acronym. 'Re' is the singular form and 'Rs' refers the plural. Indian Rupee has a symbol ₹[64] from 2010 like other global currencies such as USD, GBP, Euro, Japanese Yen. Rupee is commonly denominated in units, tens, thousands, lakh /Lac (hundred thousand), Crore (ten million) across India. In the eastern part of India, rupee is referred to as Taka. Elsewhere they are referred as roopa, rupiah etc. The Currency notes contain the value stated in 16 Indian languages.
Dearness Allowance	It is a variable portion in the salary structure. Depending upon the movement of all India consumer price index released by government, Indian Banks Association releases the rate of DA payable to employees of banks for whom IBA agrees wage settlement. Since Inflation in India is high, it follows increase in labour cost of these banks.
DRI	Indian banks were advised to earmark one percentage of their loans to low income group in 1972. Initially maximum loan amount was fixed at Rs.6500 (100 USD) just to provide funds for procurement of materials for jobs that can convert them to handmade finished products(eg. basket)or acquiring implements etc. Currently such loans can be upto twenty thousand. Interest rate is fixed at 4 per cent annually.
FDI	Investment from overseas companies in Indian companies. Foreign Direct Investment in India was liberalised gradually since FEMA was enacted in 2000. The approval is issued by Reserve Bank of India depending upon the cap fixed industry wise by government. Indian economy has been found wanting in capital funds. With globalisation accepted alike by different governments since 1990 as a future course for economic development of India, the scope for FDI is bright.
FII	Foreign Institutional Investors form now part of portfolio investors monitored by Securities Exchange Board of India, an autonomous body. There are ceilings for investments by FIIs.
Fiscal year	Indian government follows the fiscal year as 1st April to 31st March. Indian companies also follow the same period as their financial year to synchronise with the computation and payment of taxes.

---

[64]   In ms word, the symbol can be obtained by depressing keys such as 20B9 then Alt+x together.

Food advances	Government of India through Food corporation of India procures grains and other food items and distributes through authorised shops to people. There are currently 66 banks in a consortium funding approximately 8 billion USD which is known as food advance
forex reserve	Indian rupee being not a freely traded currency, most of the international trade take place in foreign currencies such as USD, Euro, GBP or Japanese yen etc., RBI is vested with the responsibility to preserve forex reserves so that sudden adverse fluctuation does not result in a run on the economy. Gold forms almost six per cent and is the second component of the reserves.
globalisation	Finding buyers abroad for local products and getting products and services at economically from abroad is the foundation of globalisation. Once India was supposed to be a flourishing economy. But Invasions spoiled the economy but resurgence can be attributed to swadeshi (use of only Indian goods) movements and restrictive trade adopted after independence. Since 1990 when the economic policies were directed towards liberalisation and globalisation, the fortune too began to return to the country. The miracle of commerce and international trade in improving the living condition, better thoughts and expansive view on matters among the population became visible in India too.
Illiterate customer	Customers those who can sign either in national language or in vernacular are considered as literate by banks. For others, banks obtain their thumb impression on bank documents and attested by a bank official. India has 272 million above seven years as illiterate as per census 2011.
juggernaut	It means something large and powerful with a bad effect. The word is understood to have its roots in the famous annual Rath (wagon) Yatra of Lord Jagannath of Puri temple in Odissa (India) and represents blind devotion and sacrifice.
knowledge workers	Those who work on information are broadly referred knowledge workers. An MIS based on accurate data that are updated on real time basis is essential to convert bank employees into knowledge workers.
KYC norms	Know your customer norms are intended to establish the identity of the customer, in the case of a bank. This is carried out by obtaining a photo id and a residence proof. This is complemented by due diligence exercise and anti-money laundering practices to prevent unaccounted money playing havoc in the nation building process.

liberalisation	National policy to liberalise control on economic activities exercised by issuing licenses usually referred as the licence raj. Since 1990, many areas have been liberalised however bank licensing continues.
lien	A lien a right to hold the securities till dues are settled. Banks use this right to set off for adjusting deposits against loan.
MCLR	Marginal cost based lending rate. A base rate worked out on a formula provided by the RBI introduced from April 2016. The components are the cost of funds, risk premium, tenor premium and spread. Prior to that, individual banks had their own base rate worked out by their own formula.
Money laundering	Funds that came to hand by illegal means are passed through some mechanism that make them accountable. Remittances received and pushing amount through bank account of someone else are the means to achieve this feat. Tax department traces them through the source of funds of suspicious transactions.
MT	Mail transfer is a remittance facility using postal mail services to communicate the particulars of beneficiary provided by the remitter to the branch where the beneficiary has the account. This has lost relevance in a CBS environment. If message for remittance is transmitted by telegram, this was called TT. Indian post has discontinued telegram services.
NABARD	National Bank for agriculture and rural development is an apex institution for loans to agriculture and other allied activities. NABARD has a pivotal role to play in persuading banks to finance agriculture and improvement of technology in farming.
Nationalisation	Nationalisation of banks refers to taking over the ownership and administrative control of an organisation by government. In two instances Government nationalised 20 banks.
NPA	Non Performing Assets are those loans and investment of banks that have stopped servicing interest and defaulted paying the dues. As regards Indian banks are concerned clear cut instructions are issued by RBI regarding identification of NPAs and provisions to be made for the impending loss.

NRI	Non resident Indians are allowed to operate bank accounts. Here Indians means those who are born in India but generally live abroad. As a definition, Non resident are those Indians who live abroad for more than 180 days. RBI issues regularly guidelines on operation of their bank accounts. Basically they are allowed to open rupee accounts that are rapatriable and non repatriable. They can also open foreign currency accounts in the form of fixed deposits. The freedom to take back deposits (repatraiability) out of India and the accountability for the exchange risk involved in those transactions distinguishes their bank accounts with bank accounts of residents.
PAN	It is an acronym for Permanant Account Number issued by Income Tax Department of government. The PAN card is considered as a proof for compliance to KYC norms by banks.
Pass book	Bank pass book is not a just statement of transactions in a saving account, but it serves as an identity too. Due to this aspect, it has not been dispensed with. Passbook contains a photo of the account holder attested by the Branch Manager.
Pay order	Pl see bankers cheque.
Pledge	It is a contract of bailment that confirms delivery for custody of an asset as security for loan. The term is commonly associated with for loans against gold ornaments in India. Unlike other contract of hypothecation, pledged goods are allowed to be sold after a reasonable notice to the depositor.
Public debt	They refer to securities floated by governments repayable on demand or after a term. The buying and sale are handled by the public debt office (PDO) managed by Reserve Bank of India as an agency function. Banks in India deal with PDO to mange investments for complying with Statutory Liquidity norms or otherwise.
RDDBFI	Recovery debt due to banks and financial institutions Act - A 1993 legislation intended to speed up recovery of bank loans. Popular Debt Recovery Tribunals function under this legislation.
RRB	Regional Rural Banks are established as a hybrid version of commercial banks and cooperative banks with the partnership of a commercial bank as sponsor, state and central government as other investors. Only a few of them were successful and for others they proved to be a burden to run the show. There are 56 of them still in operation.

RTGS	RBI manages inter bank remittance between customers of different bank accounts by using Real Time Gross Settlement System for amount above Rupees two hundred thousand (approx 3000 USD). For remittances below that, another system called NEFT (National Electronic Funds Transfer) and requests are processed in batches unlike RTGS. Around one hundred thousand bank branches are using the system with their unique id known as IFSC.
Rupay Card	is a domestic payment card comparable to internationally popular cards such as Master or Visa, promoted by the National Payment Corporation of India and marketed by Indian banks.
V SAT	Very small aperture terminal were utilised by banks at locations where satellite connections were not available for setting up ATMs and centralised banking system. To some extent expansion of India banking to remote areas were handicapped by the slow expansion of satellite and cable network to remote areas.

www.ingramcontent.com/pod-product-compliance
Lightning Source LLC
Chambersburg PA
CBHW031827170526
45157CB00001B/212